A Wise Man

A Wise Man Builds upon a Rock
by a FOOL Who Built on Sinking Sand

Erin Thiele

EncouragingMen.org

Cover Design by Dallas Thiele • NarrowRoad Publishing

A Wise Man

A Wise Man Builds upon a Rock
by a FOOL Who Built on Sinking Sand

A Manual for Men
by Erin Thiele

Published by: NarrowRoad Publishing House
POB 830
Ozark, MO 65721
U.S.A.

The materials from Restore Ministries were written for the sole purpose of encouraging women. For more information, visit us at:

EncouragingMen.net
RestsoreMinistries.net

Permission from the author has been given to those who wish to print or photocopy this book for themselves or others, strictly for encouragement and informational purposes; however, such copies or reprints cannot be sold in any form without prior written permission from the author.

Unless otherwise indicated, most Scripture verses are taken from the *New American Standard Bible* (NASB). Scripture quotations marked KJV are taken from the *King James Version* of the Bible, and Scripture quotations marked NIV are taken from the *New International Version*. Our ministry is not partial to any particular version of the Bible but **loves** them all so that we are able to help every man in any denomination who needs encouragement.

Copyright © 2019 by Erin Thiele

First Printing: 1996. Second Printing: 2000, completely revised. Third Printing: 2001, edited. Fourth Printing: 2004, edited and revised. Fifth Printing: 2005, completely revised and edited. Sixth Printing: 2014, edited. Seventh Printing: 2019, chapter 17 added.

ISBN: 1-931800-11-1
ISBN 13: 978-1-931800-11-2
Library of Congress Control Number: 2014912882

Introduction

The book that you hold in your hands is not meant to be read and put aside. It is my hope and prayer that it will give you the knowledge you need to prevent you from ever having to face infidelity or divorce. For those who have gotten this manual because of my recommendation in *How God Will Restore Your Marriage: There's Healing After Broken Vows,* I am certain that God sees your heart and is at this moment "strongly supporting" you.

It is time for *all* men (and women) to realize that *all* marriages are on sinking sand, unless they are grounded firmly on the Rock of God's Word.

As you read each chapter, you will see clearly that your dependency must be on the Lord. Scripture is all that you need to renew your mind to God's way of thinking and you must throw out other opinions from the world. Then, it is your task to rebuild your home upon the Rock by being a *doer* of the Word, not a *hearer only.*

Before rebuilding, you must have good blueprints. Your blueprints must be His Word, which you will find in the following pages. Next, you must find the Cornerstone that everything will be built around. Our Cornerstone is taking Jesus as your Lord, not just your Savior. We will cover this in Chapter Two.

With a renewed mind and the Lord's blueprint, you will then be able to rebuild your home on the Rock instead of on sinking sand. Those of you who are sitting amidst rubble because your house has fallen (through infidelity or divorce) really have the advantage. You are motivated to begin to rebuild now since basically you have nowhere to live. It will be painful, but worth every bit of effort you exert.

Those of you who are living in a home, which only creaks a little or maybe shifts when the weather changes, are comfortable, but God is trying to get your attention or you would not be holding this manual in your hands. Remember, Jesus said **when** the rains come, not *if* they come. And, He is very clear that all those whose houses are not built on the Rock will fall, and great will be their fall! Your rains and winds may come in the form of you or your wife being unfaithful, a sickness or death in the family, or financial troubles. God is faithful; He will use whatever He knows will get *your* attention.

"For I am confident of this very thing, that He who began a good work in you will perfect it until the day of Christ Jesus" (Phil. 1:6). I guarantee that all of us will have trials and tribulations in our lives; therefore, let's build our homes firmly on the Rock.

Table of Contents

1. On the Rock 6
2. Your First Love 23
3. Blessed Are the Meek 42
4. Thrusts of a Sword 58
5. Weapons of our Warfare 71
6. The Angry Man 94
7. Immoralities 111
8. Manages His Own Household 129
9. Man Alone 149
10. Various Trials 169
11. I Hate Divorce 187
12. The Fruit of the Womb 201
13. The Ministry of Reconciliation 215
14. Provide for His Own 239
15. Father's Instructions 251
16. Empty Talkers and Deceivers 284
17. Opening the Windows of Heaven 298

    Answer Key for Test Your Wisdom 314

Chapter 1

On the Rock

*Therefore everyone who hears these Words of Mine,
and acts upon them, may be compared to a wise man,
who built his house upon the rock.
And the rain descended, and the floods came,
and the winds blew, and burst against that house;
and yet it did not fall, for it had been founded upon the rock.
—Matthew 7:24*

Is your house built upon the rock? Are you sure? Because God's Word says that the rains are going to come. They may be in the form of a financial crisis, the death of a loved one, unfaithfulness, or health problems. How about your marriage; will it stand? Great is the fall of most marriages; will yours be next? Or, perhaps it has already fallen. Men, it is time for all of us to rebuild our homes firmly on the Rock of Jesus Christ–*firmly on His Word*. The ways of the world will only guarantee the fall of our home along with our hopes and plans for our families.

Do you really know what God's Word says about your responsibilities? Have you read God's blueprints and modeled your home after them? Here are a few of the questions that will be answered by Scripture in the following chapters: Should we only discipline our children for "deliberate defiance"? Why is it that most wives seem to display toward their employers those attitudes and characteristics of an ideal wife? How has the practice of birth control and sterilization actually encouraged and spread homosexuality? Is there anything wrong with divorce—in certain circumstances?

Why are insults and evil brought into our lives, and how does this relate to God's blessings? What danger is present when a wife fulfills all of her own needs, and the couple is no longer dependent upon each other? Why does Scripture tell us that we are not to be frightened by any fear? Some preachers tell us that we are commanded to be angry; is this true? Should your pastor be the spiritual leader of your family? If you put your wife first in your life, what will happen to your marriage?

Most men are so occupied with hobbies, sports, and their jobs that they spend little or no time studying God's Word. In many instances, their wives are tirelessly saturating themselves with Bible studies and seminars, yet their homes are out of order and crumbling. Have you ever wondered if your marriage will last? Are you certain that it will stand the test of time? Well, God's Word says, "Therefore let him who **thinks** he stands take heed lest he fall" (1 Cor. 10:12).

Sound doctrine? We as Christians enjoy the messages from the pulpit or Christian radio that get us all fired up for the Lord, but what about those messages that bring about conviction? Do we run from those words? A lot of preachers and speakers today need to minister to large crowds for financial reasons. The ministers tell their congregations or listeners what they *want to hear,* because it brings in the largest offerings. "For the time will come when they will not endure sound doctrine; but wanting to have their ears tickled, they will accumulate for themselves teachers in accordance to their own desires; and will turn away their ears from the Truth, and will turn aside to myths" (2 Tim. 4:3–4).

Ravenous wolves. Jesus warned us of spiritual leaders who will try to deceive us. "Beware of the false prophets, who come to you in sheep's clothing, but inwardly are ravenous wolves. You will know them by their fruits . . ." (Matt. 7:15–16). We can see the financial fruits of their ministries, yet most of their followers are perishing for a lack of knowledge. "My people are destroyed for lack of knowledge. Because you have rejected knowledge . . ." (Hos. 4:6).

Finds wisdom. If you heard a strong message entitled "Spiritual Leader," "Lusts of the Flesh," or "A Lover of Self," and it convicted you, would you embrace or run from that conviction? Not condemnation, but conviction. Do you know the difference? "My son, do not reject the discipline of the Lord, or loathe His reproof; for whom the Lord loves He reproves, even as a father, the son in whom he delights. How blessed is the man who **finds wisdom,** and the man who gains understanding. For its profit is better than the profit of silver, and its gain than fine gold" (Prov. 3:11–14).

His purpose. Satan brings condemnation to us—thoughts that make us feel hopeless. The Lord convicts us in our spirit in order to show us the things in our life that need changing. However, all guilt is not bad. On the contrary, we *should* feel guilty when we sin. If a person feels no guilt or remorse for his sin, why would he want to repent? Even the hopelessness that condemnation brings can be used for good if we turn to God for our hope. We know that we have the assurance ". . . that God causes all things to work together for good to those who love God, to those who are called according to His purpose" (Rom. 8:28). Did you know that, many times, God brings adversity into our lives to strengthen our relationship with Him? It was God who brought the many trials into Jonah's life to bring about obedience. And it was the Lord who blinded Saul in order to change him into the godly Paul. Does it really matter where the adversity is coming from as long as we allow each of these tribulations to mold us more into the Lord's image?

My ways, my thoughts. As you read through the chapters in this manual, much of what is written may seem foreign to you. Many of these truths are rarely, if ever, preached from the pulpit, discussed on Christian radio, or written about in Christian books. "For as the heavens are higher than the earth, so are My ways higher than your ways, and My thoughts than your thoughts" (Isa. 55:9). These teachings are found easily in Scripture but are often overlooked, watered down, or taken out of context to justify an opposing view or even to justify sin. "Every word of God is tested; He is a shield to those who take refuge in Him. Do not add to His Words, lest He reprove you, and you be proved a liar" (Prov. 30:5–6).

A broken and a contrite heart. Is your heart broken and contrite? It must be to receive the Truth. "The sacrifices of God are a broken spirit; **a broken and a contrite heart,** O God, Thou wilt not despise" (Ps. 51:17). This is the fertile ground that the Lord says will produce much fruit. "Hear then the parable of the sower. When anyone hears the Word of the kingdom, and does not understand it, the evil one comes and snatches away what has been sown in his heart. This is the one on whom seed was sown beside the road. And the one on whom seed was sown on the rocky places, this is the man who hears the Word, and immediately receives it with joy; yet he has no firm root in himself, but is only temporary, and when affliction or persecution arises because of the Word, immediately he falls away. And the one on whom seed was sown among the thorns, this is the man who hears the Word, and the worry of the world, and the deceitfulness of riches choke the Word, and it becomes unfruitful. And the one on whom seed was sown on the good soil, this is the man who hears the Word and understands it; who indeed bears fruit, and brings forth, some a hundredfold, some sixty, and some thirty" (Matt. 13:18–23).

Did not hear it. "But blessed are your eyes, because they see; and your ears, because they hear. For truly I say to you, that many prophets and righteous men desired to see what you see, and did not see it; and to hear what you hear, and **did not hear it**" (Matt. 13:16–17). You will need an "ear to hear." That means listening and desiring to gain the complete wisdom that the Bible has to offer.

Meditates day and night. You will need to renew your mind, to line it up with the instruction found in God's Word. Most people rely on what is popular according to the world's standards or follow the so-called "experts" in the field. Let's never forget that God is our Creator; does He not know how to deal with every circumstance or relationship He created? "But his delight is in the law of the Lord, and in His law he **meditates day and night.** And he will be like a tree firmly planted by streams of water, which yields its fruit in its season, and its leaf does not wither; *and in whatever he does, he prospers"* (Ps. 1:2–3).

Thy Word is Truth. Satan will try to tempt you into rejecting what is written in this manual. He will also try to cause division by getting you to think or say that you do not agree with the author. First of all, it doesn't matter what this author is writing or saying. What matters is what God says, since He is the Author and Creator of life. Secondly, remember that Satan will try to discourage you; division is one of his favorite tactics. If you don't believe what is written in these chapters, you have three choices: You can talk to someone *you know* will agree with you. You can just take what you want and pass over the rest like a buffet. Or *you can search the Truth*. "Sanctify them in the Truth; **Thy Word is Truth"** (John 17:17).

Seek and you shall find. "But seek for His kingdom, and these things shall be added to you" (Luke 12:31). "And I say to you, ask, and it shall be given to you; seek, and you shall find; knock, and it shall be opened to you" (Luke 11:9). Use your concordance; allow the Lord to direct you to all Truth. Memorize a verse and ruminate on it over and over in your mind. And then, one day, it will be as if a light were turned on in a dark room; you will know the Truth! It's worth the effort! You must make the time! "So teach us to number our days, that we may present to Thee a heart of wisdom" (Ps. 90:12). If we seek Him first, He promises that everything else will be given to us.

Hunger and thirst. If we are believers, Christians, then our purpose on earth is to glorify God in all that we do. Isn't that what Jesus did with His life? And, if we call ourselves Christians, we are supposed to be followers of Christ. But, are we? How do we follow Christ? Maybe you've tried to follow Christ many times before, but you stumbled and were unable to go on. If you can open your heart to God and continue to read the Scriptures that are found in the following chapters, His Word will cause you to hunger and thirst for Him and His truths. "Blessed are those who hunger and thirst for righteousness, for they shall be satisfied" (Matt. 5:6). "As the deer pants for the water brooks, so my soul pants for Thee, O God" (Ps. 42:1). What a marvelous way to feel about the Lord and His Word!

His Word. God's Holy Scriptures will be the most important words on the following pages. His Word heals. "He sent **His Word** and *healed them,* and *delivered them* from their destructions" (Ps. 107:20). His Word is the light that will illuminate the darkness. **"Thy Word** is a *lamp to my feet,* and a *light to my path"* (Ps. 119:105). His Word is Truth. "The sum of Thy Word is Truth, and every one of Thy righteous ordinances is everlasting" (Ps. 119:160). And it's the Truth that shall set you free. ". . . And you shall know the truth, and the truth shall make you free" (John 8:32).

Just do it! Once you begin to understand and accept God's truths, you must then become a doer of the Word. "For if anyone is a hearer of the Word and **not a doer,** he is like a man who looks at his natural face in a mirror; for once he has looked at himself and gone away, he has immediately forgotten what kind of person he was" (James 1:23–24).

You must put action behind what you have learned or there will never be any change in your life!

Zealous for what is good? Let this thought be prevalent in your mind: the teachings in this manual have been written to help you become a zealot (a fanatic for the Truth found in God's Word). You'll get that way when you're backed into a corner, when you're sinking and you're looking for something to save you, and when you see a real void in your life that makes your heart and your gut ache because you desperately need that void filled. If this is where you are in your life, then you too will become a zealot. Obey zealously—enthusiastically! Zealous teaching needs zealous obedience.

"And who is there to harm you if you prove **zealous for what is good?**" (1 Pet. 3:13). Jesus called for that kind of zealous obedience in His teaching while He walked on earth. "And if your hand or your foot causes you to stumble, cut it off and throw it from you; it is better for you to enter life crippled or lame, than having two hands or two feet, to be cast into the eternal fire. And if your eye causes you to stumble, pluck it out, and throw it from you. It is better for you to enter life with one eye, than having two eyes, to be cast into the fiery hell" (Matt. 18:8).

Come, follow Me. "And looking at him, Jesus felt a love for him, and said to him, 'One thing you lack: go and sell all you possess, and give to the poor, and you shall have treasure in heaven; and come, follow Me.' But at these words his face fell, and he went away grieved, for he was one who owned much property. And Jesus, looking around, said to His disciples, 'How hard it will be for those who are wealthy to enter the kingdom of God!'" (Mark 10:21–23). Are we like the rich man, unwilling to follow Jesus? How many times has He called you but you were all tied up with the things of this world, so you didn't follow?

Lay aside every encumbrance. "Therefore, since we have so great a cloud of witnesses surrounding us, let us also **lay aside** *every encumbrance,* and *the sin which so easily entangles us,* and let us run with endurance the race that is set before us . . ." (Heb. 12:1). "The night is almost gone, and the day is at hand. Let us therefore **lay aside** the *deeds of darkness* and put on the armor of light" (Rom. 13:12). ". . . In reference to your former manner of life, you **lay aside** the *old self,* which is being corrupted in accordance with the lusts of deceit . . ." (Eph. 4:22). You must make changes in your life; you must do it now and commit yourself to following Jesus Christ. When will be the next time He calls you? When will be the *last* time He calls you? Could this be your last opportunity? Ponder now this sobering verse: "Yet you do not know what your life will be like tomorrow. You are just a vapor that appears for a little while and then vanishes away" (James 4:14).

Lukewarm. God despises the lukewarm Christian. Are you on fire for Him? What does He need to do in your life to move you toward Him and His Word? "I know your deeds, that you are neither cold nor hot; I would that you were cold or hot. So because you are **lukewarm,** and neither hot nor cold, I will *spit you out of My mouth*" (Rev. 3:15–16). Make every moment, every day, count.

Spiritually poor. Are you spiritually bankrupt? If you were financially bankrupt, you'd certainly be scrambling to find the money you need to pay your bills and to feed your family, but what about the spiritual food that **you** need to share with your family?

Built his house upon the sand. Let's face it: many of us men have built our house on the sinking sand of the world's values. We put our desire for riches, fame, and position ahead of our desire to follow Christ. It's only a matter of time before this house of cards falls. We've seen the signs; we've seen other Christian brothers fall. The men who find and read this manual, whose houses have already fallen "and great was its fall," really have the advantage. They have nowhere to live, so they pick up the pieces of rubble and begin rebuilding. They have no choice to make; God made it for them. "And everyone who hears these words of Mine, and does not act upon them, will be like a foolish man, who built his house upon the sand. And the rain descended, and the floods came, and the winds blew, and burst against that house; and it fell, and great was its fall" (Matt. 7:26–27). Begin to build, step by step, board by board, your house upon the rock of Jesus Christ. Use His Word **alone** as your blueprints. Let this manual motivate you and help illuminate those areas that pertain to the circumstances of your life.

Do not be afraid of them; remember the Lord. "And he spoke in the presence of his brothers and the wealthy men. . . What are these feeble Jews doing? Are they going to restore it for themselves? Can they offer sacrifices? Can they finish in a day? Can they revive the stones from the dusty rubble, even the burned ones? . . . Even what they are building—if a fox should jump on it, he would break their stone wall down!" (Neh. 4:2). Expect ridicule and mocking as you begin to rebuild your house. Read the entire fourth chapter of Nehemiah for motivation. Highlight in your Bible those passages that explain what they did to overcome those who tried to stop them. First, they prayed when others began to ridicule them, and God gave them direction along with "a mind to work." Next, they set up a defense day and night. They were also aware of their weak points and set up extra defense in those positions. (Sounds a bit like war, doesn't it? See Chapter 5, "Weapons of Our Warfare," for more knowledge.) The leaders fought against the fear of those they were leading. "When I saw their fear, I rose and spoke to the nobles, the officials, and the rest of the people: **'Do not be afraid of them; remember the Lord** who is *great and awesome,* and fight for your brothers, your sons, your daughters, your wives, and your houses'" (Neh. 4:14). Ultimately, the enemy saw that it was *God* who was on their side.

Counsel you with My eye. Will you continue on through the following chapters with the zealous commitment needed? We really will not be able to make the changes ourselves. We are sinners; our righteousness is nothing but filthy rags. But when we allow God to work in us and through us, He will begin to make the changes from within us. "I will instruct you and teach you in the way which you should go; I will **counsel you with My eye** upon you. Do not be as the horse or as the mule which have no understanding, whose trappings include bit and bridle to hold them in check; otherwise, they will not come near to you" (Ps. 32:8–9).

According to *His* purpose. The Lord comes to us at the very time of our need. He is the one who allows us to come to the turning points in our lives, through various trials, so we will depend upon Him. It's during these times of distress that we seek Him and then He lets us find Him. Brokenness many times brings about real lifelong change. That's why we can praise Him in all things, because we have this assurance: "And we know that God causes all things to work together for good to those who love God, to those who are called according to His purpose" (Rom. 8:28).

We can see from this passage that our goal must be according to His purpose—what then is His purpose for our lives? Most of us are familiar with verse 28, but to really understand His purpose we must read the next three verses. "For whom He foreknew, He also predestined **to become conformed to the image of His Son,** that He might be the first-born among many brethren; and whom He predestined, these He also called; and whom He called, these He also justified; and whom He justified, these He also glorified. What then shall we say to these things? If God is for us, who is against us?" (Rom. 8:29–31).

Do your deeds deny Him? Do you truly love Him enough to obey Him? Are we concerned with *our purpose* in each situation in our life or *His purpose?* Where is your heart? Many times we start out in our trial with the selfish point of view in order to comfort ourselves or protect ourselves from whatever is hurting us. But as the trial or suffering continues, we begin to see more of a need for change. We develop an insight, which reveals the reason(s) why God has allowed the trial. It was possibly for our salvation or for the salvation of a loved one, but certainly the trial is for our sanctification so our deeds will stop denying Him. "They profess to know God, but by **their deeds they deny Him,** being detestable and disobedient, and worthless for any good deed" (Titus 1:16).

My heart of stone. As we look ever forward to the day of our glorification, He encourages us to be specific in our prayer life. He wants us to get to the point of crying out to Him. When will you come to this point? Will you cry out in a time of frustration, or must you get to the point of losing a loved one through death? Maybe it is merely the threat of losing the loved one that will bring you to that point. Possibly, the destruction of your marriage will make you cry out to God. We must ask ourselves, how hard is my heart? "Moreover, I will give you a new heart and put a new spirit within you; and I will remove **the heart of stone** from your flesh and give you a heart of flesh" (Ezek. 36:26). Are you willing to ask God for this heart change, "whatever it takes"?

Hardens his neck. The Lord said if you will only ask, you will receive. "Ask, and it shall be given to you; seek, and you shall find; knock, and it shall be opened to you" (Matt. 7:7). If we are truly Christians, followers of Christ, then we yearn to be closer to Him. Do you yearn? Or, are you surrounding yourself with the things that deaden that desire? If so, my friend, you are not a Christian on fire for God, but a backslider. "The backslider in heart will have his fill of his own ways . . ." (Prov. 14:14). Have you had your fill? Or must you be broken? "A man who **hardens his neck** after much reproof will *suddenly* be ***broken beyond remedy***" (Prov. 29:1).

Sorrowful to the point of repentance. In order to repent and turn away from the lukewarm life we have lived for too long, we must be sorry. "I now rejoice, not that you were made sorrowful, but that you were made **sorrowful to the point of repentance;** for you were made sorrowful according to the will of God, in order that you might not suffer loss in anything through us. For the sorrow that is according to the will of God produces a repentance without regret, leading to salvation; but the sorrow of the world produces death" (2 Cor. 7:9–10).

Destroying speculations and *every* lofty thing. What is separating you from the knowledge of God? What keeps you from reading His Word daily? If God is not first in your life, what is? Your job? Your family? Entertainment? What keeps you so busy that you are even prevented from giving God a second thought? "We are **destroying speculations and every lofty thing** raised up against the knowledge of God, and we are taking every thought captive to the obedience of Christ, and we are ready to punish all disobedience, whenever your obedience is complete" (2 Cor. 10:5–6).

Confess your sins to one another. If you are ready, if you have allowed yourself to become convicted, you are ready to change your life. Begin by confession. "Therefore, **confess your sins to one another,** and pray for one another, so that you may be healed. The effective prayer of a righteous man can accomplish much" (James 5:16). If you are not broken, you will probably put these pages down now, or continue to read them just to prove to yourself that you are the good Christian you claim to be. But we both know it will never change your life because it will never penetrate your heart. It will merely pour over you like water off a duck's back.

Do not be surprised at the fiery ordeal. These pages are written by one who was broken. God often uses other people in our lives to break us. It may be just an annoyance at first; then it escalates into complete frustration. But do we turn to Him at that point, or do we instead harden our hearts and harden our necks? God is trying to change us, to mold us. "Beloved, **do not be surprised at the fiery ordeal** among you, which comes upon you for your testing, as though some strange thing were happening to you; but to the degree that you share the sufferings of Christ, keep on rejoicing; so that also at the revelation of His glory, you may rejoice with exultation" (1 Pet. 4:12).

But, usually, we don't like the situation or the person that is bringing the trials into our lives because we can't see that *God* is behind it. We become bitter and angry with the persons or circumstances He uses. We try to break the relationships, only to find they follow us. Dear believer, it is the Lord who is trying to turn us, gently at first, and then a little more firmly. (See Chapter 10, "Various Trials," for more knowledge on the spiritual warfare that you face daily. "But if they do not hear, they shall perish by the sword, and they shall die without knowledge" (Job 36:12). "My people are destroyed for lack of knowledge. Because you have rejected knowledge, I also will reject you . . ." (Hos. 4:6).

Removed lover and friend. God oftentimes must remove a friend or our loved ones in order to put *Himself* in first place in our lives. We may be in a cold marriage or even separated or divorced. We may have children or parents who are not speaking to us. Possibly our brothers or sisters may no longer be communicating with us either. "Thou hast **removed lover and friend** far from me; my acquaintances are in darkness" (Ps. 88:18). "Thou hast put me in the lowest pit, in dark places, in the depths. Thy wrath has rested upon me, and Thou hast afflicted me with all Thy waves. *Selah*. Thou hast removed my acquaintances far from me; Thou hast made me an object of loathing to them; I am shut up and cannot go out" (Ps. 88:6–8). (*Selah is found often in the book of Psalms. When you read the word Selah, the Psalmist is asking you to ponder and think over what you just read. Reread it if you need to. What's your hurry?*)

They shall see God. But how can *I* see the Lord? First, you must have had a born again experience; then, He will begin to bring about internal purification. If we do not understand God's ways, we will become discouraged and many doubts will creep into our minds. "Blessed are the *pure in heart,* for **they shall see God**" (Matt. 5:8). God wants to be first in our lives. (See the next chapter, "Your First Love," for more knowledge.) He wants our life to reflect Jesus Christ.

They were radiant. Do you want to reflect the love and radiance of the Lord? Right now is your chance. Don't blow it, my brother in Christ. Don't turn away. Turn to Him and Him alone. Right now! "They *looked to Him* and **were radiant,** and their faces shall never be ashamed" (Ps. 34:5).

Practical Application

Hearer of the Word and not a doer. At the end of each chapter there will be either a test or practical application. "For if anyone is a **hearer of the Word and not a doer,** he is like a man who looks at his natural face in a mirror; but one who looks intently at the perfect law, the law of liberty, and abides by it, not having become a forgetful hearer but an effectual doer, this man shall be blessed in what he does" (James 1:23–24).

Against Thee, Thee only, I have sinned. The first thing we need in order to rebuild upon the Rock is to become aware of our sinfulness before God. Unless we understand that we are sinners, we cannot take another step. As you were reading this chapter, were you made aware of your sin, or did you make excuses and blame others? My friend, if you are imitating the world by rationalizing your sin and making excuses, while at the same time quickly pointing out the sin of others, you most certainly are headed for spiritual death. When you read these pages, did you think of how other men you know have fallen in certain areas but never really took a hard look at yourself?

If you are under strong conviction, please stop now, get on your knees, and ask the Holy Spirit to show **you** and convict **you** of **your** sinfulness before God. Ask Him to reveal to you your offenses through His eyes and the eyes of others whom you have offended. Begin by praying this prayer:

"Be gracious to me, O God, according to Thy lovingkindness; according to the greatness of Thy compassion blot out my transgressions. Wash me thoroughly from my iniquity, and cleanse me from my sin. For I know my transgressions, and my sin is ever before me. **Against Thee, Thee only, I have sinned,** and done what is evil in Thy sight, so that Thou art justified when Thou dost speak, and blameless when Thou dost judge. Create in me a clean heart, O God, and renew a steadfast spirit within me. Do not cast me away from Thy presence, and do not take Thy Holy Spirit from me. Restore to me the joy of Thy salvation, and sustain me with a willing spirit. Then I will teach transgressors Thy ways, and sinners will be converted to Thee. Deliver me from bloodguiltiness, O God, Thou God of my salvation; then my tongue will joyfully sing of Thy righteousness. O Lord, open my lips, that my mouth may declare Thy praise. For Thou dost not delight in sacrifice, otherwise I would give it; Thou art not pleased with burnt offering. The sacrifices of God are a broken spirit; a broken and a contrite heart, O God, Thou wilt not despise" (Ps. 51:1–17).

Confess your sins. Once we have confessed our sin before God, we need to admit we have fallen short, or confess our faults to one another. Again, if our conscience is seared (1 Tim. 4:2), we will minimize our sin and we will *never* have victory over sin in our life! "Therefore, **confess your sins** to one another, and pray for one another, so that *you may be healed*. The effective prayer of a righteous man can accomplish much" (James 5:16).

His Word healed them. It is God's Word that will change us and heal us. "He sent **His Word and healed them,** and delivered them from their destructions" (Ps. 107:20). We must begin to renew our minds. Using 3x5 cards, write down the verses from this chapter that have brought about the greatest conviction in your heart. Then, do the same with each of the following chapters. Keep these cards in your pocket and bring them out regularly as the Holy Spirit prompts you. If you are not being prompted, pray that you will be.

With God. We must not operate in the flesh. We must work "with God," moving in His direction by allowing His Spirit to direct us to do what we ought. "With men this is impossible, but **with God** all things are possible" (Matt. 19:26). "But He said, 'The things impossible with men are possible **with God**'" (Luke 18:27). Any other plan will eventually wear us out and cause us to give up. "For the one who sows to his own flesh shall from the **flesh reap corruption,** but the one who sows to the Spirit shall from the Spirit reap eternal life" (Gal. 6:8). Operating in the flesh will only bring about a temporary external change versus a permanent internal change. ". . . For the things which are seen are **temporal,** but the things which are *not seen* are **eternal"** (2 Cor. 4:18).

A righteous man falls. Be aware that stumbling and failure will come, but *you must get back up.* "For **a righteous man falls** seven times, and *rises again* . . ." (Prov. 24:16). Every man will fall, but what you do *when* you fall divides the righteous from the unrighteous! The entire tenth chapter of this book is dedicated to making us keenly aware of the trials of Christian life. But for now, let us be aware that we may be held with the cords of our sin until we hate it so much that we will be forever cured of these temptations. "His own iniquities will capture the wicked, and he will be held with the cords of his sin" (Prov. 5:22). Again, we must work "with God" because He knows best. "Woe to the one who quarrels with his Maker—an earthenware vessel among the vessels of earth! Will the clay say to the potter, 'What are you doing?'" (Isa. 45:9).

Boast about my weaknesses. And finally, once we, "through Christ," have gained the sweet victory, we must share our testimony with all those whom He brings into our lives. Some find it easy to share Jesus Christ as their Savior with every person they meet. If you are on fire like that for the Lord, praise God! Others fail to share their salvation with anyone; it is their little secret with the Lord. However, God will bring men into your life who will open a door for you to share what Christ has done for you. ". . . But sanctify Christ as *Lord in your hearts,* **always being ready** to make a defense to everyone *who asks you to give an account for the hope that is in you,* yet with gentleness and reverence . . ." (1 Pet. 3:15). Will you open your mouth? Let us retrain our lips to share God's power over sin by humbling ourselves and boasting about our weaknesses. "And He has said to me, 'My grace is sufficient for you, for power is perfected in weakness.' Most gladly, therefore, I will rather **boast about my weaknesses,** that the *power of Christ may dwell in me"* (2 Cor. 12:9).

Let the Power of Christ Dwell in Me . . . Amen and Amen!

Personal commitment: To begin to build or rebuild my home on the Rock. "Based on what I have learned from God's Word, I commit to confess my lukewarmness toward Christ and to take the proper steps to renew my mind. I commit to allow the Lord to work through me so that I may gain the sweet victory over my sinful life. I also commit to give God the praise and honor He deserves by sharing my testimony with others."

Date: _____ Signed: _____

Homework

His Word healed them. It is God's Word that will change and heal us. "He sent **His Word and healed them,** and delivered them from their destructions" (Ps. 107:20). Therefore, we must begin to renew our minds.

1. **3x5 cards.** On 3x5 cards, write down the verses from this chapter (and the following chapters) that have brought about the greatest conviction in your heart. *I write down several verses on each card and hold them together with a rubber band.* Keep these cards with you and bring them out **regularly** as the Holy Spirit prompts you. If you are not being prompted, pray that God will remind you.

2. **Healing.** If you do **not** notice a change in the way you're thinking, or you are not healing in a particular area, then it is important that you pray for the Lord to reveal what is blocking your healing. Sometimes it's wise to seek the counsel of an older man. *Often, when I have had an opportunity to confess a weakness, fear, or unconfessed sin, I finally experience a breakthrough!*

3. Share the wisdom from *this* chapter with *one other man* who seems to be searching for Truth.

Test Your Wisdom

1. Jesus warned us of spiritual leaders who would try to deceive us. How did He say that we will know who are the ravenous wolves? _____ (Matt. 7:15–16).

2. Why should we be careful to never overlook, water down, or take out of context Scripture to justify our opposing views or to justify sin? Because every Word of God is _____. We also should never _____ to His Words, lest the Lord _____ you, and you be proved a _____ (Prov. 30:5–6).

3. We need to renew our mind to line it up with what God says about everything. What is our promise *if* we meditate day and night on His Word? We will be like a tree_____ _____ by streams of water, that we will yield _____ and in whatever we do we will _____ (Ps. 1:23).

4. We never need to fear the Truth since it will set us _____ (John 8:31–32).

5. "He sent _____ _____ and _____ _____, and _____ _____ from all their destructions" (Ps. 107:20).

6. We must not just be hearers of the Word of God, we must be _____ (James 1:23).

7. God said He prefers us to be cold or hot, not **lukewarm;** but, if we are lukewarm, He warns us that He will _____ _____ _____ of His mouth (Rev. 3:15–16).

*The answers to Homework questions are at the end of this workbook.

Chapter 2

Your First Love

*But I have this against you,
that you have left your first love.
—Revelation 2:4*

Have you left your first love? Who is your first love? Is your wife, your work, your hobby, your children, or your sports your first love? Who or what is really *first* in your life? "He who loves father or mother more than Me is not worthy of Me; and he who loves son or daughter more than Me is not worthy of Me" (Matt. 10:37). The Scripture in Revelation says: "But I have this against you, that you have left your **first love**" (Rev. 2:4).

What is Jesus saying to us? He is saying that any time you put someone or something ahead of your love and your relationship with Him, you are not worthy of His love.

Seek first. You are to put Him first in your priorities, first in your day, and first in your heart. "But seek **first** His kingdom and His righteousness; and all these things shall be added unto you" (Matt. 6:33). What is the first thing you do each morning? What *should* you do first? Ask yourself these questions: Are the things that I'm doing of eternal value? Will what I do today help to increase His kingdom? Do I seek after **His** righteousness? Remember, our righteousness is like dirty rags (Isa. 64:6).

What happens when you put someone ahead of the Lord? What does He do to draw you back to Him? "Thou hast removed my acquaintances far from me; Thou hast made me an object of loathing to them" (Ps. 88:8). "Thou hast removed lover and friend far from me; my acquaintances are in darkness" (Ps. 88:18). Some men have lost their wives to another man, lost their children, and lost their jobs.

Whom do you want to please? Our goal should be to please *the Lord,* rather than to try to please our wives or anyone else in our lives. "When a man's ways are pleasing to the Lord, He makes even his enemies to be at peace with him" (Prov. 16:7). "Delight yourself in the Lord, and He will give you the desires of your heart" (Prov. 31:30).

Why not try to please my wife? That was man's first mistake. Let's look at some Scriptural facts: "When the woman saw that the tree was good for food, and that it was a delight to the eyes, and that the tree was desirable to make one wise, she took from its fruit and ate, and *she gave* also to her husband *with her,* and he ate" (Gen. 3:6). Why would Adam eat the fruit when he knew it was wrong?

Man sinned knowingly. Adam heard directly from God. In Genesis 2:17, God commanded man not to eat the fruit. The woman was not created until Genesis 2:22. We never see God commanding Eve directly. Eve was deceived; Adam knowingly sinned.

Woman was created for man. God gave Adam dominion over all living things in the garden, including Eve. Eve was created for Adam, not the other way around. "For indeed man was not created for the woman's sake, but woman for the man's sake" (1 Cor. 11:9). "Then the Lord God said, 'It is not good for the man to be alone; I will make him a helper suitable for him'" (Gen. 2:18).

Adam never stopped Eve, even though he was *with* her. ". . . And *she gave* also to her husband *with her,* and he ate" (Gen. 3:6). Why? Why did he also eat the fruit? Is it possible that Adam was trying to please Eve? Maybe he just wanted to let her do what she wanted, even though in his heart he knew it was a mistake? What about you? Do you do things just to please your wife without stopping to consider what God thinks about it? Do you many times let your wife (or your children) do things that your heart tells you are not right?

What does a man often do when things go wrong? Once caught, what does Adam do? "And the man said, 'The woman whom Thou gavest to be with me, she gave me from the tree, and I ate'" (Gen. 3:12). He blames Eve. It was her fault! The bottom line is that he also blames God! Well, there is no doubt Eve was wrong to eat the fruit. But why isn't she blamed for the fall of man if she ate it first and then gave it to Adam? Why is sin not passed down through her? "Therefore, just as through one **man** *sin entered into the world,* and death through sin, and so death spread to all men, because all sinned . . ." (Rom. 5:12).

Eve was deceived but Adam knowingly sinned. Adam was ultimately responsible and accountable before God. "Then to Adam He said, 'Because you have *listened to the voice of your wife,* and have eaten from the tree about *which I commanded you,* saying, 'You shall not eat from it . . .'" (Gen. 3:17). Men, we are ultimately responsible and accountable to God when we *"have listened to the voice of our wives"* and it was contrary to what we knew was right. When God's Word says something else, or He has directed us differently, we are to move in the *right* direction. The bottom line is for us to do what is right. "Our way" or "her way" doesn't matter; it must be God's way.

We are to be our wives' protectors. We were put over our wives for their protection, even though they may many times feel it is their curse! Because it was the woman who was deceived, God felt she was not safe from Satan's deceptive schemes and He assigned man to rule over her. Again, it is deception that we are to protect our wives from. "And it was *not Adam* who was **deceived,** but the *woman* being *quite* **deceived,** fell into transgression" (1 Tim. 2:14). As husbands and heads of our households, we are to protect our wives spiritually.

Spiritual Protection

Women in the church. "Let the *women* keep silent in the churches; for they are not permitted to speak, but let them subject themselves, just as the Law also says. And if they desire to *learn anything,* let them ask their **own husbands** at home; for it is improper for a woman to speak in church" (1 Cor. 14:34–35). Why do church services and Christian seminars seem to attract more women than men? Where are the men? If they are not in attendance, who then is leading? Men, are we capable of answering our wives' spiritual questions? Maybe they're not asking us questions because of the poor example we have set as Christian leaders.

Older women encouraging the younger women. Women need to be in their homes teaching and encouraging younger women, not in church leadership. "Older women . . . encourage the young women to love their husbands, to love their children, to be sensible, pure, workers at home, kind, being subject to their own husbands, that the Word of God may not be dishonored" (Titus 2:3).

Captivating weak women. From whom is your wife getting instruction? An older woman, or another man? What is being taught? Things that you should be teaching her? "For among them are those who enter into households and *captivate* **weak women** weighed down with sins, led on by various impulses, **always learning** and never able to come to the knowledge of the Truth" (2 Tim. 3:6). Certainly there are things your wife needs to learn from an older woman, such as the things in Titus 2:3–5, but the husband should teach his wife and be the spiritual leader in his marriage. Are you prepared for such a challenge? Have you turned over *your* spiritual leadership to the Bible study teacher and to your preacher on Sunday?

Weak women?!! If a preacher ever stood up in the pulpit and insinuated that women were weak, it would possibly divide the church. The feminist movement has indoctrinated all of us so much that we are offended by such implications. Yet God's Word says in 1 Peter 3:7, "You *husbands* likewise, live with your wives in an *understanding* way, as with a **weaker vessel,** *since she is a woman* . . ." Are we to deny the way God created a woman? If we do, we will also treat her as an equal—equally tough! But God's Word says we are to live with her differently, "in an understanding way, as with a weaker vessel, since she is a woman."

Honor her as a fellow heir. If your wife is weaker, does that make her a lower class citizen in the kingdom of God? Let's read the entire verse: "You husbands likewise, live with your wives in an understanding way, as with a weaker vessel, since she is a woman, and *grant her honor* as a **fellow heir** of the *grace of life,* so that your prayers may not be hindered" (1 Pet. 3:7). God also tells us our punishment for not granting our wives honor—our prayers will be hindered, if we do not live with her in an understanding way, as with a weaker vessel, since she is a woman!

Dressed as a harlot. "And behold, a woman comes to meet him, *dressed as a harlot* and cunning of heart. She is boisterous and rebellious; *her feet do not remain at home;* she is now in the streets, now in the squares, and lurks by every corner" (Prov. 7:10–12). Men, do you allow your daughters to dress as harlots? Do you ask your wife to dress as one, maybe in the bedroom, to satisfy the lusts of the flesh that were awakened during your dating days? Do you pressure her to look and act like the centerfolds that your eyes lusted upon before you were a Christian?

Held with the cords of your sin. Are you still held by the cords of your sin? "His own iniquities will capture the wicked, and he will be **held with the cords of his sin.** He will die for lack of instruction, and in the greatness of his folly he will go astray" (Prov. 5:22). Men, you need to get right before God. The verse just prior to this says, "For the ways of a man are before the eyes of the Lord, and **He watches** *all* his paths" (Prov. 5:21). Get it right with God. Consider confessing it to another Christian brother and have him pray for you. "Therefore, confess your sins to one another, and pray for one another, so that you may be healed. The effective prayer of a righteous man can accomplish much" (James 5:16). Then treat your wife the way God intended and release her from the bondage of *your* past sins.

I married a harlot. Maybe you would say that she was a harlot when you married her. Once you get it right with God, share with her your confession. This may lead her to repent as well. "For the unbelieving husband is sanctified through his wife, and the unbelieving wife is sanctified through her believing husband; for otherwise your children are unclean, but now they are holy" (1 Cor. 7:14). "Husbands, love your wives, just as Christ also loved the church and gave Himself up for her; that He might sanctify her, having *cleansed her* by the washing of water **with the Word,** that He might present to Himself the church in all her glory, having no spot or wrinkle or any such thing; but that *she should be holy and blameless"* (Eph. 5:25–27). God can give you both a clean start. Go to Him, confess, repent, and begin anew.

Knowing good and evil. "And the serpent said to the woman, 'You surely shall not die! For God knows that in the day you eat from it your *eyes will be opened,* and you will be like God, **knowing good and evil.'** When the woman saw that the tree was good for food, and that it was a *delight to the eyes,* and that the tree was *desirable to make one wise,* she took from its fruit and ate, and she gave also to her husband with her, and he ate" (Gen. 3:4–5). Do you want your daughters to know **good and evil?** Women seem especially drawn to seek after knowledge. But Scripture tells us that since the woman was deceived by the serpent, she needs the man's protection. Should we send our daughters to college where they will be taught the knowledge of good *and evil?* What is the ultimate reason for sending a daughter to college? What might be the consequences of that decision? It is a decision that should be weighed and prayed about earnestly, since your daughter's future is in your hands. What about our sons? Should they attend college?

Higher learning. Charles Darwin graduated from Bible college with a degree in theology (the only degree he ever obtained), but after reading a book by Charles Lawton, his faith was destroyed. We are well aware of the destruction Darwin has had on the faith of others. Can we then justify anyone going on to "higher learning" only to be indoctrinated into evil and lies? God tells us specifically what to do when confronted with evil. "And let him **turn away** from evil and do good . . ." (1 Pet. 3:11).

No worthless thing. God tells us in Psalm 101:3, "I will set no worthless thing before my eyes; I hate the work of those who fall away; it shall not fasten its grip on me." There is something very interesting in that verse. Did you notice it? Even setting *worthless* things before us can cause us to "fall away"! Could this have something to do with why there is so much rebellion in our children who are taught, day after day, worthless things, lies and evil! As the heads of our households, and those who will ultimately give an account to the Lord, God has put us in charge to protect our families. We should rethink a decision to send our children to any school that teaches worthless and evil things. And speaking of worthless things, could the Psalmist also have been prophesying about television, movies, and video games? Are we protecting our families and ourselves from these things that can cause us to fall away from God?

Wives going back to school. And what about our wives going back to college? Why are they going? Some want to go because they are bored. Many want to finish their degrees, and some who are working at menial jobs want to be able to have better jobs. Many just like education. But too many women who have come to Restore Ministries tell of how they fell into adultery in the workplace or on college campuses, and all were Christian women! Several, after being on campus, became dissatisfied with their home lives and ended up in mental and emotional conflicts. "For let not that man expect that he will receive anything from the Lord, being a **double-minded** man, unstable in all his ways" (James 1:7–8). "But let the brother of **humble circumstances** *glory* in his *high position; and let the rich man glory in his humiliation, because like flowering grass he will pass away*" (James 1:9–10). "No one can serve two masters; for either he will hate the one and love the other, or he will hold to one and despise the other. You cannot serve God and mammon" (Matt. 6:24). (In the Greek, mammon or mammon which means confidence, i.e., wealth personified.)

Talents to glorify God. If your wife feels stifled in her present circumstances, she may need encouragement as well as time to pursue learning that will ultimately "glorify God." There are talents that are found in the Proverbs 31 woman. There's also a list in Titus 2. What are your wife's gifts and talents? Make sure that **you** as her husband *allow and encourage her* to use or learn talents that will enable her to teach her daughters or other women. Have you been critical or made fun of her attempts to try a new recipe or bake bread from scratch? Have you mocked her creations when she attempted to sew? Maybe you were foolish enough to tell her that she could have bought it much cheaper. What was your reaction to the new wreath that she made for your front door or the way she rearranged the furniture? Do you thank her for the time and effort it takes to drive around to yard sales and look for bargains that save your family money?

Seek love. You may think that she is wasting time and money doing these things. She may be, but there is a loving way to handle everything. Remember, "Love never fails . . ."! (1 Cor. 13:8). Speak kindly, and then give her a specific amount of money to use when shopping. Encourage her to find women she knows who can teach her some of the things she needs to learn, like sewing, baking, and decorating. Again, remember to give her a budget of *time* and *money*. Women are naturally creative and they love a challenge. If you've been overly strict or stingy because of her past mistakes, give her some freedom. If she has been allowed to run free and there has been no accountability, tighten up a bit and begin to protect. If you don't, you will breed independence and rebellion in your daughters.

Cause to stumble. Also, women envy those women who can get away with everything; don't cause others to stumble because you are too lazy or too weak to handle possible conflict. "It would be better for him if a millstone were hung around his neck and he were thrown into the sea, than that he should cause one of these little ones to stumble" (Luke 17:2).

Restrain *her?* You may be saying, "You don't know my wife! I could never take charge of our home!" God knows your wife. "A constant dripping on a day of steady rain and a contentious woman are alike; He who would restrain her restrains the wind, and grasps oil with his right hand" (Prov. 27:15–16). But men, it's time to take control of our homes, our children, and our country. If we do what is right and let the Lord deal with our wives' reactions, we can turn our homes around. Remember, we will be held accountable for what we do or don't do. Your wife will be held accountable for submitting to God. Standing firm in our faith and doing everything **in love** will make all the difference. "Be on the alert, **stand firm in the faith,** *act like men,* be strong" (1 Cor. 16:13).

If You Love Me

After you put God first in your life, and begin to obey God's Word, then you must cast down the false doctrine that says, "You are saved by grace, so it's really okay to sin. We are no longer under the Law." Let's search the Scriptures:

Do your deeds deny Him? "They profess to know God, but their **deeds deny Him,** being detestable and disobedient and worthless for any good deed" (Titus 1:16).

Do you do what His Word says? "Why do you call Me Lord, and do not do what I say?" (Luke 6:46).

Are we to continue in sin? "What shall we say then? **Are we to continue in sin** that grace might increase? May it never be! How shall we who died to sin still live in it?" (Rom. 6:1–2).

Faith without works is dead. "What use is it, my brethren, if a man says he has faith, but he has no works? Can that faith save him?" (James 2:14). "For just as the body without the spirit is dead, so also **faith without works is dead**" (James 2:26).

I never knew you. Many believe that you can live any way you wish and then enter into heaven once you die; this is simply not true. "Many will say to Me on that day, 'Lord, Lord, did we not prophesy in Your name, and in Your name cast out demons, and in Your name perform many miracles?' And then I will declare to them, **'I never knew you;** depart from me, you who practice lawlessness'" (Matt. 7:22–23).

Confess your sins. If you have continued to sin, thinking you are saved by grace even when you walk in disobedience, do as Scripture says: "Therefore, **confess your sins** one to another, and pray for one another, so that you may be healed" (James 5:16).

Obedience to His Word

"**Wisdom** shouts in the street, she lifts her voice in the square. At the head of the noisy streets she cries out; at the entrance to the gate in the city, she utters her sayings: 'How long, O naive ones, will you love simplicity. And scoffers delight themselves in scoffing, and fools hate knowledge. *Turn* to my **reproof,** behold, I will pour out my spirit on you; I will make my words known to you. Because I called and you refused; I stretched out my hand, and no one paid attention; and you neglected all my counsel, and did not want my reproof; I will even **laugh at your calamity;** I will **mock** *when* **your dread comes,** when your dread comes on like a storm, and your calamity comes on like a whirlwind, when distress and anguish come on you.'"Then they will call on me but I will not answer; they will seek me diligently, but they will not find me, **because they hated knowledge, and did not choose the fear of the Lord.** They would not accept my counsel, they spurned all my reproof. So they shall eat of the fruit of their own way, and be satiated with their own devices. For the waywardness of the naive shall kill them, and the complacency of fools shall destroy them. **But he who listens to me shall live securely, and shall be at ease from the dread of evil**'" (Prov. 1:20–33).

Obedience comes from the *heart*. ". . . You became obedient from the **heart** to that form of teaching to which you were committed" (Rom. 6:17). And again, "For God sees not as man sees, for man looks at the outward appearance, but the Lord looks at the heart" (1 Sam. 16:7).

Obedience needs *testing*. "Do not be surprised at the fiery trial which comes upon you for your **testing**" (1 Pet. 4:12).

Obedience *purifies* your soul. "Since you have in obedience to the Truth, **purified your souls**" (1 Pet. 1:22).

Obedience gives *testimony* of who your Father is. "Obey My voice and I will be your God, and you will be My people; and you will walk in all the way in which I command you, that it may be well with you. Yet they did not obey or incline their ear, but walked in their own counsels and in the stubbornness of their evil heart, and went backward and not forward" (Jer. 7:23–24).

Your disobedience actually *praises* the wicked. "Those who forsake the law *praise the wicked,* but those who keep the law strive with them" (Prov. 28:4).

The prayers of the disobedient go unheard. "He who turns away his ear from listening to the law, even his prayer is an abomination" (Prov. 28:9).

Our Example Is Christ

He was obedient *even unto death*. "He humbled Himself by becoming obedient to the point of death, even death on a cross" (Phil. 2:5–11).

He *learned* obedience. "Although He was a Son, He *learned obedience* from the things which He suffered" (Heb. 5:7–10).

He was obedient and submissive to His authority. "My Father, if it is possible, let this cup pass from Me; yet not as I will, but Thou wilt. . . . My Father if this cannot pass away unless I drink it, Thy will be done" (Matt. 26:39, 42).

The secret to success. "All the paths of the Lord are lovingkindness and truth to those *who keep His covenant and His testimonies*. For Thy name's sake, O Lord, pardon my iniquity, for it is great. Who is the man who fears the Lord? He will instruct him in the way he should choose. His soul will abide in prosperity, and his descendants will inherit the land. The *secret of the Lord* is for *those who fear Him*" (Ps. 25:10–11).

Foolishness to him. You may be having trouble taking this all in. But I guarantee that you will never understand until you *first* obey. "But a natural man does not accept the things of the Spirit of God; for they are **foolishness to him**, and he cannot understand them, because they are spiritually appraised. But he who is spiritual appraises all things . . ." (1 Cor. 2:14–15).

Self-condemned. Unfortunately, most dispute or argue the true meaning of Scripture, which God says is to their *own* destruction. "But shun foolish controversies and genealogies and strife and disputes about the Law; for they are unprofitable and worthless. Reject a factious man after a first and second warning, knowing that such a man is perverted and is sinning, being **self-condemned**" (Titus 3:9–11).

Turn aside to myths. Instead of searching for the Truth, some want others to agree with their false ideas or compromising decisions: "But wanting to have their ears tickled, they will accumulate for themselves teachers in accordance to their own desires; and will **turn aside to myths**" (2 Tim. 4:3–4).

Obedience to Be Delivered from Our Trials

Remember that only the *blameless* will be delivered. "He who walks blamelessly will be delivered, but he who is crooked will fall all at once" (Prov. 28:18).

God watches and blesses what you do. "Thou dost recompense a man *according to his work*" (Ps. 62:12).

Watch your folly. "But let them not turn back to **folly**. Surely His *salvation* is *near* to those who fear Him" (Ps. 85:8–9).

Wisdom is needed. "He who walks **wisely** will be delivered" (Prov. 28:26).

Hear and fear. "The one who despises the Word will be in debt to it, but the one who **fears** the commandment will be rewarded" (Prov. 13:13).

Seek and follow wisdom. "He who trusts in his own heart is a fool, but he who walks wisely will be delivered" (Prov. 28:26).

Be self-disciplined in your obedience to His Word. "Do not be as the horse or as the mule which have no understanding, whose trappings include bit and bridle to hold them in check, otherwise they will not come near to you" (Ps. 32:9).

If you don't obey, He will discipline you. "The Lord has **disciplined me** severely, but He has not given me over to death" (Ps. 118:18).

God is faithful to His Word. "If his sons forsake My law, and do not walk in My judgments, if they violate My statutes, and do not keep My commandments, then I will visit their transgressions with a rod, and their iniquity with stripes" (Ps. 89:30–34).

Let us all bow our heads and pray Psalm 51 aloud: "Wash me thoroughly from my iniquity, and cleanse me from my sin. For I know my transgressions, and my sin is ever before me. Against Thee, Thee only, have I sinned, and done what is evil in Thy sight. Create in me a clean heart, O God, and renew a steadfast spirit within me. Do not take Thy Holy Spirit from me. Restore to me the joy of Thy salvation, and sustain me with a willing spirit. Then I will teach transgressors Thy ways, and sinners will be converted to Thee. The sacrifices of God are a broken spirit; a broken and contrite heart, O God, Thou will not despise."

May God be with you as you strive to be more like Christ!

Personal commitment: To put the Lord first in my life. "Based on what I have learned in Scripture, I commit to seek **first** His kingdom and His righteousness. I will show the Lord, and others, my commitment to Him by my obedience to His Word."

Date: _____ Signed: _____

"Not that I have already obtained it, or have already become perfect, but I press on, in order that I may lay hold of that for which also I was laid hold of by Christ Jesus" (Phil. 3:12).

Homework

His Word healed them. Once again, it is God's Word that will change and heal you. "He sent **His Word and healed them,** and delivered them from their destructions" (Ps. 107:20). Again, you must begin to renew your mind. Have you noticed a change in the way you're thinking? Are others commenting that you are not the same?

1. **3x5 cards.** Once more gather your 3x5 cards and write down the verses from *this* chapter that have touched your heart. Are you keeping these cards with you and bringing them out *regularly* as the Holy Spirit prompts you? Are you responding to God's promptings when He reminds you to read them?

2. **Healing.** Has God healed you in a particular area? If not, as I said before, it is important that you pray for the Lord to reveal what is blocking your healing. Have you sought the counsel of another man? Have you confessed to weaknesses, fears, or unconfessed sins? If you did, you should experience a breakthrough soon!

3. Share the wisdom from *this* chapter with *one other man* who seems to be searching for the Truth.

Test Your Wisdom

1. How were we freed from being slaves of sin? You became _____ from the _____ to the teaching of which you were _____ (Rom. 6:17).

2. Who is not worthy of the Lord? Those who _____ their _____, _____, _____, or _____ more than Him (Matt.10:37).

3. What does obedience to God's Word have to do with loving Him? Our deeds are _____, _____ and _____ of good deeds (Titus 1:16).

4. Who is our example for obedience? _____ (Phil. 2:8).

5. How did He become obedient? _____ (Heb. 5:8).

6. How can I live a blameless life and walk with integrity in my heart? By not placing a _____ thing before my eyes (Ps. 101:3), such as television, newspapers, sports pages, sports magazines, or worthless books, in lieu of (instead of) reading God's Word.

7. Who will you blame if you try to please your wife? _____ (Gen. 3:12).

The answers to Homework questions are at the end of this workbook.

Prayer Tree–A Faith Builder

A Prayer Tree is a tool for a family to use to show God's faithfulness. It has many benefits to spiritual growth that you will begin to see in yourself, as well as in your children. Make one and place it in your family room or by your kitchen table. It can be used as an evangelism tool as you share with visitors to your home how God has answered your prayers. Don't forget to offer to pray for their special needs. The Prayer Tree will help you:

1. To remember to pray.
2. To see God working in our lives and the lives of others.
3. To remember His past blessings—and count them "one by one" when you feel defeated.
4. To remember to thank Him for each trial.
5. To remember not to worry about the cares of the world.
6. To know why we need His Word to stand on.
7. To build your faith and your children's faith.

To assemble: You'll need a poster board, construction paper, scissors, glue, and markers. Then explain the following to your children:

1. Flower: "Prayer Request." Write one request on each flower. (Include the prayer requests of family and friends.)
    a. Every fruit begins as a flower.
    b. On the request make sure you include the date.
2. The Sun: "Son of God." Write Jesus, Lord, or Son on the sun.
    a. The Son gives us light and strength.
    b. Without the Son, we (the tree) will die.
3. Clouds: "Satan." Write on each raindrop the trial or affliction that your family is experiencing.
    a. Rain is necessary for growth and it is only temporary!

b. Rain could be finances, illness, things that are broken, lost or stolen, a job, or relationship problem.

c. In life we have trials, tests, and temptations that help us to seek the Lord.

4. Weeds: "Sin in our life."

    a. Repeated sin—when we don't pull it out at the roots.

    b. Unconfessed sin.

    c. Worries in our life.

    d. All the things that will choke out the blessings.

5. Fertilizer: "Scripture." Write Scripture verses on the grass area.

    a. Gives strength to the tree.

    b. God's Word is our strength.

    c. It's at the root and foundation of our faith.

6. Fruit: "Answered Prayer." Write on each fruit God's answer to your prayer.

    a. You have to wait for fruit to come in its "season."

    b. God says you will know us by our fruit.

    c. You will see how He blesses you beyond what you have even asked.

    d. Date the flower and the fruit to see how we must learn to "wait on the Lord"!

"But seek ye first the kingdom of God and His righteousness, and all these things will be added unto you" (Matt. 6:33).
"Delight yourself in the Lord and He will give you the desires of your heart"! (Ps. 37:4)

Daily Prayers

It is always best to begin your day with prayer.

"Wash me thoroughly from my iniquity, and cleanse me from my sins. For I know my transgressions, and my sin is ever before me. Against Thee, Thee only, have I sinned, and done what is evil in Thy sight, so that Thou art justified when Thou dost speak, and blameless when Thou dost judge.... Create in me a clean heart, O God, and renew a steadfast spirit within me. Do not cast me away from Thy presence, and do not take Thy Holy Spirit from me. Restore to me the joy of Thy salvation, and sustain in me a willing spirit. Then, I will teach transgressors Thy ways, and sinners will be converted to Thee" *Amen.* (Ps. 51:2–4, 10–13).

As you read the following Scriptures from God's Word, highlight these with different colors: pink for women, green for children, blue for men, and yellow for everything else that the Lord shows you. **Caution:** These Scriptures are for us, as men, and are to be used for our prayers only—not to find fault in our wives! Ask the **Lord** to show *you* what *you* need to learn from His precepts. Psalm 119:15 says, "I will meditate on Thy precepts and regard Thy ways."

Sunday	Read Genesis 2:18–25 and 3:14–19.
Monday	Read Ephesians 5:25–33.
Tuesday	Read 1 Corinthians 13 and Colossians 3:19.
Wednesday	Read Proverbs 5.
Thursday	Read 1 Peter 3:7–12 and 1 Peter 2:21–25.
Friday	Read 1 Corinthians 7:1–16.
Saturday	Read Proverbs 7.

You must also be faithful to place a "hedge of thorns" around your loved ones: "I ask you, dear heavenly Father, to rebuke and to bind Satan in the name and through the blood of the Lord Jesus Christ. I ask you, dear Father, to build a hedge of thorns around (name) so that, if anyone is of wrong influence on (name), they will lose interest in (him/her) and leave. I base this prayer on the command of your Word, for it is written: 'What God has joined together, let no man separate.' I thank You for hearing and answering my prayer. Amen."

Chapter 3

Blessed Are the Meek

*Blessed are the meek,
for they shall inherit the earth.*
—*Matthew 5:5*

Meek, in this day and age, is regarded as weak. Yet Jesus told us, "Blessed are the meek"! We husbands deal with our wives in basically two ways, either apathetically or using the "tough love" approach. In this chapter we will search God's Word to find out the Truth regarding *tough love*.

Love is . . . God gives us a description of love. See if you can find the word "tough" or any word even remotely similar. "Love is **patient,** love is kind, and is not jealous; love does not brag and is not arrogant, does not act unbecomingly; it does not seek its own, is **not provoked, does not take into account a wrong suffered,** does not rejoice in unrighteousness, but rejoices with the truth; bears all things, believes all things, hopes all things, endures all things. Love never fails . . ." (1 Cor. 13:4–8).

I command you. Another very popular statement in the church today is *love is a choice*. Read with me the following verse to see if God says we can "choose" to love. Or does God command that we do so, as followers of Christ? "This I **command** you, that you *love one another"* (John 15:17).

Do good, bless. Sometimes when our wives act in an inappropriate way, especially if they push or manipulate us, we put them in their place. This is not the time to show them love, or is it? "But I say to you who hear, **love your enemies,** *do good* to those who hate you, *bless* those who curse you, *pray* for those who mistreat you" (Luke 6:27–28). The Lord gave us three choices when dealing with those we would rather be tough with: do good unto them, bless them, or pray for them.

Love your enemies. In this passage God is even clearer. He actually admonishes those who only love the lovable. "But I say to you, **love your enemies,** and pray for those who persecute you . . . for if you love those who love you, what reward have you? Do not even the tax-gatherers do the same?" (Matt. 5:44–46).

Overcome evil with good. In the book *Love Must Be Tough,* the author tells us to cause a crisis (in other words, to take matters into our own hands). However, the Scriptures tell us that we are to leave room for His wrath. "Rejoicing in hope, persevering in tribulation, devoted to prayer. Bless those who persecute you; bless and curse not. **Never pay back evil for evil to anyone.** Never take your own revenge, beloved, but leave room for the wrath of God, for it is written, 'Vengeance is Mine, I will repay,' says the Lord. But if your enemy is hungry, feed him, and if thirsty, give him a drink; for in doing so you will heap burning coals upon his head. Do not be overcome by evil, but **overcome evil with good**" (Rom. 12:12, 14, 17, 19, 21).

You are to be perfect. Some authors, and even some pastors, have told us that God doesn't expect us to be perfect, but what did Jesus say? "Therefore, **you are to be perfect,** as your heavenly Father is perfect" (Matt. 5:48).

Kept entrusting Himself. When you feel like lashing back at your wife and you don't, it is very frustrating. Read God's explanation: "For you have been called for this purpose, since Christ also suffered for you, leaving you an example for you to follow in His steps . . . and while being reviled, **He did not revile in return;** while suffering, **He uttered no threats,** but kept entrusting Himself to Him (God) who judges righteously" (1 Pet. 2:21–23).

They shall inherit the earth. Maybe you're afraid that if you don't take matters into your own hands and take a "tough stand," others (even Christians) will tell you that you are a "wimp." Let me remind you who Jesus said are blessed. "**Blessed are the meek,** for they shall inherit the earth" (Matt. 5:5).

Does not achieve. You may recall that Jesus turned over the tables in the temple. Don't use the excuse that therefore *you* have the "right" to be angry with others. God says He is a jealous God; can we then also be jealous? "But let everyone be quick to hear, slow to speak, and slow to anger; for **the anger of man does not achieve the righteousness of God**" (James 1:19–20).

You may *not* do the things that you please. When we impulsively do or say something to our wives that is anything but meek and loving, we are walking in the flesh and are not walking in the Spirit. "But I say, walk in the Spirit, and you will not carry out the desire of the flesh. For the flesh sets its desire against the Spirit, and the Spirit against the flesh; for these are in opposition to one another, so that **you may not do the things that you please** . . . But the fruit of the Spirit is love, joy, peace, patience, kindness, goodness, faithfulness, gentleness, *self-control*" (Gal. 5:16, 17, 22–23). The old saying "do unto others as you would have them do unto you" is based on Luke 6:31. "And just as you want people to treat you, **treat them in the same way.**"

It's the kindness of God. Satan tries to deceive us into believing that confronting, and being unkind and firm, will turn the other person around. If that worked, why would God use kindness to draw us to repentance? Sinners do not go down to the altar to accept the Lord because they think that they are going to be criticized or chastised, do they? "Or do you think lightly of the riches of His kindness and forbearance and patience, not knowing that the **kindness of God** leads you to repentance?" (Rom. 2:4).

***No one* will see the Lord.** Another extremely important reason to be gentle toward your wife and others is that we are to let others see Christ in us. "Pursue peace with all men, and the sanctification without which **no one will see the Lord**" (Heb. 12:14).

Ministry of reconciliation. We are to be ambassadors for Christ in reconciliation. "Now all these things are from God, who reconciled us to Himself through Christ, and gave us the **ministry of reconciliation,** namely, that God was in Christ reconciling the world to Himself, not counting their trespasses against them, and He has committed to us the word of reconciliation. Therefore, we are **ambassadors** for Christ, as though God were entreating through us; we beg you on behalf of Christ, be reconciled to God" (2 Cor. 5:18–20). Speaking kindly and lovingly to our wives is the **only** way to work toward restoration and happiness!

You who are spiritual. This Scripture is the measuring stick for our spirituality. Can you restore your wife in a spirit of gentleness? "Brethren, even if a man is caught in any trespass, you who are spiritual, *restore such a one in a spirit of gentleness;* each one looking to yourself, **lest you too be tempted.** Bear one another's burdens, and thus fulfill the law of Christ" (Gal. 6:1–2). This Scripture warns us to be gentle to others when they have sinned against us or we will be tempted in the same trespass.

Doers of the Word. It's important that we learn the Truth and agree with what we see in Scripture, but we must not stop there. "But prove yourselves **doers of the word,** and not merely hearers who delude themselves. . . . Not having become a forgetful hearer but an effectual doer, this man shall be blessed in what he does" (James 1:22,25). "Therefore, to him who **knows the right thing to do,** and does not do it, to him it is sin" (James 4:17).

Carried away by error. God has warned us that we should not listen to or follow men who tell us something contrary to Scripture. "Be diligent to be found by Him in peace, spotless and blameless, and regard the patience of our Lord to be salvation; just as also our beloved brother Paul, according to the wisdom given him . . . in which are some things hard to understand, which the untaught and unstable distort, as they do also the rest of Scripture, to their own destruction. You therefore, beloved, knowing this beforehand, be on your guard lest, being **carried away by the error of unprincipled men,** you fall from your own steadfastness, but grow in the grace and knowledge of our Lord Jesus Christ" (2 Pet. 3:14–18).

Forgiveness

Many men do not forgive their wives because they don't fully understand the grave consequences of their lack of forgiveness. Let's search the Scriptures to see what God says about forgiving others.

The question we may ask is *why* should we forgive?

Because God forgave us. "And be kind to one another, tender-hearted, forgiving each other, just as God in **Christ also has forgiven you**" (Eph. 4:32).

Because Jesus shed His blood. Jesus shed His blood for the forgiveness of sins. "All things are cleansed with blood, and without the shedding of blood there is no forgiveness" (Heb. 9:22). "For this is my blood of the covenant, which is poured out for many *for* **forgiveness of sins**" (Matt. 26:28).

Comfort her, to relieve the *offender's* sorrow. ". . . You should rather forgive and **comfort** him, lest somehow such a one be overwhelmed by excessive sorrow. Wherefore I urge you to **reaffirm your love** for him" (2 Cor. 2:7–8). This may go against our grain, since many of us may have a history of attacking and trying to find fault with our wives.

Are we ignorant of Satan's schemes? "For if indeed what I have forgiven . . . I did it for your sakes in the presence of Christ, in order that **no advantage be taken of us by Satan;** for we are not ignorant of his schemes" (2 Cor. 2:10–11). Don't allow Satan to take advantage of either one of you by not forgiving your wife.

Forgive her from your heart. God said that He won't forgive you if you don't forgive others. "For if you forgive men for their transgressions, your heavenly Father will also forgive you, but if you do not forgive men, then your Father will **not forgive your transgressions**" (Matt. 6:14–15). "So shall My heavenly Father also do to you, if each of you do not forgive his brother *from your heart*" (Matt. 18:35). (Read all of Matthew 18: 22–35.)

But shouldn't the offender be sorry before I forgive?

Father, forgive them. Those who crucified Jesus neither asked forgiveness nor expressed sorrow for what they were doing or what they had done. As Christians, we are followers of Christ; therefore, we are to follow in His example. **"Father forgive them, for they know not what they do"** (Luke 23:34, KJV). When Stephen was being stoned he cried out just before he died, **"Lord, do not hold this sin against them!"** (Acts 7:60).

But how often does God expect us to forgive another?

Seventy times seven. When Peter asked how often he was to forgive his brother, Jesus said to him, "I do not say to you, up to seven times, but up to **seventy times seven**" (Matt. 18:22). We are to forgive others over and over without end.

Inherit a blessing. Here is a spiritual inheritance God has called us to. "Not returning evil for evil, or insult for insult, but giving a blessing instead; for *you were called* for the very purpose that you might **inherit a blessing**" (1 Pet. 3:9). Those who have ears, let them hear this call.

Forget it. Does forgiveness really mean that I forget that sin, even during an argument? "For I will forgive their iniquity, and their sin I will **remember no more**" (Jer. 31:34). "As far as the east is from the west, so far has He removed our transgressions from us" (Ps. 103:12). Do you bring up things from the past? Don't allow Satan to *use you* to condemn your wife or others who have received forgiveness by bringing up things from their past. But, you say, your wife does it all the time. Then you need to take the lead in this area also, by being a good example and her protector.

How can I *really* forgive as God has asked me to do in His Word?

Who can forgive sins? Only God can help you to forgive. You must *humble* yourself and ask Him to give you the grace. *"Who can forgive sins* but **God alone?"** (Mark 2:7). Even Jesus said it on the cross, and Steven while being stoned, **"Father,** forgive them . . ." Neither man said, **"I** forgive you."

Grace to the humble. How do I get the grace I need? "God is opposed to the proud but gives **grace to the humble.** Humble yourselves therefore under the mighty hand of God that He may exalt you at the proper time" (1 Pet. 5:5–6).

Humbled. How can I gain humility? "Because they had rebelled against the words of God, and spurned the counsel of the Most High. Therefore He **humbled** their heart *with labor;* they stumbled and there was none to help. Then they cried out to the Lord in their trouble; He saved them out of their distresses" (Ps. 107:11–13). "I **humbled** my soul *with fasting;* and my *prayer* kept returning to my bosom" (Ps. 35:13). We can work, fast, and pray to obtain humility. Sometimes the Lord may even use an illness to quiet and humble us.

When do I need to forgive those who have hurt me? Shouldn't I feel convicted first and then do it?

First be reconciled. "If therefore you are presenting your offering at the altar, and there remember that your brother has something against you, leave your offering there before the altar, and go your way; **first be reconciled to your brother,** and then come and present your offering" (Matt. 5:23–24). If you have not forgiven another, especially your wife, you need to ask for her forgiveness.

Bitterness. Not forgiving someone causes bitterness. The definition of bitterness is "poison"! "Let all **bitterness** and wrath and anger . . . be put away from you" (Eph 4:31). Not forgiving another eats away at you, *not the other person*. "The heart knows its own bitterness" (Prov. 14:10). "For He knows the secrets of the heart" (Ps. 44:21).

A Good Conscience

How important is it to have a good conscience? John F. MacArthur, Jr., has written a book entitled, *The Vanishing Conscience*. In it he deals with such topics as "misbehavior being treated as a medical problem" and "living in a guilt-free world."

A good conscience:

Stems from a pure heart. "But the goal of our instruction is love from a **pure** heart and a **good conscience** and a sincere faith" (1 Tim. 1:5).

Has been cleansed by the blood of Christ. "How much more will the blood of Christ . . . cleanse your conscience from dead works to serve the living God?" (Heb. 9:14).

Must be prayed for. "Pray for us, for we are sure that we have a **good conscience,** desiring to conduct ourselves honorably in all things" (Heb. 13:18).

Will keep others from slandering you and will inevitably reflect Christ in you. ". . . And keep a **good conscience** so that in the thing in which you are slandered, those who revile your good behavior in Christ may be put to shame" (1 Pet. 3:16).

Suffer shipwreck. Without a good conscience, you will shipwreck your faith. "Keeping faith and a **good conscience,** which some have rejected and *suffered shipwreck* in regard to their **faith"** (1 Tim. 1:19). Therefore, we must appeal to God for a good conscience. "And corresponding to that, baptism now saves you—not the removal of dirt from the flesh, but an *appeal to God* for a **good conscience**—through the resurrection of Jesus Christ . . ." (1 Pet. 3:21).

Let's begin by praying the following prayer: "Against Thee, Thee only, I have sinned, and done what is evil in Thy sight, so that Thou art justified when Thou dost speak, and blameless when Thou dost judge" (Ps. 51:4). After you have gained a pure conscience from God, you may need to continue the process by reconciling with your wife or others whom you have offended in the past; follow Matthew 5:23–24, which we read: "If therefore you are presenting your offering at the altar, and there remember that your brother has something against you, leave your offering there before the altar, and go your way; first be reconciled to your brother, and then come and present your offering."

A brother offended. When you go to reconcile with your wife, or another, be sure that you follow scriptural guidelines. You may have heard someone say that things were actually worse when they did ask for forgiveness or that it did no good. If you ask for another's forgiveness, but state it the wrong way, it may offend them and make things worse. "A **brother offended** is harder to be won than a strong city" (Prov. 18:19).

Prepare every word. Every word you say must be carefully chosen. **"Every idle word** that men shall speak they *shall give an account* thereof in the day of judgment" (Matt. 12:36). Try writing down what you are going to say. Then read **out loud** what you wrote, putting yourself in the other person's shoes and hearing it from their point of view. Does it sound accusing? Ask God to put the right words in your mouth.

I have sinned. The prodigal son prepared his words when he decided to return home: "I will get up and go to my father, and will say to him, 'Father **I have sinned** against heaven, and in your sight; I am no longer worthy to be called your son; make me as one of your hired men'" (Luke 15:18–19). Praise God—He does raise up those who are bowed down!

With many words. "When there are **many words,** transgression is unavoidable" (Prov. 10:19). "A babbling fool will be thrown down" (Prov. 10:10). Only say what *you* did; don't set the stage with something like, "When you did this, and such and such, well, then I ..."

Agree, agree, agree! "*Agree* with thine adversary quickly, while thou art in the way with him . . ." (Matt. 5:25, KJV). If the other person starts to lash out at you, do not open your mouth except to agree. "And while being reviled, He did not revile in return; while suffering He uttered *no threats* . . ." (1 Pet. 2:23).

Be sweet! Make your words sweet and kind. "**Sweetness** of speech adds persuasiveness" (Prov.16:21). "Pleasant words are a honeycomb, sweet to the soul and healing to the bones" (Prov. 16:24).

Revealing his own mind. Some men who have been guilty of infidelity in their past get right with God and then go to their wives for the purpose of unloading their own guilty feelings, not understanding that their wives will endure tremendous pain following their confession. Don't use repentance as an excuse to dump your guilt onto her. "A fool does not delight in understanding, but only in revealing his own mind" (Prov. 18:2). Confess your sin to another Christian man and make yourself accountable to him. If you are quite sure your wife already knows, suspects, or has confronted you about this sin, by all means confess. Just be discreet and leave the details out. Then be prepared to reap what you have sown by comforting her and holding her up in her pain.

Practice These Things

"For by these He has granted to us His precious and magnificent promises, in order that by them you might become partakers of the divine nature, having escaped the corruption that is in the world by lust. Now for this very reason also, applying all **diligence,** in your **faith** apply **virtue,** and to your virtue apply **knowledge;** and in your knowledge, **self-**

control, and in your self-control, **perseverance,** and in your perseverance, **godliness;** and in your godliness, **brotherly kindness,** and in your brotherly kindness, **love.** For if these qualities are yours and are increasing, they render you neither useless nor unfruitful. . . . For he who lacks these qualities is blind or short-sighted, having forgotten his purification from his former sins. . . For as long as you practice these things, you will never stumble" (2 Pet. 1:4–10).

Apply All Diligence

"He who **diligently** seeks good, seeks favor" (Prov. 11:27).

"Be **diligent** to present yourself approved to God as a workman who does not need to be ashamed, handling accurately the Word of Truth" (2 Tim. 2:15).

"I, therefore, the prisoner of the Lord, entreat you to walk in a manner worthy of the calling with which you have been called, with all humility and gentleness, with patience, showing forbearance to one another in love, being **diligent** to preserve the unity of the Spirit in the bond of peace" (Eph. 4:1–3).

In Your Faith

"**Faith** comes from hearing, and hearing by the Word of Christ" (Rom. 10:17).

"Be on the alert, stand firm in the **faith**" (1 Cor. 16:13).

"In addition to all, taking up the shield of **faith** with which you will be able to extinguish all the flaming missiles of the evil one" (Eph. 6:16).

"For just as the body without the spirit is dead, so also **faith** without works is dead" (James 2:26).

Add Virtue

"Finally brethren, whatever is true, whatever is honorable, whatever is right, whatever is pure, whatever is lovely, whatever is of good report; if there is any **virtue** and if there is any praise, think on these things" (Phil. 4:8).

"According as His divine power hath given unto us all things that pertain unto life and godliness, through the knowledge of Him that hath called us to glory and **virtue** . . ." (2 Pet. 1:3).

Apply Knowledge

"Take my instruction, and not silver, and **knowledge** rather than choicest gold" (Prov. 8:10).

"A wise man is strong, and a man of **knowledge** increases power. For by wise guidance you will wage war and in the abundance of counselors there is *victory*" (Prov. 24:5–6).

Then Self-Control

"He who is slow to anger is better than the mighty, and he **who rules his spirit,** than he who captures a city" (Prov. 16:32).

"I will **guard my ways,** that I may not sin with my tongue; I will guard my mouth as with a muzzle, while the wicked are in my presence" (Ps. 31:1). "He who corrects a scoffer gets dishonor for himself, and he who reproves a wicked man gets insults for himself. Do not reprove a scoffer, lest he hate you. Reprove a wise man and he will love you" (Prov. 9:7–9).

"Like a city that is broken into and without walls is a man who has **no control** over his spirit" (Prov. 25:28).

Then Endurance

"Knowing that the testing of your faith produces **endurance**" (James 1:3).

"And you will be hated by *all* on account of My name, but it is the one who has **endured** to the end who will be saved" (Matt. 10:22).

"But remember the former days, when, after being enlightened, you **endured** a great conflict of suffering" (Heb. 10:32).

Then Godliness

"But have nothing to do with worldly fables fit only for old women. On the contrary, discipline yourself for the purpose of **godliness;** for bodily discipline is only of little profit, but **godliness** is profitable for all things, since it holds promise for the present life and also life to come" (1 Tim. 4:7–8).

"But flee from these things, you man of God; and pursue righteousness, **godliness,** faith, love, perseverance, and gentleness" (1 Tim. 6:11).

"Instructing us to deny ungodliness and worldly desires and to live sensibly, righteously, and **godly** in the present age" (Titus 2:12).

And in Godliness, Brotherly Kindness

"To sum up, let all be harmonious, sympathetic, **brotherly,** kindhearted, and humble in spirit" (1 Pet. 3:8).

"And so, as those who have been chosen of God, holy and beloved, put on a heart of compassion, **kindness,** humility, gentleness, and patience; bearing with one another, and forgiving each other, whoever has a complaint against anyone; just as the Lord forgave you, so also should you. And beyond all these things put on *love,* which is the perfect bond of unity" (Col. 3:12–14).

And Finally, Love

"**Love** covers a multitude of sins" (1 Pet. 4:8).

"**Love** your enemies" (Matt. 5:44).

"A new *commandment* I give to you, that you **love** one another, even as I have loved you, that you **love** one another" (John 13:34).

"So husbands ought also to **love** their own wives as their own bodies. He who **loves** his own wife loves himself . . ." (Eph. 5:28).

"Nevertheless, let each individual among you also **love** his own wife even as himself . . ." (Eph. 5:33).

"**Love** is patient, **love** is kind, and is not jealous; **love** does not brag and is not arrogant, does not act unbecomingly; it does not seek its own, is not provoked, does not take into account wrong suffered, does not rejoice in unrighteousness, but rejoices in the Truth; bears all things, believes all things, hopes all things, endures all things" (1 Cor. 13:4–7).

"**Love** *never* fails . . ." (1 Cor. 13:8).

Yes, my brothers, love never fails!

Personal commitment: To desire and strive to be meek. "Based on what I have learned in Scripture, I commit to being quick to hear and slow to speak, to forgive those who have offended me, and to do what I can to reconcile with those I have offended."

Date: _____ Signed: _____

Homework

Let your mind dwell on these things. "Finally, brethren, whatever is true, whatever is honorable, whatever is right, whatever is pure, whatever is lovely, whatever is of good repute, if there is any excellence and if anything worthy of praise, let your mind dwell on these things" (Phil. 4:8).

1. **3x5 cards.** Have you been faithful to write down the verses from *each* chapter that have touched your heart? Continue to keep these cards with you and bring them out *regularly* as the Holy Spirit prompts you.

2. **Be a doer, not just a hearer.** "But one who looks intently at the perfect law, the law of liberty, and abides by it, not having become a forgetful hearer but an effectual doer, this man shall be **blessed** in what he does" (James 1:25).

3. Share *this* chapter with *one other man* who seems to be harboring a lack of forgiveness or is fond of the "tough love" approach with his wife.

Test Your Wisdom

1. Are we to love those who are difficult to love? Circle: Yes / No (Luke 6:27–28).

2. If you only love the "lovable," who are you compared to? A _____ (Matt. 5:46).

3. Circle the definitions that God does **not** use to describe "love" in 1 Corinthians 13:4–8: "Love is patient, love is kind, love is not jealous; love does not brag, love is not arrogant, love is a choice, love does not act unbecomingly; love does not seek its own, love is not provoked, love does not take into account a wrong suffered, love is tough, love does not rejoice in unrighteousness, love means never having to say you're sorry, love rejoices with the Truth, love bears all things, love believes all things, love hopes all things, love endures all things. Love never fails."

4. What leads to repentance? The _____ of _____ (Rom. 2:4).

5. What one *word* describes what type of ambassadors we are to be?

Ambassadors of _____ (2 Cor. 5:18–20). [Hint: The word is used five times in this verse.]

6. What are 5 reasons we are to forgive?

a. Because God _____ me (Eph. 4:32).

b. Because of His _____ _____ (Heb. 9:22 and Matt. 26:28).

c. To _____ and _____ our love for them (2 Cor. 2:7–8).

d. So that Satan would not _____ _____ of us (2 Cor. 2:11).

e. Because the Father will not _____ my _____ (Matt. 6:15).

7. How many times am I to forgive? (Matt. 18:35). _____X_____, or _____ times!

The answers to Homework questions are at the end of this workbook.

Blessed are the Meek

When Debbie* first met her husband Matt*, her mother told her that there was no way he could ever lead her. Her mother said, "Debbie, you are much too stubborn and pigheaded."

But after many years of marriage, the opposite was true. Matt was very kind, extremely gentle, and meek, and he had gained Debbie's admiration and respect. She said, "I just do whatever he says because I want to—and even when I don't want to, I do it anyway!" Debbie's husband obviously has many of the qualities of Christ: meekness, gentleness, and goodness.

Those who followed after our Lord did so for the "man of love" that He was. Matt, too, has gained a following—Debbie.

*Not their real names.

Chapter 4

Thrusts of a Sword

*There is one who speaks rashly like thrusts of a sword,
but the tongue of the wise brings healing.
—Proverbs 12:18*

God spoke the entire world into existence. The Lord told us that we would be judged by *every* word we speak. Yet, the world tells us to speak our minds. Let's search the Scriptures together to discover what God has to say about the tongue.

The Tongue: Small, Yet Deadly!

Set on fire by hell. "So also the **tongue** is a small part of the body, and yet it boasts of great things. Behold, how great a forest is set aflame by such a small fire! And the **tongue** *is a fire, the very world of iniquity;* the tongue is set among our members as that which *defiles the entire body,* and *sets on fire the course of our life,* and is *set on fire by hell*" (James 3:5–6).

No one can tame the tongue. "But *no one can tame* the **tongue**; it is *a restless evil and full of deadly poison*. With it we bless our Lord and Father; and with it we curse men, who have been made in the likeness of God; from the same mouth come *both blessing and cursing*. My brethren, these things ought not to be this way. Does a fountain send out from the same opening both *fresh and bitter water?*" (James 3:8–11). But thank the Lord that "nothing will be impossible with God" (Luke 1:37).

The Lord knows. Here is a sobering thought: "Even before there is a word on my **tongue,** behold, O Lord, *Thou dost know it all*" (Ps. 139:4). This should bring about great conviction. We need to watch not only what we say, but also what we think.

We need a muzzle! "I said, 'I will guard my ways, that I may *not sin* with my **tongue**; I will *guard* my **mouth** as with a *muzzle*'" (Ps. 39:1). Be careful about what you say. You may have great physical strength, but how about the strength required for self-control?

Crushes the spirit. "A *soothing* **tongue** is a *tree of life* but perversion in it crushes the spirit" (Prov. 15:4). Are the words you speak to your wife, your children, or those at your place of work soothing? Ask yourself if you have been crushing the spirit of those you are to protect.

God tells us to choose our words wisely.

Guard your mouth. How many times have you gotten into trouble by the words you have spoken? "The mouth of the righteous flows with wisdom, but the **perverted tongue** will be *cut out*" (Prov. 10:31). "There is one who **speaks rashly** like *thrusts of a sword,* but the **tongue** of the **wise** *brings healing" (*Prov. 12:18). "He who **guards his mouth** and **his tongue** guards his soul *from trouble"* (Prov. 21:23).

What proceeds out of your mouth? This statement is clear. What you say is very important. "For by **your words** you shall be *justified,* and by **your words** you shall be *condemned"* (Matt. 12:37). "It is not what enters into the mouth that defiles the man, but **what proceeds out of the mouth,** this *defiles the man"* (Matt. 15:11). ". . . *Put them all aside*: anger, wrath, malice, **slander,** and **abusive speech** . . ." (Col.3:8).

Sweetness of speech. If you have hurt your wife by what you have said or in your attitude toward her, God is faithful to offer a cure. **"Pleasant words** are a *honeycomb, sweet to the soul* and *healing to the bones"* (Prov. 16:24). **"Sweetness of speech** *increases persuasiveness"* (Prov.16:21).

Righteous lips. Is there anyone who doesn't appreciate a kind word? **"Righteous lips** are the *delight of kings,* and he who **speaks right** is *loved"* (Prov. 16:13). **"Speaking** to one another in **psalms** and **hymns** and **spiritual songs,** singing and making melody with your heart to the Lord" (Eph. 5:19).

Have you matured? Or do you still act childishly by saying things that hurt others? One of the biggest lies we learned as children was "sticks and stones may break my bones, but words will never hurt me." We probably still have not recovered from some of the words that were said to us as children. Have you hurt your wife or your children with *your* words? "When I was a child, I used to **speak as a child,** think as a child, reason as a child; when I became a man, I did away with *childish things*" (1 Cor. 13:11).

God is very specific concerning *how* we are to give an answer.

A gentle answer. When anger or wrath is directed toward us, God tells us the Christian response we must make in order to glorify Him. "A **gentle answer** turns away *wrath,* but **harsh words** stir up *anger*" (Prov. 15:1).

Ponder how to answer. Do you think before you speak? "The heart of the righteous *ponders how to answer,* but the *mouth of the wicked* **pours out evil things**" (Prov. 15:28). Do you just pour out evil on other people? If so, Scripture says you have the mouth of the wicked! "By forbearance [a proper facial expression] a ruler may be persuaded and a **soft tongue** *breaks the bone*" (Prov. 25:15). (Or "soft **answer**" in the KJV.)

Folly and shame. Do you halfway listen or cut off the other person before he or she has had a chance to finish speaking or asking you a question? "He who gives an **answer before he hears,** it is *folly* and *shame* to him" (Prov. 18:13). Give your wife an opportunity to get everything off her chest. Ask her questions so you are sure you understand what she is trying to tell you and why. Is she in need of empathy? Give her a listening and understanding ear. Or, perhaps she needs help discerning something that just "talking it out" will accomplish. Many times your wife doesn't want you to fix her problems; she just needs understanding and encouragement. This sometimes takes a lot of patience. But, patience is the proof of your love. Are you doing all you can to be patient with your wife? Prove your love for her by being patient and understanding.

Washed with the Word. Do you bless your wife with God's Word and with your loving, edifying words? If not, then you are not experiencing the blessing of a holy and blameless wife. "Husbands, love your wives, just as Christ also loved the church and gave Himself up for her; that He might sanctify her, having cleansed her by the *washing* of water **with the Word** that He might present to Himself the church in all her glory, having no spot or wrinkle or any such thing; but that she should be holy and blameless" (Eph. 5:25).

Beware of *how much* you say.

Many words. When there is a lot of talking and discussing, transgression (a violation of God's Law) cannot be avoided. "With **many words** *transgression is unavoidable*" (Prov. 10:19). As the leader, properly direct lengthy discussions to a conclusion. This does not mean that you are to cut your wife off when it's her turn, or drop a hurtful "bomb" and then say the matter is finished. Be sure you understand her and make sure she knows you do by giving her a positive and loving response. If you don't think you agree, tell her you need time to pray about it. Then do just that.

Guards his mouth. Others tell us to speak our minds and to share what we think—but God says: "A *man of understanding* keeps **silent**" (Prov. 11:12). And, "One who **guards** his mouth *preserves his life;* one who **opens it** *comes to ruin"* (Prov. 13:3).

Considered wise. God actually says that we practice wisdom and are considered prudent when we say nothing. "Even a fool, when he **keeps silent,** is *considered wise*. When he **closes his lips** he is *counted as prudent"* (Prov. 17:28).

Anything more. "But let your statement be, '**Yes, yes**' or '**No, no**'— *anything beyond* these is *of evil"* (Matt. 5:37). Nod your head up and down when your wife is talking to you. She will spend much less time trying to be heard and understood if you keep your eyes and mind on her, rather than watching the TV or reading the paper.

Empty chatter. "Guard what has been entrusted to you, avoiding **worldly** and empty chatter, and the **opposing arguments** of what is *falsely* called *'knowledge'*—which some have professed and thus *gone astray from the faith"* (1 Tim. 6:20). You don't need to argue your point; just state your decision based on prayer and God's leading. However, you must resist using your authority to get your own way; your decision *must* be of the Lord's leading. When your wife sees that your heart is striving to follow the right way, the Lord's way, then she will stop trying to control or manipulate you.

We are also instructed to be content and not to grumble.

Do all things . . . "Do all things without **grumbling or disputing**" (Phil. 2:14). Do you find yourself often grumbling about a task before you do it? If it's something you should be doing, do it and don't grumble or dispute it! Yet, if you are being "railroaded" into doing something you don't think you should, don't do it. Remember the mess it got Adam (and all of us) into. "Then to Adam He said, 'Because you have listened to the voice of your wife, and have eaten from the tree about which I commanded you . . .'" (Gen. 3:1). "Therefore, to one who knows the right thing to do, and does not do it, to him it is sin" (James 4:17).

Whatever the circumstances. Are you someone who has to complain about everything that happens to you? You must learn contentment. "Not that I speak from want; for I have *learned* to be **content** in *whatever circumstances* I am" (Phil. 4:11). Are you setting a good example for your wife and children? Are you as the head of your household demonstrating to your family how to be content in the midst of trials, or how to be a grumbler and complainer?

Great gain. Godliness and contentment must go hand in hand. "But *godliness* is actually a means of great gain, when *accompanied* by **contentment**" (1 Tim. 6:6).

Content? ". . . being **content** with *what you have;* for He Himself has said, 'I will never desert you, nor will I ever forsake you'" (Heb. 13:5). Are you satisfied with what you have? Or are you constantly trying to upgrade all your "toys" and possessions?

Do not crush the spirit. Proverbs tells us that our speech can crush our wives' spirits. "A soothing tongue is a tree of life, but *perversion* (or "obstinance") in it **crushes the spirit**" (Prov.15:4).

Is arguing *good* for marriage?

A dry morsel. Some "experts" say that arguing can actually be good for a marriage. What does God say? "Better is a dry morsel and *quietness* with it, than a house full of feasting with **strife**" (Prov. 17:1). Strife is defined as a prolonged struggle for power or superiority. There should be no struggle for power or superiority if each one in the family knows his or her role, and each one concentrates on fulfilling that role. Strife comes when these duties are neglected, or when each person is too busy seeing to it that the other person is doing what they should do.

On the subject of quietness—be sure your children are quiet and under *your* control! It's not only your wife's responsibility to keep them quiet; your presence should warrant respect and silence. (See Chapter 14, "Father's Instructions.")

Abandon the quarrel. Do you abandon the quarrel, or do you fight until you win? "The beginning of **strife** is like letting out water, so *abandon* the **quarrel** before it breaks out" (Prov. 17:14). Again, you do not need to struggle, argue, or prove yourself to be the head of your home. God has given you the position of leadership. This is not a place of pride or arrogance; your head-ship is to be used to guide, protect, and manage your family wisely under God's direction.

Any fool will quarrel. "A *fool's lips* bring **strife,** and his mouth calls for blows" (Prov. 18:6). Your wife may even take a swing at you if your words are extremely painful to her. Of course, she is no match. This could then become an abusive situation. Remember, *abandon* the **quarrel** before it breaks out! She is wrong for throwing a punch, or maybe even starting the verbal fighting, but you are to be the leader and savior of the body. "For the husband is the **head** of the wife, as Christ also is the head of the church, He Himself being the **Savior** of the body" (Eph. 5:23). Remember, ". . . *any fool* will **quarrel!**" (Prov. 20:3).

Dealt treacherously. ". . . The Lord has been a witness between you and the wife of your youth, against whom you have **dealt treacherously,** though she is your companion and your wife by covenant. But **not one** has done so who has a **remnant** of the **Spirit.** And what did that one do while he was seeking a godly offspring? Take heed then, to your spirit, and let no one deal treacherously against the wife of your youth" (Mal. 2:14–15).

If you have dealt treacherously with your wife, then God is saying to you that you have not even a remnant of His Spirit! Very sobering. Let's each take a hard look at ourselves and get right with God and our wives.

Covers his garment with wrong. "'For I hate divorce,' says the Lord, the God of Israel, 'and him who **covers his garment with wrong,**' says the Lord of hosts. 'So take heed to your spirit, that you do not deal treacherously'" (Mal. 2:16). *Treacherously* in the Hebrew translation is defined as "to deal deceitfully or unfaithfully, offend, transgress, or depart." *To cover your garment with wrong* is defined as "one who is violent, unjust, cruel, an oppressor." Many men are in a physical battle or emotional battle with their wives. We have all seen or known women who try to act as tough as men, but are they? Can they ever be? In sports that require strength, can men and women ever compete fairly? Of course not. God gives us an outward appearance to show us women and men were created differently. Have you ever been witness to a successful businesswoman who gave way to tears? Why are we shocked when this happens? Because we have been fooled by her outward appearance into thinking that she was every bit as tough as a man. It is the hope of this ministry that your wife, after reading the *Workbook for Women,* will decide to seek a gentle and quiet spirit and allow herself to be the weaker vessel. How will you respond? Will you crush her or cherish her? (See Proverbs 15:4 and Ephesians 5:29.)

What is so important about agreeing with others, especially my wife?

Agree. Agree with your wife and others, especially when they are hurt or upset. **"Agree** with thine **adversary** quickly, while thou art in the way with him . . ."** (Matt. 5:25, KJV). Listening and nodding your head will help a lot when someone is angry or frustrated. So many times we play the "devil's advocate," trying to show someone the other side. (The name alone should warn us of probable consequences!) Give the other person a chance to share their thoughts, feelings, and frustrations. Get on their side. Don't fuel the fire. Later, when they feel they have been heard and understood, they *may* be receptive to your pointing out a different view.

When you are humble enough to show another person understanding, especially when that person is out of control, you are reaching spiritual maturity.

Divided against itself. Satan does all he can to illuminate the areas where you *don't agree* so he can divide and conquer your family. "Any kingdom divided against itself is laid waste; and any city or house divided against itself shall not stand" (Matt. 12:25). And in Luke, "Any kingdom divided against itself is laid waste; and a house divided against itself falls" (Luke 11:17). "Keeping away from **strife** is *an honor* for a man, but any *fool* will **quarrel**" (Prov. 20:3).

Agreement. This verse will show you why disagreement between Christian couples is so important to Satan. "Again I say to you, that if two of you agree on earth about anything that they may ask, it shall be done for them by My Father who is in heaven" (Matt. 18:19). When we don't agree as a couple, we actually cancel each other out. For instance, if you are voting for opposing political candidates, you might as well stay home. "But refuse *foolish and ignorant speculations* knowing that they *produce* **quarrels.** And the Lord's bond-servant must not be **quarrelsome,** but be kind to all, able to teach, patient when wronged" (2 Tim. 2:23).

Deeds of the flesh are evident. It is evident to other Christians and certainly to God when the way we act is of a fleshly nature. "Deeds of the flesh are evident . . . **strife,** jealousy, **outbursts of anger, disputes, dissensions,** envying . . ." (Gal. 5:19–21). "If any one advocates a different doctrine and **does not agree with sound words,** those of our *Lord Jesus Christ,* and with the **doctrine conforming to godliness,** he is conceited and understands nothing; but he has a morbid interest in controversial questions and **disputes** about words, out of which arise envy, **strife, abusive language,** evil suspicions, and **constant friction** between men of depraved mind and deprived of the truth . . ." (1 Tim. 6:3–5).

Fruit of the Spirit. "But the fruit of the Spirit is love, joy, peace, patience, kindness, goodness, faithfulness, gentleness, self-control; against such things there is no law" (Gal. 5:22). "Urge bondslaves to be subject to their own masters in everything, to be well-pleasing, not **argumentative"** (Titus 2:9). As a Christian, you are Jesus' bondslave; He bought you with a price. You are not your wife's bondslave. You, as

Christ's bondslave, need to be pleasing to *Him*. You can be patient with others, yet firm in your faith. Do not think that you must give in to your wife's desires; stand for what is right. And, *abandon* the **quarrel** before it breaks out. You need not prove yourself, or get your wife to agree with your way of thinking; just be firm and loving in your decisions as the head of your family, and be "*quick to hear,* slow to speak, and slow to anger" (James 1:19).

Slow to anger. You have heard some say that, since Jesus was angry and turned over the tables in the temple, we can be angry. James 1:19–20 says, "But let everyone be quick to hear; *slow to speak,* and *slow to anger;* for the **anger of man** does *not achieve* the **righteousness of God."** (See Chapter 6, "The Angry Man," for more knowledge.)

Again, agree! You must try to find the area of *agreement* instead of the point of *disagreement.* "Again I say that if two of you **agree** on earth about anything that they may ask, it shall be done for them by My Father who is in heaven" (Matt. 18:19). Take charge of a disagreement—nod your head, find the points you agree on, and state them to her out loud. Wives want to be heard; everyone does. That's why people get louder and begin screaming or yelling their point; they want to be heard and understood. Take time to consider the areas that you agree on and move in that direction.

What does God think of a lying tongue, besides the fact that He hates it?

The Lord hates. Let's read on in Proverbs that tells us much about lying. "There are six things which the Lord hates, yes, seven which are an abomination to Him: haughty eyes, a **lying tongue,** and hands that *shed innocent blood* (abortionists) . . ." (Prov. 6:16–17). God not only hates lying and thinks it's an abomination, but also lists a lying tongue alongside an abortionist!

Deceitful. "*Deliver my soul,* O Lord, from **lying** lips, from a **deceitful** tongue" (Ps. 120:2). When someone, possibly your wife, catches you in a lie (or what you call "a fib"), do you deny it? Are you truthful? Do you debate about exactly what you said and try to twist the truth to your favor?

Remember, the word *deceitful* is in the definition of dealing treacherously with your wife.

Father of lies. And lastly, we *never* want to **lie** since the *devil* is the father of lies and lying is an **abomination** to God. "You are of your *father the devil,* and you want to do the desires of your father. He was a murderer from the beginning, and *does not stand in the truth,* because *there is no truth in him.* Whenever he speaks a **lie,** *he speaks from his own nature;* for he is a **liar,** and the *father* of **lies**" (John 8:44). Remember, it's the Truth that sets you free!

Your tongue will be much harder to control if you've been drinking.

Not wise. "Wine is a mocker, strong drink a **brawler,** and whoever is *intoxicated* by it is *not wise"* (Prov. 20:1). The problem here is the person who is intoxicated by the effects of alcohol. Drinking alcohol is not in itself a sin. It is the evil that you speak, and other consequences—the effects of drinking too much.

Utter perverse things. "Who has woe? Who has sorrow? Who has **contentions?** Who has complaining? Who has wounds without cause? Who has redness of eyes? Those who linger long over wine, those who go to taste mixed wine. Do not look on the wine when it is red, when it sparkles in the cup, when it goes down smoothly; at the last it bites like a serpent, and stings like a viper. Your eyes will see strange things, and your mind will **utter perverse things.** And you will be like one who lies down in the middle of the sea, or like one who lies down on the top of a mast. 'They struck me, but I did not become ill; they beat me, but I did not know it. When shall I awake? I will seek another drink'" (Prov. 23:29–35). A person who drinks a lot is not an "alcoholic." Drinking to excess is not a disease; it's a sin. Confess your sin if you are held by the cords of alcohol. If you stumble, continue to confess and cry out to God for deliverance.

Proceeds out. "Not what enters into the mouth defiles the man, but what proceeds **out of the mouth,** this defiles the man" (Matt. 15:11). If what you are putting into yourself (alcohol) is causing your lips to transgress, then maybe you should stop. Ask your wife or others who are close to you—anyone who loves you enough to tell you the truth. ". . . They will accumulate for themselves teachers in accordance to their own desires . . ." (2 Tim. 4:3). Certainly you wouldn't choose someone who has a weakness for alcohol to help you find the Truth, would you? ". . . The Truth shall make you free" (John 8:32).

To Sum Up

1. Be aware of **how much** you say—with **many words** *transgression is unavoidable*. Instead, let your communication be **"Yes, yes"** or **"No, no"**—*anything more* than this will lead to *evil*.

2. Be **careful** *what* you say—by **your words** you'll be *justified* and by **your words** you'll be *condemned!*

3. Do not argue—**agree** with your **adversary** *quickly!*

4. Answer properly. Give a **gentle answer, ponder** (think awhile) **how to answer,** and **don't answer before you listen** for it is *folly* and *shame!*

5. Then *learn* to **be content** in *whatever circumstances* you are in.

6. If healing is needed, remember, **pleasant words** are a *honeycomb, sweet to the soul* and *healing to the bones,* and **sweetness** of speech adds persuasiveness.

7. The rule of thumb that will help to guide you is this—whatever is easy for us to do in the flesh, it is *of the flesh*. Whatever is difficult to do and requires us to draw on the Holy Spirit's strength is *walking in the Spirit*.

8. You must **walk in the Spirit** and stop doing whatever you please. "But I say, walk by the Spirit, and you will not carry out the desire of the flesh. . . . *These are in **opposition** to one another*, so that *you **may not** do the things that you please*" (Gal. 5:16–17).

Let us all strive to appear wise by keeping silent. Let our words be loving and patient.

Let us love our wives as Christ loves His church by **washing our wives in the Word.**

Personal commitment: To open my mouth with wisdom and healing.
"Based on what I have learned from God's Word, I commit to remain patient, to wait before I answer, and to be sweet in all my words, especially to my wife and children."

Date: _____ Signed: _____

Homework

1. **3x5 cards.** Men, please use your 3x5 cards and write down the verses from *this* chapter. You will never be changed from the "old man" to the "new creation" without constantly being bathed in His Word. "Therefore if any man be in Christ, he is a new creature: old things are passed away; behold, all things are become new" (2 Cor. 5:17, KJV).

2. Are you keeping these cards with you and bringing them out *regularly* as the Holy Spirit prompts you? **If not, why not?**

3. Share the wisdom from *this* chapter with *one other man* who speaks harshly to his wife and children. Make sure you are first to share your weakness in this area.

Test Your Wisdom

1. What do a fool's lips call for? _____ (Prov. 18:6).

2. How does God say we are to answer? _____ (Prov.15:1) and with a _____ _____ (Prov.25:15).

3. Who waits before answering? _____ (Prov. 15:28).

4. What is it to us if we don't hear a matter out before answering? It is _____ and _____ to us (Prov. 18:13).

5. What must I learn from my circumstances? To be _____ (Phil. 4:11).

6. I cannot excuse my anger by the fact that Jesus turned over the tables in the temple, since James 1:19–20 says, "But let everyone be quick to hear, *slow to speak,* and *slow to anger*; for the _____ _____ _____ does *not achieve* the righteousness of God."

7. Where do lies originate? _____ (John 8:44). Then, if I lie, I am like my _____ the _____.

*The answers to Homework questions are at the end of this workbook.

Chapter 5

Weapons of our Warfare

*For though we walk in the flesh,
we do not war according to the flesh,
for the weapons of our warfare are not of the flesh,
but divinely powerful for the destruction of fortresses.
—2 Corinthians 10:4*

In our vastly changing world, we men are bombarded with so many mixed messages regarding what men are to be like and how we are to act. The feminists have convinced both men and women that if we take authority over our households or protect our wives we are "chauvinist pigs." In contrast, at the movie theater, it seems there is always at least one movie that portrays the brutal violence of men against their enemies. Amidst this confusion, it is a welcome relief to have the Bible and the Holy Scriptures to guide us, renew our minds with the Truth, and therefore transform us.

Satan has set his main attack on our homes; this is the "front line." When there is trouble at home, especially with our wives, it causes us to be totally ineffective in our lives. Some men will run from the front lines by finding solace in their jobs, in sports, in hobbies, or in the arms of another woman. *Let's face the battle head on* with the weapons God has given us through Christ's death on the cross. Let's learn how we can use the "weapons of our warfare" to pull down some of the walls that have divided our homes.

When I am having trouble with my wife, what should I do?

We must go to the top; we must go to our heavenly Father and appeal to *Him*.

First, examine yourself and your motives. "Search me, O God, and know my heart; try me and know my anxious thoughts, and see if there be any hurtful way in me . . ." (Ps. 139:23–24).

Next, turn over, *through prayer alone,* **your wife to God.** You must understand that you are not responsible for what your wife does or does not do; she is accountable to God for her actions. "But each one is **tempted** when he is carried away and enticed by his *own lust*" (James 1:14).

Get out of her way. "How blessed is the man who does not walk in the counsel of the wicked, **nor stand in the path of sinners** . . . but his delight is in the law of the Lord, and in His law he meditates day and night" (Ps. 1:1). Because you are her authority, explain *clearly* to your wife what you want her to do. But, if she rebels, get out of her way! The second line tells us what we are *to do*—meditate on His Word. Leave your wife to God; God must be the One to make changes in your wife. Who got your attention and made the changes in you? God. If God did this with you, isn't He more than able to change your wife?

Stop riding her about it; *pray about it!* You can help to heal your home with your prayers. "Therefore, confess your sins to one another, and *pray* for one another, so that you may be healed. The effective *prayer* of a righteous man can accomplish much" (James 5:16).

Have the proper attitude. "Let no one look down on your youthfulness, but rather in speech, conduct, love, faith, and purity, show yourself an example of those who believe" (1 Tim. 4:12).

Overcome all evil with good. Be careful how you react to evil *when* it occurs: "Do not be *overcome with evil,* but **overcome evil with good**" (Rom. 12:21). And it *may* occur: ". . . knowing that the **testing of your faith** produces *endurance"* (James 1:3). Take this opportunity to pray a blessing over your wife: ". . . not returning evil for evil, or insult for insult, but *giving a blessing instead;* for you were called for the very purpose that you might inherit a blessing" (1 Pet. 3:9).

Concentrate on loving the unlovable! When you love and give honor to your wife, even when she is unlovable and unkind, you are showing her unconditional love. "For if you love those who love you, what reward have you? Do not even the tax-gatherers do the same?" (Matt. 5:46). Give God your hurts, rather than returning evil or insults. He will help you love your wife regardless of her actions toward you.

The ministry of reconciliation. As children of God, we are to be ambassadors of God's love and that will draw others to the Lord. "Therefore we are **ambassadors** *for* **Christ** . . . and [he] gave us the **ministry of reconciliation** . . . *not counting their trespasses against them,* and he has committed the word of reconciliation" (2 Cor. 5:18–20). Are you counting your wrongs suffered? Remember, God's mercies are new every morning. Are your mercies toward your wife new every morning?

Our first mission field. You may ask yourself, "Why should I minister to my wife and my family?" The Lord gives us our homes as the first "mission field." We may want to rush ahead of God before we are really ready. As husbands and fathers, we are to minister *at home first!* ". . . if any man be above reproach, the husband of one wife, having children who believe, not accused of dissipation or rebellion. For the overseer must be above reproach as God's steward, not self-willed, not quick-tempered, not addicted to wine, not pugnacious, not fond of sordid gain, but hospitable, loving what is good, sensible, just, devout, self-controlled, holding fast the faithful word which is in accordance with the teaching, that he may be able both to exhort in sound doctrine and to refute those who contradict" (Titus 1:6–9). Once we become effective "missionaries" in our own home, we then can be effective with others.

God wants *us* to learn contentment *before* He'll change our wives. To prove the point further, let's examine Paul's life. "Not that I speak from want; for I have **learned to be content** in whatever circumstances I am. I know how to get along with humble means, and I also know how to live in prosperity; in any and every circumstance I have **learned the secret** of being filled and going hungry, both of having abundance and suffering need." He goes on to say (the verse you hear so often), "I can do all things through Him who strengthens me" (Phil. 4:11–13).

You must battle in the proper way. Do what God says—it *will* work! "To sum up, let all be harmonious, sympathetic, brotherly, kindhearted, and humble in spirit; not returning *evil for evil,* or *insult for insult,* but **giving a blessing instead;** for you were called for the very purpose that you might **inherit a blessing"** (1 Pet. 3:8).

This is a spiritual battle. "Do you think that I cannot appeal to My Father, and He will *at once* put at My disposal more than twelve legions of angels" (Matt. 26:52). Our heavenly Father will call on the angels to battle on your behalf in the "heavenlies" where the "real battle" is waging. "For our struggle is **not against flesh and blood,** but against the rulers, against the powers, against the world forces of wickedness **in the heavenly places"** (Eph. 6:12). Pray Psalm 91 over your family.

Your wife is not the enemy. "Do you not know when you present yourselves to someone as slaves of obedience, you are slaves of the one whom you obey, either of sin resulting in death, or of obedience resulting in righteousness?" (Rom. 6:16). When sin abounds in someone's life, that person is really just a slave of the devil. We may think the one who sins is awful, but so are we if we continue to react with vengeance. Remember, that belongs to God alone! "For though we walk in the flesh, we do not war according to the flesh, for the **weapons of our warfare** are not of the flesh, but **divinely powerful** for the *destruction of fortresses"* (2 Cor. 10:4). Wouldn't you rather get at the root cause, not just at the symptom?

Word of warning. *Never* open up or share with any woman your troubles at home or tell another woman that your wife just "doesn't understand." If you do, you are like an ox being led to slaughter! Even though they may be very nice, married, not your type, or any other excuse Satan is telling you (or you are telling yourself), it is not "safe" to talk to another woman! Satan doesn't care who he uses to destroy your home. *Never confide or share anything* with *another woman!* "Be of sober spirit, be on the alert. Your adversary, the devil, prowls about like a roaring lion, **seeking *someone* to devour"** (1 Pet. 5:8). (See "Because of Immoralities" for more knowledge.)

Boast about your weaknesses. If you see or hear of a situation with another married man who is falling into this trap, share this Truth with him. Don't judge him. Care enough to turn back your brother. "My brethren, if any among you strays from the T""'ruth, and one turns him back, let him know that he who turns a sinner from the error of his way will save his soul from death, and will cover a multitude of sins" (James 5:19–20). Let him confide in you. Then, open up to him your failings or temptations, humbly. "And He has said to me, 'My grace is sufficient for you, for power is perfected in weakness.' Most gladly, therefore, I will rather **boast about my weaknesses,** that the *power of Christ* may dwell in me" (2 Cor. 12:9).

Be committed. Be committed regardless of the consequences and leave the results to God. "If it be so, our God whom we serve is able to deliver us from the furnace of blazing fire; and He will deliver us out of your hand, O king. But even if He does not, let it be known to you, O king, that we are not going to serve your gods or worship the golden image that you have set up" (Dan. 3:17). These youths believed God would deliver them, but, regardless of the consequences, they had resolved that they would not compromise, even if it meant death in the furnace. These young men were determined to do what they knew God wanted them to do and left the results in God's hands. The youths didn't die, but the cords that bound them were removed by their walking in the fire. Do you have cords (of sin or anxiety) that are binding you? God will deliver you. **Let's prepare for the battle that will win the war in our homes!**

Preparing for War by Putting on Your Armor

The schemes of the devil. "Finally, be strong in the Lord and in the strength of His might. Put on the full armor of God, that you may be able to stand firm against the schemes of the devil" (Eph. 6:10–11). Remember the real enemy is Satan—not your wife.

The full armor of God. "For our struggle is not against flesh and blood, but against the rulers, against the powers, against the world forces of this darkness, against the spiritual forces of wickedness in the heavenly places. Therefore, take up the full armor of God, that you may be able to resist in the evil day" (Eph. 6:12–13). You must resist the *fear* that causes you to run to something or someone else or to just give up! **Stand firm.**

Stand firm. "Stand firm therefore, having girded your loins with Truth . . ." (Eph. 6:14). People talk about "stepping out in faith." It may be best to stop moving and just stand firm! It may be the difference between trusting and tempting God. Sometimes we feel as though we are taking a "step of faith," but we are actually throwing ourselves off a cliff. Our convictions should enable us to "stand" for what is right. If God brings adversity into our lives, our *stand* will be the testimony. Yet, sometimes we are asked to step out and walk on water, as Peter was asked to do. Discernment is needed here. Usually our "flesh" brings about urgency. God usually says wait.

His righteousness. "And having put on the breastplate of righteousness . . ." (Eph. 6:14). God is talking about His righteousness, not yours. He tells us in His Word that our righteousness is nothing but "filthy rags."

Walk in peace. "And having shod your feet with the preparation of the gospel of peace . . ." (Eph. 6:15). It says in Matthew, "Blessed are the peacemakers!" And in 1 Peter 3, it says to "be prepared to give an account of the hope that is within you yet with patience and gentleness." We are to wait until the "door" is opened and then proceed with great gentleness and patience.

The shield of faith. "In addition to all, taking up the shield of faith with which you will be able to *extinguish all the flaming missiles* of the evil one" (Eph. 6:16). You must have faith, not in yourself or someone else, but faith in God, in Him alone! Circumstance has nothing to do with faith. Believe His Word alone for the Truth about your situation.

Helmet of salvation. "And take the helmet of salvation . . ." (Eph. 6:17). You must be saved; you must be one of His children to really win a difficult spiritual battle. It's as easy as talking to God right now. Just tell Him in your own words that you need Him now. Ask the Lord to make Himself real to you. Give Him your life, a life that is messed up, and ask the Lord to make it new. Tell Him that you will do whatever He asks, since He is now your Lord. Ask Him to "save you" from your situation and from the eternal torment that is waiting for all those who do not accept His gift of eternal life with Him in heaven. Thank Him for His death on the cross and His resurrection. You can now believe that you will no longer live alone; God will always be with you and you will spend eternity in heaven.

Sword of the Spirit. "And the sword of the Spirit which is the Word of God" (Eph. 6:17). If you search His Word for the Truth concerning your situation, then you will have something to stand on. When the battle is the Lord's, the victory is ours! Write down, on 3x5 cards, the Scriptures you'll need to help you in your battle. Keep them with you at all times, either in your briefcase or in your car. When you feel an attack coming on, like anger or anxiety, cry out to God. "Cease striving and know that I am God . . ." (Ps. 46:10). Stand firm in faith and wait for God.

Pray at all times. "With all prayer and petition pray at all times in the Spirit" (Eph. 6:18). Pray from deep in your spirit. Have a designated time or times of prayer. God desires to hear from us and prayer is our form of communication.

Be on the alert. "And with this in view, be on the alert with all perseverance and petition for all the saints" (Eph. 6:18). Pray for another person each time anxiety overwhelms you. Pray this verse for them: "Most gladly therefore, I will rather boast about my weaknesses, that the power of Christ may dwell in me. Therefore I am well content with weaknesses, with insults, with distresses, with persecutions, with difficulties, for Christ's sake; for when I am weak, then I am strong" (Phil. 12:9–10).

Pray for those who persecute you. God also asked that we pray for our enemies—every one of them! Pray for them and ask God to show you what He wants you to do to bless them. It wasn't until after Job prayed for his "so-called" friends that God restored what Job had lost. "And the Lord restored the fortunes of Job when he prayed for his friends, and the Lord increased all that Job had twofold" (Job 42:10). "But I say to you, love your enemies, and pray for those who persecute you." He goes on to tell you why: "in order that you may be sons of your Father who is in heaven" (Matt. 5:44–45).

Know God's Word

His Word will not come back void. You must know and learn God's Word. You need to set out to find the blessed promises of God. These principles we have been learning are from His Word, and when we speak His Word to Him by prayer, it will not come back void. That is His promise to you! "So shall My Word be which goes forth from My mouth;

it shall not return to Me void [empty], without **accomplishing** what I desire and without **succeeding** in the matter for which I sent it" (Isa. 55:11). His desire is that you may overcome the evils in this world. You must pray His Word. If you accept no imitations or counterfeits, then you can expect to receive the guaranteed promises of God! Amen!

Search for God's promises throughout your Bible. Seek understanding. God says if you seek you will find. God's Word gives wisdom. "And I say to you, ask, and it shall be given to you; **seek,** and *you shall find;* knock, and it shall be opened to you" (Luke 11:9). Once you've found God's Truth, then you can apply it to your life. "By **wisdom** a house is *built,* and by **understanding** it is *established;* and by **knowledge** the *rooms are filled* with all *precious* and *pleasant riches"* (Prov. 24:3–4).

Read them with delight and mark them in your Bible. "Delight yourself in the Lord; and He will give you the desires of your heart" (Ps. 37:4). Take the time to mark these passages for quick reference in times of distress or when leading another to the Truth. What did Jesus answer when Satan was trying to tempt Him? "And Jesus answered him, 'It is written... It is written... For it is written....'" (Luke 4:4, 8, 10). When the devil assaults you again, come against him with "It is written . . . It is written . . . For it is written . . ."!

Memorize. Meditate day and night. Memorize the promises you find in your Bible so that the blessed assurance of them may sink into your soul. You must learn and know God's promises if you ever want to depend on Him alone. "But his delight is in the law of the Lord, and in His law he meditates day and night. And he will be like a tree firmly planted by streams of water, which yields its fruit in its season, and its leaf does not wither; and in whatever he does, he prospers" (Ps. 1:2).

Spiritual Warfare by Taking Your Thoughts Captive

Your battle may be won or lost in your mind. So take your thoughts captive! "We are **destroying speculations** and every lofty thing raised up against the knowledge of God, and we are **taking every thought captive** to the obedience of Christ, and we are ready to punish all disobedience, whenever your obedience is complete" (2 Cor. 10:5–6). Don't play into the enemy's hands. Don't entertain evil thoughts; take your thoughts captive!

Overcome evil with good. Satan knows that if he can divide, he can conquer. Most of us play right into his hands, the hands of the enemy. Scripture tells us, "Do not be overcome by evil, but **overcome evil with good"** (Rom. 12:21).

No matter how bad things seem—God *is* in control. Our comfort is in knowing that God is in control, not us, and certainly not Satan. "Simon, Simon, behold, Satan has *demanded permission* to sift you like wheat; but I have prayed for you, that your faith may not fail; and you, when *once you have turned again,* strengthen your brothers" (Luke 22:31–32).

Sifting. Jesus knew the future outcome, yet Peter still had to go through the "sifting" to be ready for God's calling on his life. Will you be ready when He calls you? "And let endurance have its perfect result, that you may be **perfect and complete,** *lacking in nothing"* (James 1:4).

The Keys of Heaven

Jesus gave us the keys of heaven to "bind up" the evil and "loose" the good. "I will give you the *keys* of the kingdom of *heaven;* and whatever you shall **bind** on earth shall be bound in heaven, and whatever you shall loose on earth shall be **loosed** in heaven" (Matt. 16:19).

Remove the evil. You must first bind the "strong man"—that is, the spirit that has a hold on the person you are praying for. "But *no one* can enter the strong man's house . . . unless he *first* **binds the strong man** . . ." (Mark 3:27).

Replace the evil with good. This is very important! "When the unclean spirit goes out of a man, it passes through waterless places seeking rest, and not finding any, it says, '*I will return to my house from which I came.*' And when it comes, it finds it swept and put in order. Then it goes and takes along seven other spirits more evil than itself, and they go in and live there; and the last state of that man becomes *worse than the first"* (Luke 11:24–26).

Replace the lies with the Truth—the Truth that is **only** found in His Word. Unless what you hear, what you read, or what someone tells you matches up with a principle in God's Word, it is a lie!

Replace the "arm of the flesh" with the "Lord." Replace trusting in "the arm of the flesh" (yourself, a friend, or whomever) with trusting in the Lord. "Finally, be strong in the Lord, and in the strength of His might" (Eph. 6:10). "Thus says the Lord, **cursed** is the man who trusts in mankind and makes **flesh his strength,** and whose heart turns away from the Lord. . . . Blessed is the man who trusts in the Lord and whose trust is the Lord" (Jer. 17:5, 7).

Replace running away from God with—running *to* Him! "God is our refuge and our strength, a very present help in time of trouble" (Ps. 46:1). Run to the book of Psalms! *Read the Psalms that correspond to the date plus 30 (30, 60, 90, etc.), then read the chapter of Proverbs that corresponds to the date. (e.g., on the 5th of the month you would read the 5th, 35th, 65th, 95th, 125th Psalms and the 5th chapter of Proverbs). An easy way to remember is to write where to turn on the bottom of the Psalm (e.g., on the bottom of the 6th Psalm you would write 36, then on the bottom of the 36th you would write 66, and so on. When you get to the 126th Psalm, you would write Proverbs 6.) Psalm 119 is reserved for the 31st day of the month.*

Replace complaining to another with crying out to Him! He promises to hear you and lift you up immediately! But you *must* cry out! Don't think to yourself, "Well, God hasn't helped me in the past!" If He didn't help, it's simply because you didn't ask or you weren't patient. **"Ask,** and it shall be given to you; **seek,** and you shall find; knock, and it shall be opened to you" (Matt. 7:7).

What "Condition" Is Needed to Be Heard

Your desire needs to be His will. Jesus' condition is that "If you abide in Me, and My Words abide in you, ask whatever you wish, and it shall be done for you" (John 15:7). When your heart rests in Jesus alone, *your will* is centered in *His will,* and this is truly making Him Lord of your life. To know His will, you need to know His Word.

The condition for the blessing. Each promise given by God has a condition for receiving that blessing. Many will claim a portion of the Scripture and omit the condition. Others claim the Scripture and choose to ignore the condition.

Condition: "Believe on the Lord Jesus . . ."

> Promise: ". . . and you shall be saved" (Acts 16:31).

Condition: "Delight yourself in the Lord . . ."

> Promise: ". . . and He will give you the desires of your heart" (Ps. 37:4).

Condition: "Train up a child in the way he should go . . ."

> Promise: ". . . even when he is old he will not depart from it" (Prov. 22:6).

Promise: ". . . God causes all things to work together for good . . .

> Condition: ". . . to those who love God, to those who are called according to His purpose" (Rom. 8:28).

Called by My name. ". . . And [if] My people who are **called by My name** humble themselves and pray, and seek My face, and turn from their wicked ways, then I will hear from heaven, will forgive their sin, and will heal their land" (2 Chron. 7:14). Once you cry out to Him, you will be called by Christ's name. A Christian is a *"follower* of Christ." Remember, you must be one of His children. Talk to God right now.

Humble yourself. ". . . And [if] My people who are called by My name **humble themselves** and pray, and seek My face, and turn from their wicked ways, then I will hear from heaven, will forgive their sin, and will heal their land" (2 Chron. 7:14). Self-willed, haughty people sometimes understand the Word without the Spirit, but to know the mind of God we need to wait **humbly** on God's Spirit.

Humility will be tested. ". . . He might **humble** you, **testing** you, to know *what was in your heart,* whether you would *keep His commandments* or not" (Deut. 8:2).

Humility will save you. "When you are *cast down,* you will *speak with confidence,* and the **humble** person He will *save*" (Job 22:29).

Humility will strengthen your heart. "O Lord, Thou hast *heard* the *desire* of the **humble;** Thou wilt *strengthen their heart,* Thou wilt *incline Thine ear* . . ." (Ps. 10:17).

He teaches and leads the humble. "He *leads* the **humble** in justice, and He *teaches* the **humble** *His way*" (Ps. 25:9).

Only the humble will inherit the land. "But the **humble** will *inherit the land* . . ." (Ps. 37:11).

The humble will be exalted. "He has brought down rulers from their thrones, and has **exalted** those who were **humble**" (Luke 1:52).

Only the humble will be given grace. "But He gives a greater grace. Therefore it says, 'God is opposed to the proud, but *gives grace* to the **humble.**' Humble yourselves in the presence of the Lord, and He will exalt you" (James 4:6, 10).

Humility is rooted in the spirit. "To sum up, let all be harmonious, sympathetic, brotherly, kindhearted, and **humble in spirit** . . ." (1 Pet. 3:8).

Walk in the Spirit. Being filled with the Holy Spirit will enable you to walk in the Spirit, not in sin and fleshly desires. Many churches are enthusiastically "Spirit-filled." In 1 Corinthians Chapter 13, "love" is said to be superior to having the gift of tongues. Any talent or blessing we receive sometimes can cause us to become prideful. When you judge another's importance or measure their spirituality by whether or not they display spiritual gifts, you set yourself up for the fall of pride. "And *do not judge* and you will not be judged . . ." (Luke 6:37).

"And I will put **My Spirit** within you and *cause* you to **walk** *in My statutes,* and you will be careful to *observe My ordinances*" (Ezek. 36:27).

". . . **Walk by the Spirit,** and you will not carry out the *desire of the flesh*" (Gal. 5:16).

5. Weapons of our Warfare

Pray. ". . . And [if] My people who are called by My name humble themselves **and pray,** and seek My face and turn from their wicked ways, then I will hear from heaven, will forgive their sin, and will heal their land" (2 Chron. 7:14).

Wait. When the battle is the Lord's, the victory is ours! Just like with all real wars, not all the battles are won by the same side, so do not be discouraged if you have fallen short and made mistakes. We have comfort in knowing that He hears us immediately—but there *is* a battle being waged. In the book of Daniel, an angel spoke to him and gave us these insights: ". . . From the **first day** that you **set your heart** on understanding this and on **humbling yourself** before God, *your words were heard,* and I have come in response to your words. But the prince of Persia was withstanding me for **twenty-one days"** (Dan. 10:12–13). It may take some time to win the battles; do not become weary. "But as for you, brethren, do not grow weary of doing good" (2 Thess. 3:13).

His timing. One thing you must understand—God seems to work on one thing at a time. We must work *with* Him in His timing. This does not mean we need to *wait to pray;* it only means we need to wait for God to change the situation at the proper time. Thank God that He doesn't dump (through conviction) all our sins on top of us all at once! Just use the time when you're waiting to pray. If you don't understand this very important point, you may become weary and unable to overcome. "He that **overcomes** shall **inherit** *all* **things"** (Rev. 21:7).

Two or three gathered. Find two other men who will pray with you. "But Moses' hands were heavy. Then they took a stone and put it under him, and he sat on it; and Aaron and Hur supported his hands, one on one side and one on the other. Thus his hands were steady until the sun set . . . When Moses held his hand up, than Israel prevailed, and when he let his hand down Amalek (the enemy) prevailed" (Exod. 17:11–12). Find **two** other *men* (not a woman, unless it is your wife) to hold you up so you won't become too weary. Pray and ask God to help you find two others who are like-minded.

The power of three. "And if **one** can *overpower him* who is alone, **two** can *resist* him. A cord of **three** strands is not quickly *torn apart"* (Eccl. 4:12).

To lift the other up. "**Two** are *better* than **one** because they have a *good return for their labor*. For if either of them *falls*, the *one will lift up his companion*. But woe to the one who falls when there is not another to lift him up" (Eccl. 4:9–10).

He is there with you. "For where **two or three** have *gathered* together in My name, there I am in their midst" (Matt. 18:20). "Then Nebuchadnezzar the king was astounded and stood up in haste; he responded and said to his high officials, 'Was it not **three men** we cast bound into the midst of the fire?' They answered and said to the king, 'Certainly, O king.' He answered and said, 'Look! I see **four men** loosed and walking about in the midst of the fire without harm, and the appearance of the **fourth** is like a *son of the gods!*'" (Dan. 3:24). You are never alone!

Agreement. "Again I say to you, that if **two** of you *agree* on earth about **anything** that they may ask, it shall be done for them by My Father who is in heaven" (Matt. 18:19).

Pray for one another. "Therefore, confess your sins to one another, and *pray for one another,* so that you may be healed. The effective prayer of a righteous man can accomplish much" (James 5:16). Confession to a like-minded man is the best method of obtaining a pure heart.

Seek My face. ". . . And [if] My people who are called by My name humble themselves and pray, and **seek My face,** and turn from their wicked ways, then I will hear from heaven, will forgive their sin, and will heal their land" (2 Chron. 7:14).

"They **looked to Him** and were **radiant,** and their faces shall never be ashamed" (Ps. 34:5).

Turn from your wicked ways. ". . . And [if] My people who are called by My name humble themselves and pray, and seek My face, and **turn from their wicked ways,** then I will hear from heaven, will forgive their sin, and will heal their land" (2 Chron. 7:14). Scriptures are not only for the head; they are for the heart and the will. To get the real impact of Scripture, we must surrender our lives and our wills to the leading of the Spirit. We must be willing to be made over.

Whom does the Lord hear? Whom does the Lord deliver? "The eyes of the Lord are toward the **righteous,** and His ears are *open* to **their cry**" (Ps. 34:15). "The **righteous** cry and the *Lord hears,* and delivers them out of all **their troubles**" (Ps. 34:17).

Whom will He not answer? When you are in sin, God will not answer, even if you do cry out to Him. "Then they will cry out to the Lord, but *He will not answer them.* Instead, He will hide His face from them at that time, because they have **practiced evil deeds**" (Mic. 3:4).

We all have sinned. We all have sinned and come short of the glory of God, but God sent His Son. "For you first, God raised up His Servant, and **sent Him** to bless you by *turning* every one of you from your **wicked ways**" (Acts 3:26).

To obey is better than sacrifice. "Behold, to **obey is better than sacrifice,** and to heed than the fat of rams. For rebellion is as the sin of divination, and insubordination is as iniquity and idolatry" (1 Sam. 15:22). Do you know the right thing to do, yet you do not do it? Obey! "Therefore, to one who knows the right thing to do, and does not do it, to him it is sin" (James 4:17).

Begin by praying Psalm 51:2–4. "Wash me thoroughly from my iniquity, and cleanse me from my sin. For I know my transgressions, and my sin is ever before me. Against Thee, Thee only, I have sinned, and done what is evil in Thy sight, So that Thou art justified when Thou dost speak, and blameless when Thou dost judge."

When do you give up praying? Never! We have a wonderful example of the fact that God does not always mean "no" when we haven't received an answer to our prayer. Read Matthew 15:22 and see how the Canaanite woman continued to beg Jesus for her daughter's healing. The result of her faith: ". . . Then Jesus answered and said to her, 'O woman, your faith is great; be it done for you as you wish.' And her daughter was healed at once."

The battle for the soul. Are you unequally yoked? Read this quote taken from John Rice's book *Prayer, Asking and Receiving*. He is talking about a wife praying for her husband, but certainly it can be applied to you, praying for your wife. "If a Christian wife is out-and-out for God . .

. she can win her husband more quickly than anyone else. Pray this simple prayer of confession. Mean it from your very soul. Acknowledge in these words, your failure, your barrenness, your shallowness as a Christian, and your lack of bearing fruit. Pray it now in your heart. I beseech you today, go beg for it, plead for it, with confession, with tears, with travail of soul, until God answers from heaven." Remember, you have the promise that ". . . you will be saved, you and all your household" (Acts 11:14). Remember, **the unbelieving wife is sanctified through her believing husband.** "For the unbelieving husband is sanctified through his wife, and the unbelieving wife is sanctified through her believing husband . . . For how do you know, O husband, whether you will save your wife?" (1 Cor. 7:14).

Faith

Peter, an example of faith. Read the account of Peter in Matthew 14 starting at verse 22. Jesus asked Peter to walk on water. If He asks you to walk on water, will you get out of the boat? Notice that when Peter cries out to Jesus, it is always followed by the word *immediately*. Immediately, Jesus spoke to them and told them to take courage. And then later when Peter began to sink, he cried out to the Lord, and *"immediately* Jesus stretched out His hand and took hold of him"! (Matt. 14:31).

Fear. A question we must ask ourselves is, "Why did Peter sink?" "But seeing the wind, he became afraid" (Matt. 14:30). If you look at your situation and at the battle that is raging against you, you will sink! Peter took his eyes off the Lord and the result was fear! It says, "he became afraid." If you take your eyes off the Lord, you, too, will become fearful.

Your testimony. How did the others in the boat react? (Did you forget there were others who didn't get out of the boat?) It says, "And those who were in the boat worshiped Him saying, 'You are certainly God's Son!'" (Matt. 14:33). Are you willing to allow God to use you to show His goodness, His lovingkindness, His protection, to draw others to Him? There is a great reward! This is evangelism. Others will come to you when they are having trouble because they have seen your peace, despite your circumstances.

The wind stopped. "And when they got into the boat, the wind stopped" (Matt. 14:32). Your trials and battles will not go on forever. Peter was tested in order to be made strong enough to be the "rock" of which Jesus had spoken. Satan (and others working for him) will tell you that you will stay in your affliction unless you run away, give in, or give up. But God never intended for us to remain *in* "the valley of the shadow of death." In Psalm 23:4, it says that we go *"through* the valley of the shadow of death." Satan wants us to believe that we must *live there!* He wants to paint a "hopeless" picture! God is our hope. And, hope is our faith in His Word that has been sown in our hearts.

Abraham. We can look to Abraham for a second example of faith. When he was about 90 years old and still without the child God had promised him, "he hoped against hope" (Rom. 4:18). Isn't that good? Even when all hope was gone, he continued to believe God and take Him at His Word. We must do the same.

If you lack faith. If you lack faith, you need to ask God for it, since there is a constant spiritual battle going on, waged by Satan, to destroy your faith. "Fight the good **fight of faith** . . ." (1 Tim. 6:12). "I have fought the **good fight,** I have finished the course, I have kept the **faith** . . ." (2 Tim. 4:7). Without the people's faith, even Jesus' power was inhibited. "And He (Jesus) could do **no miracle** there except that He laid His hands upon a few sick people and healed them. And He wondered at their **unbelief**" (Mark 6:5).

Act on the faith that you do have. "And He said to them, 'Because of the littleness of your faith; for truly I say to you, if you have **faith as a mustard seed,** you shall say to this mountain, 'Move from here to there,' and it shall move; and *nothing* shall be impossible to you'" (Matt. 17:20).

Imitators of faith. We would do well to imitate those in Scripture who exhibited faith. (You can find the "Hall of Faith" in Hebrews, Chapter 11.) We need to act on God's promises by being "**imitators** of those who through **faith and patience** *inherit the promises"* (Heb. 6:12).

Double-minded or doubting. You must not be double-minded. Your mind must not waver or doubt God. "But let him **ask in faith** *without any doubting,* for the one who doubts is like the surf of the sea driven and tossed by the wind. For let not that man expect that he will receive anything from the Lord, being a double-minded man, *unstable in all his ways"* (James 1:6–8).

Faith without works. "But someone may well say, 'You have faith, and I have works; show me your faith without the works, and I will *show you my faith by my works*'" (James 2:18). Show others that you have faith by your actions. If you have trouble in your home, don't just *say* you believe that it will be healed, *act* like it. "But are you willing to recognize, *you foolish fellow*, that **faith without works is useless?**" (James 2:20).

Things not seen. Many may ask you if you *see* any change. Share these Scriptures with them. "Now **faith** is the assurance of things **hoped for,** the conviction of *things not seen"* (Heb. 11:1). ". . . For we walk by faith, not by sight . . ." (2 Cor. 5:7).

The Word. How can we gain faith, or increase our faith? "So **faith** *comes from hearing,* and *hearing by the* **Word** *of Christ"* (Rom. 10:17). Read His Word and surround yourself with faithful *men.*

Obedience. Don't forget that obedience to God is paramount to victory. Don't forget what Jesus said: "Not everyone who says to Me, 'Lord, Lord,' will enter the kingdom of heaven; but he who does the will of My Father who is in heaven" (Matt. 7:21).

In God's will. If you are experiencing conviction in your heart and are feeling that you are not in God's will, that you do not keep His commandments, and that you do not ask for things according to His will, then, of course, you will have no confidence, no faith to receive your request from the Lord. Ask God to direct your paths and to change your will to His will ". . . Yet not what I will, but what Thou wilt" (Mark 14:36).

Prayer *and* **fasting.** Jesus told His apostles, "But this kind does not go out *except* by **prayer and fasting**" (Matt. 17:21). If you have been praying fervently and have purified your ways, then fasting may be called for. There are different lengths of fasts.

One-day fast. The day fast begins in the evening after your evening meal. You drink only water until the 24-hour period is complete; then you eat the next day's evening meal. You pray during this time for your petition. This fast can be done a couple of times a week.

Three-day fast. Esther fasted "for favor" from her husband, the king. She fasted three days "for favor." "Go, assemble all the Jews who are found in Susa, and **fast** for me; do not eat or drink for *three days,* night or day. I and my maidens also will **fast** in the same way" (Esther 4:16).

Seven-day fast. Seven days seems to represent completion. "Now it came about when I heard these words, I sat down and wept and mourned **for days;** and **I was fasting and praying** before the God of heaven" (Neh. 1:4). Usually it will be during great sorrow that you are "called" to fast for seven days. When you are hungry or weak, use that time for prayer and reading His Word.

A gloomy face. Keep as quiet about your fast as possible. During the fast, you are not to complain or draw attention to yourself. "And whenever you **fast,** do not put on **a gloomy face** as the *hypocrites* do, for they neglect their appearance *in order to be seen* fasting by men. Truly I say to you, they have their *reward in full.* But you, when you fast, anoint your head, and wash your face so *that you may not be seen fasting by men,* but by your Father who is in secret; and *your Father who sees in secret will repay you"* (Matt. 6:16–18).

The Lord will fight your battles. Stand and see! Once you have prayed according to what we have been reading throughout Scripture, then do as it says—"You need not *fight* in this **battle;** station yourselves, *stand and see* the salvation of the Lord on your behalf" (2 Chron. 20:17).

No one should boast. God says we are a stubborn people! When a battle is won or when the war is over, let us boast only in Him. Let us remain humble. "For by grace you have been saved through faith; and that not of yourselves, it is the **gift of God;** not as a result of works, that *no one should boast"* (Eph. 2:8–9). "Do not say in your heart . . . 'Because of **my righteousness** the Lord has brought me in to possess this land,' but because of the wickedness . . . that the Lord is dispossessing them before you. It is not for your righteousness or for the **uprightness of your heart** that you are going to possess their land, but *because* of *the wickedness* of these . . . for you are a **stubborn people** . . . You have been rebellious against the Lord" (Deut. 9:4–7). We all have sinned and come short of the glory of God, so let us remember that when the battle is won, our righteousness is nothing but filthy rags. "But we are all as an unclean thing, and all our righteousness is as **filthy rags;** and we all do fade as a leaf; and our iniquities, like the wind, have taken us away" (Isa. 64:6, KJV).

Intensity of your trials is a sign that you are close to victory. Your trials may intensify when you are close to gaining the victory. "For this reason, **rejoice,** O heavens and you who dwell in them. Woe to the earth and the sea, because the devil has come down to you, having great wrath, *knowing* that he has only a **short time**" (Rev. 12:12). **Let's begin our commitment by praying His Word** . . .

"Dear heavenly Father, I enter into my prayer closet, and, now that I have shut the door, I pray to you, my Father, in secret. As you see me here in secret, you will reward me openly. It is written 'all things you ask in prayer, believing, you shall receive' (Matt. 21:22).

"O God, Thou art my God; early will I seek Thee. My soul longs for Thee in a dry and thirsty land, where no water is. Lord, there is no one besides Thee to help in the battle between the powerful and those who have no strength; so help us, O Lord our God, for we trust in Thee, and in Thy name have come against this multitude. O Lord, Thou art my God; let not man prevail against Thee.

"Your eyes Lord, move to and fro throughout the whole earth that you may strongly support those hearts whose are completely Yours. Search my heart.

"For though we walk in the flesh, we do not war after the flesh, for the weapons of our warfare are not carnal, but mighty through God to the pulling down of strongholds. Casting down imaginations and every high thing that exalts itself against the knowledge of God, and bringing into captivity every thought to the obedience of Christ, you have readiness to revenge all disobedience when your obedience is fulfilled.

"O let the evil of the wicked come to an end, but establish the righteous. I shall not be afraid of evil tidings; my heart is fixed, trusting in the Lord. My heart is established, I shall not be afraid, until I see my desire come upon the enemy.

"Let my fountain be blessed, and let me rejoice with the wife of my youth. For why should I be exhilarated with an adulteress, and embrace the bosom of a foreigner? My own iniquities will capture the wicked, and I will be held with the cords of my sin. I will die for lack of instruction, and in the greatness of my folly I will go astray. The ways of a man are before the eyes of the Lord and he watches all his paths.

"Abraham, who hoped against hope, believed in hope, and was not weak in faith, staggered not at the promise of God through unbelief, but was strong in faith, giving glory to God. He was fully persuaded that what God had promised, He was able to perform.

"We are saved by hope, but hope that is seen is not hope. For what man seeth, why doth he yet hope for it? But if we hope for what we see not, then do we with patience wait for it. I would have fainted unless I had believed I would see the goodness of the Lord in the land of the living. Wait on the Lord; be of good courage, and He will strengthen thine heart, yes, wait on the Lord. They that wait upon the Lord shall renew their strength; they shall mount up with wings as eagles; they shall run and not be weary; and they shall walk and not faint.

"For since the beginning of the world men have not heard, nor perceived by the ear, neither hath the eye seen, O God, besides Thee, what He hath prepared for Him who waiteth for Him. Surely goodness and mercy shall follow me all the days of my life and I will dwell in the house of the Lord forever. Amen."

May God Grant You Victory

Personal commitment: To pray to our Father in heaven rather than retreat from the battle line or use the arm of the flesh. "Based on what I have learned from God's Word, I commit to bathing all my desires and concerns in prayer. I acknowledge that the only way to win my battles is by knowing and applying His Word to my life."

Date: _____ Signed: _____

"Not that I have already obtained it, or have already become perfect, but I press on, in order that I may lay hold of that for which also I was laid hold of by Christ Jesus" (Phil. 3:12).

Homework

What can you do that will ensure victory in each and every crisis and marital dispute in your life? **You can pray!**

1. If you have been faithful to write down the verses from *each* chapter that have touched you and you have read them often, then His Word is now hidden in your heart. Use these cards to pray the Word during frustrating situations, and also to guide your wife spiritually with love and prayer.

2. **Be a doer, not just a hearer.** "But one who looks intently at the perfect law, the law of liberty, and abides by it, not having become a forgetful hearer but an effectual doer, this man shall be **blessed** in what he does" (James 1:25).

3. Share the wisdom from *this* chapter with *one other man* who is battling in the flesh. Make sure that you "boast" about your weaknesses first!

Test Your Wisdom

1. When dealing with a difficult situation with your wife, it is important to remember that she is not the enemy. "Do you not know when you present yourselves to someone as _____ of obedience, you are _____ of the one whom you obey, either of sin resulting in death, or of _____ resulting in _____?" (Rom. 6:16).

2. Jesus gave us the keys of heaven. "I will give you the _____ of the kingdom of _____; and whatever you shall _____ on earth shall be bound in heaven, and whatever you shall loose on earth shall be _____ in heaven" (Matt. 16:19).

3. When your wife is disobedient to the Word of God, you must love her by being _____ with her (1 Cor. 13:4), since love never _____! (1 Cor. 13:8).

4. The Word tells us that our obedience to God is paramount to victory. "Not _____ who says to Me, 'Lord, Lord,' will enter the kingdom of heaven; but he who does the _____ of My Father who is in heaven. And then I will declare to them, 'I never knew you; Depart form Me, you who _____ _____'" (Matt. 7:21, 23).

5. We must continually remind ourselves of those who overcame and thus received the abundant life God promised. "But resist him, _____ _____ _____ _____, knowing that the _____ _____ of suffering are being accomplished by your brethren who are in the world" (1 Pet. 5:9).

6. When people ask us if we *see* any change in the things we are hoping and praying for, we must remember that "_____ is the assurance of things _____ _____, the conviction of *things not seen*" (Heb. 11:1).

7. "But this kind does not go out *except* by _____ and _____" (Matt. 17:21).

The answers to Homework questions are at the end of this workbook.

Chapter 6

The Angry Man

*He who is slow to anger is better than the mighty,
and he who rules his spirit, than he who captures a city.
—Proverbs 16:32*

Ask yourself, "Am I an angry man?" If you answered "No," what if someone were to ask your wife, your children, or those at your workplace if you were an angry man? Would they also say "No"? *Anger* is mentioned 266 times in the Bible. The majority of these passages are written in regard to God's anger toward those who sinned repeatedly without repenting. The word *angry* is mentioned 87 times. Some preachers tell us that we are commanded to be angry. Is this true? Let's search for the wisdom of God in His Word regarding anger.

Angry Men in Scripture

Angry Cain. There are many accounts of angry men in Scripture and the consequences suffered by those who could not overcome their anger. They kept trying to "rise above" their anger. Satan deceived them, because to overcome anger you must bow down with humility. ". . . But for Cain and for his offering He had no regard. So Cain became *very angry* and his countenance fell. Then the Lord said to Cain, 'Why are you angry? And why has your countenance fallen? If you do well, will not your countenance be lifted up? And if you do not do well, sin is crouching at the door; and its desire is for you, but you must master it'" (Gen. 4:5). It was Cain's pride that made him envious and angry towards his brother.

Moses. Moses was a man whom God used mightily. Yet it was his anger that often got in his way. "But they did not listen to Moses . . . and Moses was angry with them" (Exod. 16:20). Many times he was angered by the disobedience and sinfulness of those he was to lead to the Promised Land. Do you ever get angry with those whom you have been assigned to lead?

"An angry man stirs up strife, and a hot-tempered man *abounds* in transgression" (Prov. 29:22).

"But **Moses** searched carefully for the goat of the sin offering, and behold, it had been burned up! So he was **angry** with Aaron's surviving sons . . ." (Lev. 10:16).

"Then **Moses** became **very angry** and said to the Lord, 'Do not regard their offering! I have not taken a single donkey from them, nor have I done harm to any of them'" (Num. 16:15).

"And **Moses** was **angry** with the officers of the army . . ." (Num. 31:14).

"And all these your servants will come down to me and bow themselves before me, saying, 'Go out, you and all the people who follow you,' and after that I will go out. And he went out from Pharaoh in **hot anger**" (Exod. 11:8).

"And it came about, as soon as Moses came near the camp, that he saw the calf and the dancing; and Moses' **anger burned,** and *he threw* the tablets from his hands and shattered them at the foot of the mountain" (Exod. 32:19). Men, have you ever thrown anything when you were angry? Don't make the mistake of using Moses' anger as an excuse for your own anger. The truth is that God did use him mightily in spite of his weakness in this area; but to excuse sin is placing yourself on dangerous ground. By the way, is anger the only sin in your life, or are there other sins such as immorality, covetousness, drunkenness, or carousing? "But you, why do you judge your brother? Or you again, why do you regard your brother with contempt? For we shall all stand before the judgment seat of God" (Rom. 14:10).

"And Aaron said, 'Do not let the **anger** of my lord burn; you know the people yourself, that they are prone to evil'" (Exod. 32:22). All those in our homes are prone to evil. They need our prayers to help keep their paths straight; battle *for* them in the proper way. Teach them to battle in the proper way. "For our struggle is not against flesh and blood, but against the rulers, against the powers, against the world forces of this darkness, against the spiritual forces of wickedness in the heavenly places" (Eph. 6:12). If they (or you) are unsaved, they (or you) are slaves of sin. "Do you not know that when you present yourselves to someone as slaves for obedience, you are slaves of the one whom you obey, either of sin resulting in death, or of obedience resulting in righteousness?" (Rom. 6:16).

Moses was a man blessed by God in many ways, but his anger caused him to miss the blessing of going into the Promised Land.

Angry Jonah. "But it greatly displeased **Jonah**, and **he became angry**" (Jon. 4:1).

"And the Lord said [to Jonah], 'Do you have *good reason* to be **angry?**'" (Jon. 4:4). Many times, after you calm down, aren't you surprised when you realize how stupid it was to get so angry over something so small and insignificant?

What did Jesus say about being angry? "But I say to you that everyone who is **angry** with his brother shall be guilty before the court; and whoever shall say to his brother, 'Raca,' shall be guilty before the supreme court; and whoever shall say, 'You fool,' shall be guilty enough to go into the fiery hell" (Matt. 5:22). Was Jesus just talking about being angry with a brother? No. He was talking about being angry with anyone, even your wife or your children. Does that mean that you are guilty enough for hell? Yes, it does. But, if we are Christians, Christ saved us from the consequences of our sin because He continues to cleanse us from our sins.

"If we confess our sins, He is faithful and righteous to forgive us our sins and to cleanse us from all unrighteousness" (1 John 1:9). The verse says *if* we confess. The question then is, if you have a problem with anger, have you confessed this sin to the Lord *your* Savior? Have you confessed it to those whom you have offended? "Raca" is a word that means "worthless" in Greek. Have you ever told your wife or children, in so many words, that they were worthless? You are guilty of fiery hell, unless you repent. If you think that you will lose their respect by asking them to forgive you, try it and see. They may just give you the respect that you've been desiring from them.

Angry tempers. "For I am afraid that perhaps when I come I may find you to be not what I wish and may be found by you to be not what you wish; that perhaps there may be strife, jealousy, **angry tempers,** disputes, slanders, gossip, arrogance, disturbances . . ." (2 Cor. 12:20). What would your brothers in Christ find if they walked unannounced into your home or office?

Commanded to be angry? Many preachers have used the following verse to tell those who want to have their ears tickled that we are actually commanded to be angry. Taken out of context this would seem true. Yet, when searching for the Truth, you need only to read the entire verse: "Be **angry,** and yet *do not sin;* do not let the sun go down on your **anger,** and *do not give the devil an opportunity* . . . Let no unwholesome word proceed from your mouth, but only such a word as is good for edification according to the need of the moment, that it may give grace to those who hear . . . And *do not grieve the Holy Spirit* of God . . . Let all bitterness, and wrath, and **anger,** and clamor, and slander *be put away from you,* along with all malice. And be *kind to one another, tender-hearted, forgiving each other,* just as God in Christ also has forgiven you" (Eph. 4:26–32). Anger is a natural reaction when someone offends us, or should we say a *fleshly reaction*. But as followers of Christ, we are asked to walk in the Spirit! "But I say, walk by the Spirit, and you will not carry out the desire of the flesh" (Gal. 5:16).

Walk in love. "Therefore be imitators of God, as beloved children; and **walk in love,** just as Christ also loved you, and gave Himself up for us, an offering and a sacrifice to God as a fragrant aroma" (Eph. 5:1).

Family scattered. "Cursed be their **anger,** for it is fierce; and their wrath, for it is cruel. I will disperse them in Jacob, and scatter them in Israel" (Gen. 49:7). Has your family been scattered? Do your children go outside or to a friend's house to play when you are home because they are fearful of your anger? Are your teens or young adults gone because of your anger? "And **fathers,** *do not provoke your children to* **anger;** but bring them up in the discipline and *instruction* of the Lord" (Eph. 6:4). (See Chapter 14, "Father's Instructions.")

Slow to Anger

God tells us that He is slow to anger. "Then the Lord passed by in front of him and proclaimed, 'The Lord, *the Lord God,* compassionate and gracious, **slow to anger,** and *abounding in lovingkindness* and Truth . . .'" (Exod. 34:6).

"The Lord is **slow to anger** and *abundant in lovingkindness,* forgiving iniquity and transgression . . ." (Num. 14:18).

"The Lord is gracious and merciful; **slow to anger** and *great in lovingkindness"* (Ps. 145:8).

Slow or quick to anger—which one are you? God describes the difference between a man who follows God and one who does not.

Do you exalt folly? If you are quick-tempered you do. "He who is **slow to anger** has great understanding, but he who is **quick-tempered** *exalts folly"* (Prov. 14:29).

Do you stir up strife or do you pacify contentions? "A **hot-tempered man** stirs up strife, but the **slow to anger** pacifies contention" (Prov. 15:18).

Are you better than the mighty? "He who is **slow to anger** is *better than the mighty,* and he who **rules his spirit,** than he who captures a city" (Prov. 16:32).

The anger of man does not achieve the righteousness of God. "This you know, my beloved brethren. But let everyone be quick to hear, slow to speak, and **slow to anger;** for the **anger of man** *does not achieve the righteousness of God"* (James 1:19).

How to Gain Control of Your Anger

By having discretion. "A man's *discretion* makes him **slow to anger,** and it is his glory to overlook a transgression" (Prov. 19:11). How do you gain discretion? "I, **wisdom,** dwell with prudence, and I *find* knowledge and **discretion"** (Prov. 8:12).

By having wisdom. "Scorners set a city aflame, but **wise men** *turn away* **anger"** (Prov. 29:8). Where do you find wisdom? You find it in your *fear of the Lord.* "The *fear of the Lord* is the beginning of **wisdom** . . ." (Ps. 111:10).

Is this you in your home? "The **terror** of a *king* is like the growling of a lion; he who provokes him to **anger** *forfeits his own life"* (Prov. 20:2).

Anger produces strife. "For the churning of milk produces butter, and pressing the nose brings forth blood; so the *churning* of **anger** *produces strife"* (Prov. 30:33). Does your anger churn constantly inside you? Is everyone expected to walk on eggshells because you may blow up any minute? "Better is a dry morsel and quietness with it than a house full of feasting with **strife**" (Prov. 17:1).

Are you "practicing" the deeds of the flesh or the fruits of the Spirit? "Now the **deeds of the flesh** *are evident,* which are: immorality, impurity, sensuality, idolatry, sorcery, enmities, **strife,** jealousy, **outbursts of anger,** *disputes*, *dissensions*, *factions*, envying, drunkenness, carousing, and things like these, of which I forewarn you just as I have forewarned you that *those who* **practice** *such things shall not inherit the kingdom of God.* But the fruit of the Spirit is love, joy, peace, patience, kindness, goodness, faithfulness, gentleness, self-control; against such things there is no law" (Gal. 5:19–23).

Quarrelsome Spirit

Do you have a quarrelsome spirit? "But refuse foolish and ignorant *speculations* knowing they produce **quarrels.** And the Lord's bondservant must not be **quarrelsome** but be *kind to all,* able to teach, *patient when wronged"* (2 Tim. 2:23). Are you a "know it all"? Or do you have a contrary comment for many of the things others say? God tells us to "agree with thine adversary quickly while thou art in the way with him, lest at any time thine adversary deliver thee to the judge" (Matt. 5:25, KJV).

Are you argumentative? "Urge bondslaves to be subject to their own masters in everything, to be well-pleasing, not argumentative" (Titus 2:9). Are you Jesus' bondslave? Has He bought you with a price? Then you owe it to *Him* to be well-pleasing.

Is there strife in your home? Again, "Better is a dry morsel and quietness with it than a house full of feasting and **strife**" (Prov. 17:1). Are your children loud and unruly? (See Chapter 14, "Father's Instructions," for "My people are destroyed for lack of knowledge. Because you have rejected knowledge . . ." (Hos. 4:6).)

Do you ever quarrel with your wife? "The beginning of strife is like letting out of water, so *abandon* the **quarrel** before it breaks out" (Prov. 17:14). The world, and so-called experts in marriage, tell us that a good fight is actually healthy for the marriage—*don't you believe it!*

Was I Not Joking?

Are you a madman? One of the most common snares that men fall into is joking with others when in public. Do you tease your wife about her weaknesses or sometimes about things that she has confided in you? "Like a *madman* who throws firebrands, arrows, and death, so is the man who **deceives** his neighbor [or his wife], and says, **'Was I not joking?'"** (Prov. 26:18–19).

Empty words, silly talk, or coarse jesting. "But do not let immorality or any impurity or greed even be named among you, as is proper among saints; and there must be no filthiness and **silly talk,** or **coarse jesting,** *which are not fitting,* but rather *giving of thanks.* For this you know with certainty, that no immoral or impure person or covetous man, who is an idolater, has an inheritance in the kingdom of Christ and God. Let no one deceive you with **empty words,** for because of these things the *wrath of God* comes upon the *sons of disobedience.* Therefore *do not be partakers with them;* for you were formerly darkness, but now you are light in the Lord; walk as children of light (for the fruit of the light consists in all goodness and righteousness and Truth), trying to learn what is *pleasing to the Lord.* And do not participate in the unfruitful deeds of darkness, but instead even *expose them;* for it is *disgraceful* even to *speak of the things* which are done by them in secret. But all things become visible when they are *exposed by the light,* for everything that becomes visible is light" (Eph. 5:3–13).

Speak as a child. Do you joke, jest, talk silliness, or waste your words with nonsense? Is what you say pleasing to the Lord? Most women hate to be teased. Some are good sports about it; most are not. As a boy, you may have practiced your jokes and talking nonsense with your friends when you were in school or in sports. You probably practiced your teasing on the outcasts at school and more than likely with your brothers or sisters. "When I was a child, I used to **speak as a child,** think as a child, reason as a child; when I became a man, I did away with childish things" (1 Cor. 13:11). Now that you are a man, put away your childish ways, "trying to learn what is *pleasing to the Lord.*"

Expose them. When other men start joking about their wives, or other empty words are spoken, walk away from these situations or keep silent. When others see the difference in you, they may ask you about it. Expose them to the light of Truth. ". . . But sanctify Christ as Lord in your hearts, *always being ready to make a defense to everyone who asks you to give an account for the hope that is in you,* yet with **gentleness and reverence;** and keep a good conscience so that in the thing in which you are slandered, those who revile your good behavior in Christ may be put to shame. For it is better, if God should will it so, that you suffer for doing what is right rather than for doing what is wrong" (1 Pet. 3:15–17).

A slanderer. You must never expose to others a weakness in your wife, nor tell others something your wife told to you in confidence. Remember, "A slanderer *separates intimate friends"* (Prov. 16:28).

The definition of a slanderer in the Strong's Concordance is *rakiyl* (raw-keel), a talebearer.

Others may think you're funny, but God knows your heart. "Whoever secretly **slanders** his neighbor, him *I will destroy"* (Ps. 101:5). "It is a terrifying thing to fall into the hands of the living God" (Heb. 10:31).

Let's all put this type of talk away from us. "Let all bitterness and wrath and anger and clamor and **slander** *be put away from you,* along with all malice" (Eph. 4:31).

The Source of Your Anger . . . Pride!

"Now I, Nebuchadnezzar, praise, exalt, and honor the King of heaven, for all *His* works are true and *His* ways just, and *He* is able to *humble those who walk in **pride"*** (Dan. 4:37).

Why are so many men angry? Is it because Christian men imitate the world and the world's thinking? Almost all the books we read, the counselors we seek, and the classes we attend do not reflect God's Word, which is *pure* and *uncompromising.* Instead the church continues to present us with a Christianized worldly view.

Poison dipped in chocolate is still poison! Men, the deadly worldly views are more dangerous when they are dipped in Christianity because we eat it right up! We have been brainwashed into thinking that "self-love" and "self-esteem" are good things; yet, these attitudes are the root of our problem. It's the "know-it-all" who argues and wants his own way, because he knows (actually thinks) he is right. And when he is wrong, his self-esteem needs to be protected. There is never a humble word or an "I'm sorry." The angry man has been conditioned to think that to make an apology would be too humiliating—a sign of weakness. His "self-love" will train him to continue to climb up on his pedestal of pride, only to fall again and again.

What is the cure? "And when they came to Marah, they could not drink the waters of Marah, for they were bitter; therefore it was named Marah" (Exod. 15:23). Moses threw a tree into the water, a representation of the cross of Calvary. You must also throw the cross into your sea of bitterness. Christ died to free you from all sin, including anger, pride, and self-absorbed behavior.

Here is God's prescription. God told us that if we, as a nation, would *humble* ourselves, seek His face, and turn from our wicked ways, He would heal our land. Instead, we "walk in the counsel of the wicked" (Ps. 1:1) and we "trust in mankind" (Jer. 17:5). This is why we will have *superficial* healing! "The brokenness of His people is healed superficially" (Jer. 8:11).

Psychology in the church. It is extremely dangerous for Christians to act as if man's ideas or psychology is God's Word. It is also dangerous to use God's Word to promote current worldly views in the church. "'The prophet who has a dream may relate his dream, but let him who has My Word speak My Word in Truth. What does straw have in common with grain?' declares the Lord ... 'Behold, I am against the prophets,' declares the Lord, 'who use their tongues and declare, "the Lord declares."'" (Jer. 23:28, 30, 31). What does psychology (straw) have in common with God's Word (grain)?

Self-esteem

Are you training and encouraging your children to have self-esteem? The word "self-esteem" should make a Christian cringe since it is just another word for "pride." This is a wolf's word in sheep's clothing! You will soon witness a child who acts so arrogant and self-absorbed that others won't even like him. It is absurd to think that a child needs to be built up to feel good about himself, as if a child isn't completely self-absorbed already! From birth, a child wants his own way, so he cries. Won't a two-year-old scream and pitch a fit until he gets what he wants?

Building your child's self-esteem. There are books and books and more books written for Christians by Christians, but many of the teachings are *not* what God teaches in His Word. Let's look at what God tells us about building our self-esteem or our children's self-esteem. Let's find out why we should be careful not to say, "I have my *pride!*" and "I am so *proud* of you."

Pride is a sin. Pride was the first sin ever committed by the angel Lucifer, who later became Satan. "Your heart was lifted up because of your beauty; you corrupted your wisdom by reason of your splendor. I (God) cast you to the ground" (Ezek. 28:17). Satan also said, "I will make myself like the Most High" (Isa. 14:14). Yet, we praise our children for their beauty, and we teach our children to "go for the top," to "reach for the stars," and to "believe in yourself."

"Self-esteem" began as a lie, formed by twisting Scripture. Satan used Scripture when he tempted Jesus in the desert; he uses it today. He just twists it a little and makes it a half-truth. But we know that anything that is half-true is a lie, lest we forget Abraham and Sarah ("she is my sister," Gen. 12:19).

"Love your neighbor as yourself" (Matt. 22:39). Those who have psychology degrees will try to tell you that this verse means you have to love yourself before you can love anyone else. In other words, "self-love" is needed first because some of us, or most of us, hate ourselves. Is this the Truth or a lie? It is a lie! Why—because it contradicts God's Word. "For **no one** *ever hated* his own flesh, but nourishes and cherishes it . . ." (Eph. 5:29).

Jesus teaches that if we are *humble* we will be blessed. We are to think of others as more important than ourselves. Those who contemplate or threaten suicide are told by the world that they *hate* themselves, but that contradicts the Word of God. Remember, God said, **"No one** ever hated his own flesh!" Satan blinds them with pain until they are not thinking clearly. If there is a "spirit of death" in your home, see if this sin has been passed down from a family member. A person who threatens suicide is crying out for help. Help them with love and comfort. Share the Truth. Satan wants them to feel hopeless—give them some hope! (See Chapter 10, "Various Trials.") Then encourage them to pray with "thanksgiving," thanking God for *everything,* including the trials, "knowing they are working together for good" (Rom. 8:28).

Selfishness or empty conceit. "Do nothing from selfishness or empty conceit, but with *humility of mind* let each of you regard one another as more important than himself; do not merely look out for your own personal interests, but also for the interests of others" (Phil. 2:3). "Blessed are the *humble* [gentle, meek] for they shall inherit the earth" (Matt. 5:5). These verses of Scripture are so contrary to the way Christians speak these days because of the influence of psychology among believers. If this complacency to God's Word does not cause you to shudder, it should!

The last will be first. Many teach their children that being first should be their goal and that we cannot please anyone unless we please ourselves. The Truth is, "But many who are first will be last; and the last first" (Matt. 19:30). "If anyone wants to be first, he shall be last of all, and servant of all" (Mark 9:35). Help your children to attain Christlikeness by sharing these verses instead of rambling off the worldly clichés we have all heard!

The world tells us to speak well of ourselves, but Jesus said, "And whoever exalts himself shall be humbled; and whoever humbles himself shall be exalted" (Matt. 23:12).

Learn from Nebuchadnezzar—his grandson didn't. Nebuchadnezzar (see this section's opening Scripture), who was proud of his power and wealth, was made to be like the cattle of the field and to eat grass. Yet his grandson chose to exalt himself. "Yet you, his son, Belshazzar, have not **humbled** your heart, even though you knew all this, but you have exalted yourself . . ." (Dan. 5:22–23).

Pride is evil—it will cause God to humble you. You may think that certain things you go through are humiliating, but God means it for your good. He doesn't want to humiliate you; He wants to humble you. "For from within, out of the heart of men proceed the evil . . . pride" (Mark 7:21). "For all that is in the world, the lust of the flesh, and the lust of the eyes, and the **boastful *pride* of life,** *is not of the Father,* but is from the world" (1 John 2:16). **Pride is not of God!**

Why do you boast? "For who regards you as superior? And what do you have that you did not receive? But if you did receive it, **why do you boast** . . .?" (1 Cor. 4:7).

Instead we are to die to self. "For you have died and your life is hidden with Christ in God" (Col. 3:3). ". . . He died for all that they who live should no longer live for themselves, but for Him who died and rose again on their behalf" (2 Cor. 5:15).

As we humble ourselves, then God is free to exalt us. ". . . Clothe yourselves with *humility* toward one another, for God is **opposed** to the *proud,* but gives **grace** to the *humble. Humble* yourselves, therefore, under the mighty hand of God, that *He may exalt you* at the proper time . . ." (1 Pet. 5:5–6). "God is opposed to the proud, but gives grace to the *humble . . . Humble* yourselves in the presence of the Lord, and *He will exalt you*" (James 4:6, 11). "I can do all things *through Christ* who strengthens me" (Phil. 4:13). Exalt Christ above yourself.

Always and in all things, Jesus should be our example in the way that He walked on this earth. "Have this attitude [humility] in yourselves which was also in Christ Jesus, who, although He existed in the form of God, did not regard equality with God a thing to be grasped, but *emptied* **Him*self,*** taking the form of a bond-servant, and being made in the likeness of men. And being found in appearance as a man, He *humbled* Himself by becoming obedient to the point of death, even death on a cross. Therefore also God highly *exalted* Him and bestowed on Him the name which is above every name" (Phil. 2:5–9).

What shall we do if we have been prideful?

Learn from the Lord. "Take My yoke upon you, and *learn from* **Me,** for I am gentle and *humble* in heart . . ." (Matt. 11:29).

Boast in the Lord. "But *he who boasts,* let him **boast in the Lord.** For *not* he who commends *himself* is approved, but **whom the Lord commends"** (2 Cor. 10:17–18).

Don't praise yourself. "Let *another praise* you and **not your own mouth;** a stranger and not your own lips" (Prov. 27:2).

And if you don't humble yourself?

"Woe to those who are wise in their own eyes and clever in their own eyes" (Isa. 5:21).

"Do you see a man *wise in his own eyes?* There is **more hope for a fool** than for him" (Prov. 26:12).

"For anyone who thinks he is something when *he is nothing,* **he deceives himself"** (Gal. 6:3).

"Surely *God will not listen to vanity,* neither will the Almighty regard it" (Job 35:13).

"An *arrogant man* stirs up **strife,** but he who trusts in the Lord will prosper. He who *trusts in his own heart* is a **fool,** but he who walks wisely will be delivered" (Prov. 28:25–26).

"And He said to them, 'You are those who justify yourselves in the sight of men, but God knows your hearts; for that which is *highly esteemed* among men is **detestable** in the sight of God'" (Luke 16:15). "And He *humbled* you and let you be hungry . . ." (Deut. 8:3).

Can you see anywhere in Scripture where God instructs us to build up our self-esteem? Or do you find anywhere in Scripture where God instructs us to teach our children to have self-esteem? Are we to pride ourselves in what we have done, or made, or accomplished? What will our flattering do to others, especially our children?

How do we Begin to Change?

Confess your sins. "Therefore, confess your sins to one another, and pray for one another, so that you may be healed. The effective prayer of a righteous man can accomplish much" (James 5:16). Pray for an opportunity to talk to your wife so you can ask for forgiveness for your anger. Don't ramble on and on, justifying yourself or blaming her for your anger. Just tell her honestly that God has convicted you of being angry and argumentative. Tell her that with the *Lord's* help you can change. Give her a kiss, and then go and ask your children's forgiveness and explain to your children how God is going to help you to change. Each time you blow up, confess to those who have been hurt by your anger. Continue to ask for forgiveness.

First **be reconciled.** If you don't feel "led" to go and get things right with your wife and children, never go back into church. "If therefore you are presenting your offering at the altar, and there remember that your brother has something against you, leave your offering there before the altar, and go your way; *first* be reconciled to your brother, *and then* come and present your offering" (Matt. 5:23–24).

Grace to the humble. Humble yourself; don't be too proud to admit that you are an angry man. "God is opposed to the proud, but gives grace to the humble. Humble yourselves, therefore, under the mighty hand of God, that *He* may exalt you at the proper time" (1 Pet. 5:5–6).

Stumbles. This verse separates the men from the boys, or, actually, the righteous from the wicked. Which one will you prove to be? "For a righteous **man** falls **seven times,** and *rises again,* but the wicked stumble in time of calamity" (Prov. 24:16). You will stumble even after you humble yourself and confess your past failures. "Therefore let him who thinks he stands take heed lest he fall" (1 Cor. 10:12). The only way to be victorious is to continue to get up again and confess over and over again. Each confession will bring about more humility; therefore, more grace will abound. This will lead to victory over this area of sin in your life.

Personal commitment: To put away my angry ways. "Based on what I have learned from God's Word, I commit to refuse the excusing of my anger and the blaming of others for it. I commit to renew my mind daily and to be a doer of the Word by putting away my angry ways."

Date: _____ Signed: _____

"Not that I have already obtained it, or have already become perfect, but I press on, in order that I may lay hold of that for which also I was laid hold of by Christ Jesus" (Phil. 3:12).

Homework

Let your mind dwell on these things. "Finally, brethren, whatever is true, whatever is honorable, whatever is right, whatever is pure, whatever is lovely, whatever is of good repute, if there is any excellence and if anything worthy of praise, let your mind dwell on these things" (Phil. 4:8).

1. **3x5 cards.** Write down the verses from *this* chapter that have touched your heart. Then continue to keep these cards with you and bring them out *regularly* as the Holy Spirit prompts you.

2. **Be a doer, not just a hearer.** "But one who looks intently at the perfect law, the law of liberty, and abides by it, not having become a forgetful hearer but an effectual doer, this man shall be **blessed** in what he does" (James 1:25).

3. Share the wisdom from *this* chapter with *one other* **angry man** who might be searching for the Truth.

Test Your Wisdom

1. Write down the last time that you should have "abandoned the quarrel" before the quarrel broke out.

_____

_____

_____.

Remember, Matthew 5:25 says, "Agree *quickly!*"

2. Circle your answers:

a) "Better is a dry morsel with quietness" (Prov. 17:1). Is your house loud? Do you frequently yell at your wife and children?   Yes / No

b) "I will set no worthless thing before my eyes" (Ps.101:3). Do you set yourself or your children down in front of the television for hours?   Yes / No

c) Have you prayed and asked God to forgive you for your anger and asked to help you as you renew your mind?   Yes / No

d) Have you gone to your wife and your children to ask their forgiveness for your angry ways?   Yes / No Read 1 John 1:6.

3. If your wife has also been prone to anger, it's because she has _____ with a man given to anger and has _____ _____ _____! (Prov. 22:24–25).

4. When we are a poor example to our wives and children, the Lord said in Mark 9:42, ". . . Whoever causes one of these little ones who believe to stumble, it would be better for him if, with a heavy millstone _____ around his neck, he had been _____ into the sea."

5. "If therefore you are presenting your offering at the altar, and there remember that your brother has something against you, leave your

offering there before the altar, and go your way; _____ to your brother, and then_____ and present your offering" (Matt. 5:23–24).

6. "But do not let immorality or any impurity or greed even be named among you, as is proper among saints; and there must be no filthiness and _____ _____, or _____ _____, *which are not fitting*, but rather *giving of thanks*" (Eph. 5:3).

7. "Let no one deceive you with _____ _____, for because of these things the *wrath of God* comes upon the *sons of disobedience*" (Eph. 5:6).

The answers to Homework questions are at the end of this workbook.

Chapter 7

Immoralities

*But because of immoralities,
let each man have his own wife,
and let each woman have her own husband.
—1 Corinthians 7:2*

There are so many men who fall into the sin of immorality. Christian men are falling at an overwhelming rate. The Bible documents that this sin of immorality has been plaguing men all throughout history. Why? Let us look to Scripture for the answers. What can we learn from those who fell and those who remained steadfast?

The foundation, bought with a price. The foundation of our faith and following God's Word always comes down to one key element—who we are in Christ Jesus. "For you have been **bought with a price:** *therefore* **glorify God in** *your body"* (1 Cor. 6:20).

Not to touch a woman. "Now concerning the things about which you wrote, it is **good for a man** *not to touch a woman"* (1 Cor. 7:1).

But because of immoralities. "But because of immoralities, *let each man* **have his own wife,** and let each woman have her own husband" (1 Cor. 7:2).

Authority over her own body. "Let the husband fulfill his duty to his wife, and likewise also the wife to her husband. The wife does not have authority over her own body, but the husband does; and likewise also the husband does not have authority over his own body, but the wife does" (1 Cor. 7:3–4). We as men see these verses and think, "Great, now I've got the proof I need!" Yes, we have the written proof that our wives are to be submissive to our advances, but what else is this verse telling us? Are you fulfilling and meeting her needs? Do you speak with love toward her consistently during the day so that her heart will long to be with you?

Or must intimacy be her "duty" to you and a burden she must bear? ". . . that He might sanctify her, having cleansed her by the washing of water with the word . . ." (Eph. 5:26). Have you cleansed your wife with kind words lately?

Lack of self-control. "Stop depriving one another, *except by agreement* for a time, that you may devote yourselves to prayer, and come together again lest Satan tempt you because of your lack of self-control" (1 Cor. 7:3).

Loves himself. Would your wife say that you love her or yourself more? Is your purpose in life based upon giving to others or getting for yourself? "So husbands ought also to **love their own wives** *as their own bodies*. He who loves his own wife **loves himself** . . ." (Eph. 5:28). If you are dissatisfied with your intimacy with your wife, could it be because you have forgotten an important lesson Jesus taught us: **"Give, and it will be given to you;** good measure, pressed down, shaken together, running over, they will pour into your lap. For by your standard of measure it will be measured to you in return" (Luke 6:38). This is a rewarding principle that should be applied to all areas of your life.

Cherishes. ". . . For no one ever hated his own flesh, but nourishes and **cherishes it,** just as Christ also does the church, because we are members of His body" (Eph. 5:29–30). The definition of cherish is to hold dear, to nurture. Do you hold your wife dearly; do you nurture her with your loving and kind words?

Biblical Examples of Moral Purity

Daniel was innocent—free from guilt or sin. Daniel is an example of an innocent man. We are very much aware of his life of continual testing, but because of his **innocence** *God delivered him.* "My God sent His angel and shut the lions' mouths, and they have not harmed me, inasmuch as I was found **innocent** before Him, and also toward you, O king, I have committed no crime" (Dan. 6:22).

Job was blameless—free from fault. Job is an example of a blameless man who pleased God. "And the Lord said to Satan, 'Have you considered My servant Job? For there is no one like him on the earth, a *blameless* and upright man, **fearing God** and **turning away from evil**'" (Job 1:8). What was the secret to Job's blameless life?

He feared the Lord. "He will *bless those* who **fear the Lord,** the small together with the great" (Ps. 115:13).

He turned from evil. "And let him **turn away from evil** and *do good*" (1 Pet. 3:11). When you remove something sinful from your life, you must replace it with something good. (See also "Weapons of our Warfare" for more knowledge: "For my people perish for a lack of knowledge," Hos. 4:6.)

Therefore, Job was blessed by God. "*Blessed* are those whose way is **blameless**" (Ps. 119:1).

We are also very much aware of Job and his difficult circumstances. "Then his wife said to him, 'Do you still hold fast your integrity? Curse God and die!'" (Job 2:9). A non-supporting spouse, such as Job had, should not deter us from these guidelines.

Job's secret. How was Job able to stay morally pure even after he had lost everything and was bound to a contentious wife? "I have made a **covenant with my eyes;** how then could I gaze at a virgin? . . . If my step has turned from the way, or my *heart followed my eyes* . . ." (Job 31:1–7). Let us also look at: "To *keep you* from the evil woman, from the smooth tongue of the **adulteress.** Do not desire her beauty in your heart, nor let her *catch you* with her **eye**lids" (Prov. 6:24–25).

There is danger in making eye contact with those who we are trying to avoid. But, you say, I have never been unfaithful to my wife! ". . . But I say to you, that everyone who **looks on a woman** to *lust for her* **has committed adultery** with her already in his heart" (Matt. 5:28). How many women do you suppose you have looked at since you first became aware of the opposite sex? How much pornography have you consumed? If this is the cord of sin that is holding you, Satan knows he can keep you ineffective in your Christian walk, keep you and your wife in continuous struggles, and keep you in bondage as one of his slaves!

Job said, "Does He (God) not see my ways, and number all my steps? If I have walked with falsehood, and my foot has hastened after deceit, let

Him weigh me with accurate scales, and let God know my integrity" (Job 31:4–6). Are you a man of integrity?

What does His Word say about adultery?

Adultery is one of the Ten Commandments. The *seventh* commandment of the Ten Commandments is "Thou shalt not commit adultery" (Exod. 20:14). In the *seventh* chapter of Proverbs, we learn in detail the ways of the adulteress. This chapter of *A Wise Man* is also number *seven*. When you are in need of renewing your mind you will now be able to quickly find the food for your soul, "to keep you from the strange woman."

God will eventually bring on His wrath. "Therefore consider the members of your earthly body as dead to immorality, impurity, passion, evil desire, and greed, which amounts to idolatry. For on account of these things the **wrath of God** *will come"* (Col. 3:5–6). It doesn't say *"may come"* — it says *"will come"!* "For we know Him who said, 'Vengeance is mine, I will repay, and again, the Lord will judge His people. It is a **terrifying thing** to fall into the hands of the living God'" (Heb. 10:30–31). If you have gotten away with hidden sins so far, it is only because we serve a merciful God who has given you time to repent. If this is convicting you, repent now — don't wait another day! "For nothing is hidden that shall not become evident, nor anything secret that shall not be known and come to light" (Luke 8:17).

The adulteress flatters. Hopefully you haven't fallen into the sin of adultery. However, the Bible warns us that the adulteress is out there in the streets flattering us and appealing to our egos. "To deliver you from the strange woman, from the adulteress who *flatters* with her words . . ." (Prov. 2:16). "That they may keep you from an adulteress, from the foreigner who *flatters* with her words" (Prov. 7:5). What we as men need from our wives is edification. What's the difference between flattering and edifying? When someone flatters, their motivation is to get something from that person. One who edifies, or builds up, is motivated by giving — expecting nothing in return. Two women can be saying basically the same thing, yet their hearts are different.

When your secretary or co-worker flatters you, watch out! "With her **many persuasions** *she entices him;* with her **flattering lips** *she seduces him.* **Suddenly** he follows her, as an ox goes to the slaughter, or as one in fetters to the discipline of a fool, until an arrow pierces through his liver; as a bird hastens to the snare, so he does not know that it will cost him his life" (Prov. 7:21–23). But, you may say, "Those words make me feel so good, and I haven't heard them for so long from my wife!"

Then you need to ask your wife out on a date. As long as you are alive, you should be dating your wife at least once a week. Ask her out; don't just assume you are going out. Court her throughout the week with your kind and loving words as you both anticipate "date night."

Be sure you have a plan; don't make her have to figure out what the two of you are going to do. Keep in mind that it doesn't matter where you go or how much money you spend; *it's being together*. If your wife has been deprived of going out somewhere nice or she hasn't bought a new dress in ages, anticipate this need and offer it to her before she has to ask (or even hint). Just remember what you did years ago to get her; this will guide you in how to keep her. Once you give out of the fullness of your heart, unselfishly, it will return to you. Your motivation cannot be to give only to get, but rather, to give expecting nothing in return.

What can we learn from Scripture to keep us from the adulteress?

Her speech entices men. "For the *lips* of an adulteress drip honey and *smoother than oil* is her *speech;* but in the end she is bitter as wormwood, sharp as a two-edged sword. Her feet go down to death, her steps lay hold of Sheol. She does not ponder the path of life; *her ways are unstable, she does not know it*" (Prov. 5:3–6).

She uses her speech to pull men into certain spiritual death. "With her many persuasions *she entices him;* with her flattering lips *she seduces him.* **Suddenly** he follows her as an ox goes to slaughter. So he does not know it will cost him his life" (Prov. 7:21–23). Many wives whose husbands have fallen into the pit of adultery have reported that they warned their husbands of the enticing adulteress, yet they did not listen!

Once again, it is her speech that pulls a man into adultery. "That they may keep you from an adulteress, from the foreigner who *flatters with her words*" (Prov. 7:5).

The adulteress will cause a man to suffer financially. "To keep you from the evil woman, from the *smooth tongue of the adulteress*. Do not desire her beauty in your heart, do not let her catch you with her eyelids. For on account of a harlot one is *reduced to a loaf of bread,* and an adulteress hunts for the precious life. Can a man take fire to his bosom, and his clothes not be burned? The one who commits adultery with a woman *is lacking sense;* he who would destroy himself does it. Wounds and disgrace he will find, and his reproach will not be blotted out" (Prov. 6:24–33). How many seemingly intelligent men have found wounds and disgrace from this temporary pleasure?

And again God says that the adulterer will suffer financially. "He who keeps company with harlots *wastes his wealth*" (Prov. 29:3). Many men think they are too successful for this to ever happen to them. God's Word applies to all. Every man will finally end up in a financial collapse. And men, your wife and children will also suffer financial collapse. Many middle and upper-middle class women who are married to adulterers have found themselves in line collecting food stamps!

Where do most men meet these adulteresses? She is usually found at or connected with his place of work. "A woman comes to meet him, dressed as a harlot and cunning of heart, *she is boisterous and rebellious; her feet do not remain at home*" (Prov. 7:5). "For the harlot is a deep pit, and an adulterous woman is a narrow well. She lurks as a *robber,* and *increases the faithless* among man" (Prov. 23:28). The adulteress is almost always the working woman, whether she is married or not. Most men have left their wives for women who are not as attractive as their wives and aren't even their "type." It is their job that keeps them in close contact.

Many persuasions. Men, when you share your problems with another woman, she'll just "reel you in." Sometimes it's *her* sad situation that is shared and you feel sorry for her, and again, she "reels you in." "With her **many persuasions** she entices him; with her flattering lips she seduces him. **Suddenly** he follows her, as an ox goes to the slaughter, or as one in fetters to the discipline of a fool . . ." (Prov. 7:21). Men, you need no female friend, *period*. It doesn't matter if you never felt attracted to her; it doesn't matter if she is fat or much too old or even a complete slob!

In Restore Ministries, we have seen every one of these types lead a seemingly sane and intelligent man to slaughter! I will say it again: you have no business carrying on personal conversations with any woman other than your wife, whether it be in person, by phone, or over the internet! It is a trap of the devil to be avoided at all costs, even if it means finding a new job! "And if your right eye makes you stumble, tear it out, and throw it from you; for it is better for you that one of the parts of your body perish, than for your whole body to be thrown into hell. And if your right hand makes you stumble, cut it off, and throw it from you; for it is better for you that one of the parts of your body perish, than for your whole body to go into hell" (Matt. 5:29–30).

The adulteress is deceived into thinking that she has done *nothing* wrong. "This is the way of an adulterous woman: she eats and wipes her mouth, and says, *'I have done nothing wrong'*" (Prov. 30:20). The excuse of the adulteress is that she is innocent because the husband was so miserable or he had nothing in common with his wife, even though they may have spent twenty-five years together or raised a houseful of children! But God said, "Charm is deceitful and beauty is vain, but a woman who **fears the Lord,** she shall be praised" (Prov. 31:30). If your wife is not interested in a sinful type of fun, thank the Lord for your wife; "she (should) be praised" (Prov. 31:28).

The adulteress is an enemy of God! "You adulteresses, do you not know that friendship with the world is hostility with God? Therefore, whoever wishes to be a friend of the world makes himself *an enemy of God*" (James 4:4). Men, as Christians we should not associate with anyone who God says is an enemy of His.

God will give time to repent and then cause great tribulation! "And I gave her time to repent; and she does not want to repent of her immorality. Behold, I will *cast her upon a bed of sickness,* and those who commit adultery with her into *great tribulation,* unless they repent of her deeds" (Rev. 2:22). We have seen this testimony often in our ministry. The adulterous men are in "great tribulation." We have also seen at least four cases in which the adulterous woman, who would not repent, after a time was stricken with a significant illness (i.e., lupus, cancer). In addition we know of two cases where a child of the adulterous woman died. "And I will *kill her children* with *pestilence;* and all the churches will know that I am He who searches the minds and hearts; and I will give to each one of you according to your deeds" (Rev. 2:23). One woman lost a child to what the doctors said was a "parasite." We also know of another case where the adulterous woman (a professing Christian) continued to pursue in boldness another woman's husband after many warnings. Her oldest son died of a brain tumor.

Adultery is a spiritual battle raged against the flesh. This battle must be fought and won in the Spirit. Please read Chapter 5, "Weapons of our Warfare." to understand more about spiritual warfare. Please ignore and resist the temptation to fight this in the flesh. *It is a spiritual battle. It must be fought and won in the Spirit.*

How can I guard myself from falling into adultery?

What can I do to guard myself against the pit of adultery? First acknowledge that you are not above this sin just because you haven't fallen. "Therefore let him who thinks he stands take heed lest he fall" (1 Cor. 10:12). It is God's hand and His mercy that have saved you thus far! "For by grace you have been saved through faith; and that *not of yourselves,* it is the gift of God; not as a result of works, that *no one should boast"* (Eph. 2:8–9).

A man of excellence, Paul. "And this I [Paul] pray, that your love may abound still more and more in *real knowledge* and in *all discernment,* so that you may approve the things that are **excellent,** in order to be sincere and **blameless** until the day of Christ" (Phil. 1:9–10). What did Paul attribute to an excellent, sincere, and blameless life? It was real knowledge and discernment.

Real knowledge. Paul tells us to get real knowledge—knowledge of what is good, not the trivia that today's world is so preoccupied with, and not the knowledge of evil that the newspaper so vividly teaches us. Pore over the Scriptures, reread this chapter many times, mark your Bible, and hide God's Word in your heart. "Thy Word have I hid in mine heart, that I might not sin against Thee" (Ps. 119:11, KJV). It must be the hidden treasure of your heart. "Thy Word I have **treasured** in my heart, that I may not sin against Thee" (Ps. 119:11).

All discernment. We learned from 1 Peter to "turn from evil." (This action takes all discernment, which we will also study later in this chapter.)

Undefiled: without spot. Men, most of us are also fathers, and as fathers it is our responsibility to help our daughters to remain morally pure. The woman in Song of Solomon was committed to purity. You want that for your daughters, but isn't your wife someone's daughter, sister, granddaughter, or niece? Song of Solomon 6:9: "My dove, my **undefiled** is but one . . ." Our example as Christians, "followers of Christ," is Jesus Himself who was described as "innocent and undefiled." "For it is fitting that we should have such a high priest [Jesus], holy, innocent, **undefiled** . . ." (Heb. 7:26).

Virtuous woman. "Who can find a **virtuous** woman?" (Prov. 31:10, KJV). Today, virginity has almost become extinct. Since a woman is to be *untouched,* dating must be out of the question. If you do the research, you will find that when dating became the norm, morality in our country plummeted. Dating is a 20th-century invention. As a father, rethink this idea of dating in light of the rotten fruit that has resulted from this dangerous practice. Encourage courting and save the dating until after the marriage. Also, be very careful of church youth groups and youth camps. The most important way to renew your mind is to eliminate the label "teen" or "teenager." Instead, refer to your daughter as a young woman or a young lady. If you want her to grow up properly, her time should be spent with her mother, and her friends should be her mother's friends and other godly women. Undoubtedly one of the most important relationships is *your* relationship with your daughter. Would you say you have a relationship? How good is it? Do you two have a deep love for one another? Do you have her heart now? If so, keep it and protect it until you give her hand in marriage. If you don't have a close relationship with your daughter(s), begin now to win her heart by spending time with her, listening to her, and showing her understanding.

Virgin: a woman untouched. The priests in the Bible were to take a virgin because of what impurity would do to their children. "And he [the priest] shall take a wife in her **virginity**—that he may not profane his offspring . . ." (Lev. 21:13). Men, if you intend to have a godly heritage, you must keep your daughters protected from those who would steal their virginity and therefore steal your godly heritage. How can you possibly accomplish this enormous task in this day and age?

There are many books on the subject of courtship versus dating. Another way of gaining the knowledge you'll need to guide your family is by talking to men whose daughters have remained morally pure. Now, we all know that some "appear" pure; some may even boast of their pureness because they have not yet "gone all the way." God tells us that a true virgin is untouched. Your wife is probably a good judge; we men are usually "snowed." Are you taking on your responsibility to protect your daughter properly? You *are* ultimately responsible! If your wife and/or your daughter are fighting you concerning *your* protection of them, stand firm, now! You can't get back your daughter's virginity once it is gone.

Why would any young man want a virtuous woman? Because "a **virtuous** woman is a *crown* to her husband . . ." (Prov. 12:4 KJV). The NASB states it as: "An **excellent** wife is the *crown* of her husband . . ." (Prov. 12:4). Do you want the Truth about the virtuous woman?

Virtue: excellence. An example of an excellent and virtuous woman in the Bible is Ruth: "And now, my daughter, do not fear. I will do for you whatever you ask, for all my people in the city know that you are a woman of **excellence**" (Ruth 3:11). Can your sons ever hope to find this type of wife? "An **excellent** wife, who can find?" (Prov. 31:10). Are you training your sons to stay away from the adulterous woman and the harlot? Or has your lack of training or example left them wide open to the seductions of a "Delilah"? What are your hopes for your sons? Do you care? Or are you too involved in your work or sports?

Difficult times will come. "But realize this, that in the **last days** *difficult times* will come. *For men will be* **lovers of self,** lovers of money, boastful, arrogant, revilers, disobedient to parents, **ungrateful, unholy, unloving,** irreconcilable, malicious gossips, *without* **self-control,** brutal, haters of good, treacherous, reckless, conceited, **lovers of pleasure rather than lovers of God;** holding to a *form of godliness, although they have* **denied**

its power; and avoid such men as these. For among them are those who *enter into households* and **captivate weak women** weighed down with sins, led on by various impulses, always learning and never able to come to the knowledge of the Truth" (2 Tim. 3:1–7).

Is this a description of you? Have you put pressure on your wife to live the sinful ways of the world to satisfy your lusts? Have you told her that this will keep you from adultery? The world tells us that a wife should act as a harlot—before and after the marriage. Even Christian books on marriage encourage a woman to act as a harlot or a "mistress." This will not keep us from adultery. The opposite is true. How do we know?

Because of the fruits! "You will know them by their fruits" (Matt. 7:16). What are the fruits of our wives imitating harlots and their ways? Aren't there *more* men in adultery than ever before? Doesn't adultery run rampant even in the church? If our wives participate in lingerie parties, shop at stores like Victoria's Secret, or have their picture taken at Glamour Shots (so they can look like they posed for Playboy) to try to keep and please us, then they are imitating harlots and their ways. Even Wal-Mart, the all-American store, displays and sells articles that could only have been purchased in Frederick's of Hollywood just a few years ago! Let us remember: "You adulteresses, do you not know that the *friendship of the world* is hostility toward God? Therefore whoever wishes to be a friend of the world **makes himself** an *enemy of God"* (James 4:4).

The marriage bed. Next time you are tempted to buy, or encourage your wife to buy, an article of clothing that a harlot would wear, ask yourself if you are not setting her up as an adulteress and you for certain unfaithfulness. Let us rather rise above those in the world as well as those who are being deceived in the church. When you commit yourself to keeping your bed undefiled, God will reward you and your wife with more pleasurable intimacy than you can ever imagine. "Let marriage be held in honor among all, and let **the marriage bed** be *undefiled* . . ." (Heb. 13:4). Of course trials and temptations will come your way; but, if you are steadfast, the reward will be close at hand.

Warning: Never tell your son to look at a woman who is indecently dressed or attractive; you are encouraging him to lust. Even if you don't tell him to look, he will follow your example; do you look? Some men unconsciously look without even thinking. Men, start thinking about it and consciously look away! It shames your wife if you look at another woman whether she is with you or not.

Joseph's discretion. The definition of discretion is *action* based upon caution. Discretion in the thesaurus is: attentive, careful, cautious, considerate, **discerning,** prudent. Many godly men have fallen into the pit of adultery, both today and in Biblical times. One of the men in Scripture who did not fall was Joseph. Let's look at this situation with the boss's wife to learn "action based upon caution."

Discerning and wise. Because of Joseph's life of trials and tribulations, he acquired discernment as well as wisdom. "So Pharaoh said to Joseph, 'Since God has informed you of all this, there is no one so **discerning and wise** as you are'" (Gen. 41:39).

"And it came about after these events that his master's wife looked with desire at Joseph, and she said, 'Lie with me.' But he refused and said to his master's wife, '. . . How then could I do this great evil, and **sin against God?**'" (Gen. 39:7). Joseph could discern that sin is always against God. David remembered this after his sin of adultery. "*Against Thee,* **Thee only,** I have sinned, and done what is evil in Thy sight, so that Thou art justified when Thou dost speak, and blameless when Thou dost judge" (Ps. 51:4). If you think that your wife deserves your unfaithfulness because of her coldness or because you never can get along, think again— "*Against God,* **God only**" have you sinned!

"Now it happened one day that he went into the house to do his work, and **none of the men of the household was there inside**" (Gen. 39:11). Billy Graham has stated that he is never with another woman alone, period! He says that sometimes it is quite difficult, but it is well worth the trouble or inconvenience it causes. He never is alone in a car, alone in his office, or alone in a restaurant with a woman. One time he said that a woman was assigned to pick him up from the airport for one of his speaking engagements. He called the church to see if other arrangements could be made. When they couldn't, he took a cab. Maybe you feel that this is going to extremes, but the proof is in the fruits. Wouldn't Satan just love to destroy this man's ministry the way he has destroyed so many others! How many pastors have run off with one of their flock? How many men have left with their secretaries? Come on, men—this is war! Cover yourself; don't leave your guard down and yourself wide open for an attack!

"And she caught him by his garment, saying, 'Lie with me!' And he left his garment in her hand and **fled,** and went outside" (Gen. 39:12). **"Flee immorality.** Every other sin that a man commits is outside the body, but the immoral man sins against his own body" (1 Cor. 6:18). Men, don't wait until you must run out naked, literally or figuratively! When you come across a situation that could possibly become a problem, flee!!! This is no time to stand firm. Move, get another job, ask for a transfer, or fire her. If you don't, you are making a terrible mistake.

"When she saw that he had left his garment in her hand, and had fled outside, she called to the men of her household, and said to them, 'See, he has brought in a Hebrew to us to make sport of us; he came in to me to lie with me, and I screamed.' And it came about when he heard that I raised my voice and screamed, that he left his garment beside me and fled, and went outside. So she left his garment beside her until his master came home" (Gen. 39:13). If you lie with another woman, or even get close to lying with another woman, she will someday, somehow, tell others *everything*.

In Restore Ministries, we have heard numerous accounts of the adulteress calling the wife to tell her every little perverted detail. This usually happens when the husband is trying to break away from his sin of adultery; the adulteress feels rejected and responds in this manner. (Have you noticed that this manual has never called adultery an "affair"? Adultery is not an affair; the word "affair" connotes a party. This is no party, not for *anyone* involved. Adultery is a sin that brings great pain and destruction to the lives of everyone concerned. It also destroys the Christian testimony by making a mockery of God and His Word if the adulterer has proclaimed himself to be a Christian.)

"So is the one who goes in to his neighbor's wife; whoever touches her will not go unpunished . . ." (Prov. 6:29). "The one who commits adultery with a woman is lacking sense; he who would destroy himself does it. Wounds and disgrace he will find, and his reproach will not be blotted out. For jealousy enrages a man, and he will not spare in the day of vengeance. He will not accept any ransom, nor will he be content though you give many gifts" (Prov. 6:32–35).

Discretion (defined as prudence, discerning caution) is certainly what is needed. God tells us that if we lack discretion, we can acquire it by reading the book of Proverbs. "[The Proverbs] . . . give prudence to the naive, to the youth knowledge and **discretion**" (Prov. 1:4). Read the Proverbs daily, one chapter for each day of the month (e.g., on the twelfth day of the month, read the twelfth chapter of Proverbs.)

And by having discretion, you are protected. **"Discretion** will *guard* you, understanding will watch over you, to deliver you from the way of evil . . ." (Prov. 2:11–12).

Discretion is also the lifeline to your soul. "My son, do not let them depart from your sight; keep sound wisdom and **discretion,** so they will be *life to your soul* and adornment to your neck. Then you will walk in your way securely and your foot will not stumble. When you lie down you will not be afraid and your sleep will be sweet" (Prov. 3:21–22).

The foundation for discretion is **wisdom** and **understanding.** When you have obtained them, you will be able to use discretion. "My son, give attention to my *wisdom,* incline your *ear* to my *understanding;* then you may observe **discretion,** and your lips may reserve knowledge" (Prov. 5:1–2).

If I have fallen into adultery, can I ever be truly forgiven?

What did Jesus say? Jesus said to the woman caught in adultery, "Did no one condemn you? . . . Neither do I condemn you; go your way. *From now on, sin no more"* (John 8:10–11). Sin, any sin that is confessed and truly repented for, will be forgiven by God. Jesus paid the price for all our sins by going to the cross. But remember, Jesus not only forgave, He also said, "From now on, sin no more."

Don't be quick to judge other men who are struggling or have fallen. Jesus also said to the people who wanted this woman in adultery punished, "He who is without sin among you, cast the first stone" (John 8:7). Are you without sin; are you ready to cast the first stone at others because you haven't physically committed adultery? "If we say that we have no sin, we are deceiving ourselves, and the Truth is not in us" (1

John 1:8). As we have seen, truthfully most of us have committed adultery in the light of the Scripture **"Everyone who looks on a woman** to *lust for her* **has committed adultery."**

When God refers to adulterers and fornicators, He says, "And such *were* some of you; but you were washed, but you were *sanctified,* but you were justified in the name of the Lord Jesus Christ and in the Spirit of our God" (1 Cor. 6:11).

Most important is repentance. Repentance means turning away from the evil and doing good. Most men remain in the sin of adultery because they are in too deep. They somehow feel responsible for the adulterous woman. Many times they are more loyal to her than to their own wives and families! Here is a biblical explanation for this behavior: "His own iniquities will capture the wicked, and he will be held with the cords of his sin" (Prov. 5:22). Many men try to get away from their immoral situation, but the sinful cords of lust and selfishness hold them. "And do not participate in the unfruitful deeds of darkness, but instead even expose them . . . But all things become visible when they are exposed by the light . . ." (Eph. 5:11–13).

To rid yourself of sin, you must expose it to the light—the light of Scripture and the light of Truth. Your loyalty *must* be to the Lord and to the wife of your youth. But what about the other woman whom you have basically used? What do you suppose your wife would say to do with your adulteress? You must break all contact with her—forever! You were probably very rude and unkind to your wife back when you were deceived into thinking you didn't want her anymore. You've got to be just as firm with the adulteress and cut the situation off immediately! Don't ever meet or talk again; walk away from any conversations and hang up when you hear her voice. If you don't repent and handle it in this way, you will fall again, and again, and again. Stand up and be a man of God now, or you will probably pay the price for your sin and lack of guts in hell!

"Don't be overcome with evil, but overcome evil with good" (Rom. 12:21). God specifically asked His prophet Hosea to remarry his wife Gomer, even after she was blatantly unfaithful to him. "For she is not my wife, and I am not her husband . . . Then she will say, 'I will go back to my first husband, for it was better for me then than now.' Then the Lord said to me [Hosea], 'Go again, love a woman who is loved by her husband, yet an adulteress'" (Hos. 2:2–3:1). God used the story of Hosea and Gomer to show His commitment to His own. This love story of Hosea and Gomer is written in story form in *How to Save Your Marriage Alone*. (See the recommended reading.)

Another example is found in Luke 15:30. The older son said to his father, ". . . But when this son of yours came, who devoured your wealth with harlots, you killed the fattened calf for him" (Luke 15:30). The father said to his older son, "But we had to be merry and rejoice, for this brother of yours **was dead** and has begun to live, and was lost and has been found" (Luke 15:32). There *is* true forgiveness for you if you have been unfaithful, certainly from God and eventually from your wife. If you are not experiencing forgiveness, you must make sure you have been humble in your repentance and have placed your ability to overcome this sin in *His* strength. Your part is to be obedient by breaking the relationship and keeping away from *any contact* with the adulteress. If this means moving, changing jobs, or whatever, *do it!*

Can I ever trust myself again? No. God said to trust *Him* and Him alone. "Cursed is the man who trusts mankind and makes flesh his strength . . . Blessed is the man who trusts in the Lord and whose trust is the Lord" (Jer.17:5–7).

What can I do to work *with* God? "And looking upon them Jesus said to them, 'With men this is impossible, but with God all things are possible'" (Matt. 19:26). Here is a Scriptural formula that can help you battle temptation. "Keep watching and praying, that you may not come into temptation; the spirit is willing, but the flesh is weak" (Mark 14:38). God may allow many tests to come into our lives, to be sure, but when God heals, *it is finished*. Keep in mind though, if you sow in the flesh, you will reap in the flesh! "For the one who sows to his own flesh shall from the flesh reap corruption, but the one who sows to the Spirit shall from the Spirit reap eternal life" (Gal. 6:8). Spiritual blessings have no sorrow added to them: "It is the *blessing of the Lord* that makes rich, and He adds **no sorrow to it**" (Prov. 10:22).

Personal Commitment: To consistently be aware of the possible traps of immorality in my life. "Based on what I have just learned from God's Word, I strive to be morally pure. I will remove items that would cause me to stumble. And more importantly I will remove myself from situations that I should flee from regardless of the trouble or inconvenience it may cause and regardless of what others may think."

Date: _____ Signed: _____

"Not that I have already obtained it, or have already become perfect, but I press on, in order that I may lay hold of that for which also I was laid hold of by Christ Jesus" (Phil. 3:12).

Homework

Let your mind dwell on these things. "Finally, brethren, whatever is true, whatever is honorable, whatever is right, whatever is pure, whatever is lovely, whatever is of good repute, if there is any excellence, and if anything worthy of praise, let your mind dwell on these things" (Phil. 4:8).

1. **3x5 cards.** Are you faithful to write down the verses from *each* chapter that has touched your heart? Continue to keep these cards with you and bring them out *regularly* as the Holy Spirit prompts you.

2. **Hide His Word to save you from sin.** "Thy Word have I hid in mine heart, that I might not sin against Thee" (Ps. 119:11, KJV). The verses that are in the Test Your Wisdom section deal with the adulterous woman. They are a *must* for you to memorize.

3. Share the wisdom from *this* chapter with *one other man* who has no idea of the dangers and enticements of an adulterous woman. Make sure that you have first removed the log from your eye, so that you can help remove his speck.

Test Your Wisdom

1. What are the three secrets of a blameless life? "And let him _____ _____ from evil and *do good*" (1 Pet. 3:11). "*Blessed* are those whose way is _____" (Ps. 119:1).

2. What is the consequence of your son not marrying a virgin, or your daughter not being a virgin when she marries? "And he shall take a wife in her **virginity**… that he may not _____ his offspring…" (Lev. 21:13–15).

3. Let's list the characteristics of an adulterous woman: "To keep you from the evil woman, from the smooth tongue of the adulteress" (Prov. 6:24). "But in the end she is _____ as wormwood, _____ as a two-edged sword. She does not ponder the path of life; her ways are _____, she does not know it" (Prov. 5:4–6).

4. "With her many persuasions she _____ him; with her _____ lips, she _____ him" (Prov. 7:21).

5. "She is _____ and _____; her feet do not _____ at _____" (Prov. 7:11).

6. She doesn't admit her mistakes. "This is the way of an adulterous woman; she eats and wipes her mouth and says, 'I have done _____ _____'" (Prov. 30:20).

7. "You adulteresses, do you not know that the friendship of _____ _____ is hostility toward God? Therefore, whoever wishes to be a friend of the world makes himself an _____ of _____" (James 4:4).

*The answers to Homework questions are at the end of this workbook.

Chapter 8

Manages His Own Household

*He must be one who manages his own household well . . .
but if a man does not know how to manage his own household,
how will he take care of the church of God?*
—1 Timothy 3:4–5

Many men feel it is their responsibility to punish or chastise another who sins, especially their wives. Scripture teaches us differently and tells us that we will realize adverse consequences for these prideful actions. The husband is to be the authority over the wife, this is true, but what if the wife rebels? Are we then to punish her as we do our children? Proverbs 10:12 says, "Hatred stirs up strife, but love covers all transgressions." And 1 Peter 4:8 says, "Above all, keep fervent in your love for one another, because love covers a multitude of sins."

Discipline. Discipline is referred to 90 times in the Old Testament. Discipline, Scripture says, is for training, correcting, and punishing. God is the Father, and we are His children. Christ's relationship with the church is to be our example of a proper husband and wife relationship. "For the husband is the head of the wife, as Christ also is the head of the church, He Himself being the Savior of the body" (Eph. 5:23). Then what does Christ do to discipline the church? We see no discipline from Christ; all discipline comes from God our Father. Instead, from our Lord Jesus, we see the epitome of love. "Husbands, love your wives, just as Christ also loved the church and gave Himself up for her . . ." (Eph. 5:25). This love is what draws us to Him; it speaks to our hearts and is the reason why we desire to obey Him. "But as the church is subject to Christ, so also the wives ought to be to their husbands in everything" (Eph. 5:24).

Proverbs. References to discipline are found 36 times in Proverbs and are almost always used to give us instruction concerning the parent-child relationship. Though there are many Scriptures that refer to husbands and their wives in the Bible, none instructs the husband to discipline, chastise, or punish his wife.

Know the love. Paul followed our Lord's example and lived out love for those in the church. He wrote, "For out of much affliction and anguish of heart I wrote to you with many tears; not that you should be made sorrowful, but that you **might know the love which I have especially for you** . . . You should rather *forgive and comfort* him, lest somehow such a one be overwhelmed by excessive sorrow. Wherefore I urge you to reaffirm your love for him" (2 Cor. 2:4–7). *This is so important!* "He heals the brokenhearted . . ." (Ps. 147:3).

Encouraged to love. But, aren't women also commanded to love their husbands? No, they are to be encouraged to love their husbands and their children by older "Titus women." "Older women likewise are to be reverent in their behavior . . . teaching what is good, that they may *encourage* the young women to love their husbands, to love their children . . ." (Titus 2:3–4). The feminist movement has changed the way everyone thinks. Unless what you are talking about or referring to is *unisex,* it is **not** "politically correct." This has resulted in pastors, Christian radio and television shows, and Christian publications being extremely careful not to violate this new way of thinking. But God said, "But from the beginning of creation, God made them *male and female"* (Mark 10:6). We need to teach our sons and daughters to understand and be pleased with their distinct male and female differences, since that is how God created them.

Honor and obey. Children are also never commanded to love their mothers or fathers; they are commanded to honor and obey. "Children, obey your parents in the Lord, for this is right" (Eph. 6:1). "Honor your father and your mother, as the Lord your God has commanded you . . ." (Deut. 5:16). Children are commanded 15 times in the Bible to honor their parents. It is the fifth of the Ten Commandments. Are you training your children to follow this commandment? Could your behavior be causing them to stumble? "It would be *better for him if* a millstone were hung around his neck, and he were thrown into the sea, than that he should cause one of these little ones to stumble" (Luke 17:2). Are you a drunkard, a sluggard, or a lover of self whose sole purpose is to play? (See Chapter 14, "Father's Instructions," for more knowledge.)

Grant her honor. "You husbands likewise, live with your wives in an understanding way, as with a weaker vessel, since she is a woman; and **grant her honor** as a fellow heir of the grace of life, so that your prayers may not be hindered" (1 Pet. 3:7).

Love your wife. Wives are commanded to submit to and respect their husbands. They are not commanded to love or honor us. Yet we husbands are *commanded* to love and **honor** our wives.

Love your own wife as yourself. "Nevertheless let each individual among you also **love his own wife** even **as himself;** and let the wife see to it that she respect her husband" (Eph. 5:33).

Love your wives. "Husbands, **love your wives,** just as Christ also loved the church and gave Himself up for her . . ." (Eph. 5:25).

Love your own wife. "So husbands ought also to **love their own wives** as their own bodies. He who loves his own wife loves himself . . ." (Eph. 5:28). Does this mean we are to love ourselves before we can love our wives? No. God tells us that we all love ourselves: "He who loves his own wife loves himself; for **no one ever** *hated his own flesh,* but nourishes and cherishes it, just as Christ also does the church . . ." (Eph. 5:29). If you love yourself more than you ought then you are just an example of man in the last days: "But realize this, that in the last days difficult times will come. For men will be **lovers of self** . . ." (2 Tim. 3:1).

Love your wife. "Husbands, **love your wives,** and do not be embittered against them" (Col. 3:19).

We love, because He first loved us. The foundation of love is found in 1 John 4:19: "We love, because He first loved us." Christ's example toward us is what we should follow. "For you have been called for this purpose . . . leaving you an example for you to follow in His steps" (1 Pet. 2:2). A wife cannot give love without *being loved first.*

When we give our love first, only then can our wives learn to love us. Love motivates submission and respect. In the same way, when we grow more in love with our Lord, we are motivated to righteous living. Does your wife respect, love, and submit to you? If not, could it be due to an inadequate expression of your love for her? Your love is evident in the way you look at your wife, in the loving words you speak to her, in your loving touch, and in the time you spend with her. Does your wife *feel* your love?

Also, notice that loving words came before loving touch. Men, we have a habit of not speaking the loving words that our wife wants to hear, but we expect her to respond to our touch. Our wives may be begging us (in their hearts) to say that we love them. Some of us say we love them and yet don't talk to them. Is your wife constantly begging to talk with you? "Talk—meaning that you actually participate and share in the conversation. Learn to be a good listener first, and then comment on what *she* has said. If you see a man who is not receiving affection from his wife, you can be sure he is not showing her proper love.

If you love her, show her. Stop pretending that you love her just because you provide for her or because you tell her. "For let not that *man expect* that he will **receive anything** from the Lord, being a *double-minded* man, unstable in all his ways" (James 1:8). Love is an action. Let's look at 1 Corinthians chapter 13 to find out more about love.

What then is love? Thousands of authors, play writers, and movie directors have provided us with what *they* think love is. Let us go to the Author of Love for the true description: "And if I have the gift of prophecy, and know all mysteries and all knowledge; and if I have all faith, so as to remove mountains, but do not have **love,** *I am nothing*. And if I give all my possessions to feed the poor, and if I deliver my body to be burned, but do not have **love,** *it profits me nothing*. Love is **patient,** love is **kind,** and is **not jealous;** love does not brag and is not arrogant, does **not act unbecomingly;** it does not **seek its own,** is **not provoked,** does not take into account a wrong suffered, does not rejoice in unrighteousness, but rejoices with the Truth; **bears all things, believes all things, hopes all things, endures all things. Love never fails"** (1 Cor. 13:2–8). Love is more than just saying that you love your wife; it is your actions or reactions towards her. Let's find out more about acting out our love.

Love Never Fails

Love is patient. Patience, which seems to be in short supply with many of us men, is a reaction and it is, therefore, very important that we learn to react to our wives with patience. "And we urge you, brethren . . . *encourage* the fainthearted, *help* the weak, be **patient** with all men" (1 Thess. 5:14). Did you notice that this verse also says to "help the weak"?

Men, are you guilty of not helping your wife with tasks she needs done because of your laziness? God gave physical strength to you that He did not give to your wife. Women who have husbands who don't help them will usually resort to all kinds of ways to get the job done. They will either learn to do it themselves, ask a neighbor, or wait for their sons to grow strong enough to help them. Isn't that pathetic?

Of course, many of us are quick to accuse our wives of nagging us when they remind us about something we promised to do days, weeks, months, or even years ago. We may even laugh about this behavior with our friends. And then we wonder what happened when our wives become bitter! "Hope deferred makes the heart sick, but desire fulfilled is a tree of life" (Prov. 13:12).

Our next step is usually to judge that bitterness in our wives as sin. Brother, are you quick to judge your wife? "Do not judge lest you be judged. For in the way you judge, you will be judged; and by your standard of measure, it will be measured to you. And why do you look at the speck that is in your brother's eye, but do not notice the log that is in your own eye? Or how can you say to your brother, 'Let me take the speck out of your eye,' and behold, the log is in your own eye? You hypocrite, first take the log out of your own eye, and then you will see clearly to take the speck out of your brother's eye" (Matt. 7:1–5). God did not command your wife not to be bitter toward you, but He *did* command *you* not to be bitter toward her. **"Husbands,** love your wives, and do not be **embittered** *against them"* (Col. 3:19).

Love is kind. We seem to forget that kindness goes a long way when dealing with our wives. Isn't that why your wife married you? Would she choose to marry someone who would later be unkind to her? "And the Lord's bond-servant must not be quarrelsome, but be **kind** to all, able to teach, patient when wronged . . ." (2 Tim. 2:24). When you are having a conversation with your wife, give her your full attention, look into her eyes, and speak to her in a kind and gentle way. Most of us don't listen or comment on what our wives are saying; then we suddenly bark out our response. Non-participation will usually result in our wives yelling at us.

Does your wife seem to repeat the same thing over and over again? When this happens, you obviously have not shown her that you've heard her by answering her, nodding your head, grunting, or whatever. Men, we know we are all too often "zoned out," in "another world." We feel it's our right to come home to find peace and quiet; it's our place to relax, unwind. We don't want to be bothered by listening to another thing, do we? Men, make sure you tune in to your wife rather than the television or the newspaper. Of course our excuse is that "She will never leave me alone until she gets her own way. She doesn't just want me to listen!" Try listening, commenting, and responding during your conversations with her and see what happens. Our wives are supposed to be under our authority and our protection. Let's not make it so hard for them to be under our authority and be obedient to God's Word.

Again, we've got to remember that women are different than men. They don't just "get to the point"; they tend to take the "scenic route" in the conversation. Yet, we are still commanded to be patient and understanding with them. "You husbands likewise, live with your wives in an **understanding way,** as with a weaker vessel, since she is a woman; and grant her honor as a fellow heir of the grace of life, so that your prayers may not be hindered" (1 Pet. 3:7). When your wife doesn't feel you understand, she'll either tell you so, or she'll go away broken. "A joyful heart is good medicine, but a **broken spirit** dries up the bones" (Prov. 17:22). "The spirit of a man can endure his sickness, but a **broken spirit** *who can bear?"* (Prov. 18:14). How has her countenance been lately? "A joyful heart makes a cheerful face, *but when the heart is sad,* the **spirit is broken"** (Prov. 15:13).

Love does not act unbecomingly. Acting unbecomingly has become commonplace in too many of our homes. Major "scenes" or "ranting and ravings" go on all too often. Do you have control over your spirit? Love your wife enough to control *your* spirit. Don't expect your wife to control *her* spirit until you can control your own. "Like a city that is broken into and without walls is a man who has **no control over his spirit"** (Prov. 25:28). You are her leader; she is the weaker vessel.

Love does not seek its own. Men in today's society are encouraged to "do their own thing" and to "just do it." Not long ago, that attitude would have been considered selfish and self-centered. God's Word brings us back to the truth: selfishness will reap only sorrow and regrets. "Do nothing from selfishness or empty conceit, but with humility of mind let each of you regard one another as **more important than himself . . .**" (Phil. 2:3). Consider the responsibility you have to manage your household, to love your wife, and to instruct and train your children. If we are doing all that God commands, then how can we have so much free time to play sports, watch television, hunt, or tinker with hobbies? It is, obviously, because we are seeking our own interests and dumping many of *our* responsibilities on our wives.

Love is not provoked. How short is your fuse? Are you quick to fly off the handle? Is most of what you say expressed in a raised voice? "A hot-tempered man stirs up strife, but the **slow to anger** pacifies contention" (Prov. 15:18). "He who is **slow to anger** is better than the mighty, and he who rules his spirit, than he who captures a city" (Prov. 16:32). "A man's *discretion* makes him **slow to anger,** and it is his glory to overlook a transgression" (Prov. 19:11). We must learn to control our emotions and practice discretion when we are offended or disappointed. Those who are born into royalty are taught from an early age to control their feelings and emotions in public. We are adopted children of *the King!* We should therefore act accordingly in the presence of others, especially our wives.

Love bears all things. The burdens we bear as husbands and fathers can sometimes seem overwhelming; don't be too proud to run to Him. "Blessed be the Lord, who daily **bears our burden,** the God who is our salvation. Selah" (Ps. 68:19). "For this finds favor, if for the sake of conscience toward God a *man* **bears up under sorrows** when *suffering unjustly"* (1 Pet. 2:19). Many men run to their wives for help. Others run to another woman, to the bottle, or to drugs for help. Remember to run to Him and Him alone!

Love believes all things. Sometimes following Scripture, when it comes to dealing with our wives, takes a lot of faith, but God promises us that we will not be disappointed! ". . . For *with the heart* man **believes,** resulting in righteousness, and with the mouth he confesses, resulting in salvation" (Rom. 10:10). For the Scripture says, ". . . Whoever believes *in Him* will not be *disappointed"* (Rom. 10:11). Trust in our Creator and the Author of life for a real change!

Love hopes all things. Would you describe yourself as a positive or negative person? Perhaps you are able to fool others into believing you are a very upbeat person, but what would your wife say if she were asked to describe you? Do you have faith? That is what a positive attitude is—faith. "Now **faith** is the assurance of things **hoped for,** the conviction of things not seen" (Heb. 11:1). "Know that **wisdom** is thus for your soul; if you find it, then there will be a future, and your **hope** will not be cut off" (Prov. 24:14).

If you are lacking faith, seek God's Word, pore over it, and meditate on it. "How blessed is the man who does not walk in the counsel of the wicked, nor stand in the path of sinners, nor sit in the seat of scoffers! But his delight is in the law of the Lord, and in His law he **meditates day and night.** And he will be like a tree firmly planted by streams of water, which yields its fruit in its season, and its leaf does not wither; and in *whatever he does,* **he prospers"** (Ps. 1:1).

Love endures all things. When we feel we are at the end of our rope, God encourages us to hang on to Him. "But the one who **endures to the end,** he shall be saved" (Matt. 24:13). "And you will be hated by all on account of My name, but the one who **endures to the end,** he shall be saved" (Mark 13:13). Most of us endure certain types of hardships, without complaint, like a man should. But if we examine ourselves we may find areas where we are unable to "endure," areas in our lives where we are we acting like babies, or quitters.

Men, we need to act like men; we must be examples for our sons, daughters, wives, and this effeminate-accepting society. We've got to demonstrate, through our example, what the Scriptures say. "Be on the alert, stand firm in the faith, **act like men,** be strong" (1 Cor. 16:13). "Or do you not know that the unrighteous shall not inherit the kingdom of God? Do not be deceived; neither fornicators, nor idolaters, nor adulterers, **nor effeminate,** nor homosexuals, nor thieves, nor covetous, nor drunkards, nor revilers, nor swindlers, shall inherit the kingdom of God" (1 Cor. 6:9–10).

Love *never* fails. This is one of God's greatest promises that His love for us, and our love for others, especially our wives, will never fail! "Hatred stirs up strife, but **love** covers all transgressions" (Prov. 10:12). There is a proper order for everything, since God is a God of order. We need only look at the perfect order of the universe, the perfect order of the seasons and the days to see God's way of order. God has also set up the order of authority: "But I want you to understand that Christ is the head of every man, and the man is the head of a woman, and God is the head of Christ" (1 Cor. 11:3). So God is over Christ, Christ is over man, man is over woman, and parents are over children. The interesting thing to note is that all love is to be given from above, not from beneath. The love is initiated by the authority figure, and, if given properly, it is responded to and reciprocated by those under authority. "The one who does not love does not know God, for **God is love**" (1 John 4:8).

God is the origin of love. "But God demonstrates His own **love** toward us, in that while we were yet sinners, **Christ** died for us" (Rom. 5:8). God states His love for us and also demonstrates His love for us. We, in the same way, must tell our wives that we love them and then demonstrate it with our actions as stated in 1 Corinthians 13. But how are we to possess the proper love for our wives? ". . . and to know the **love of Christ** which surpasses knowledge, that you may be filled up to all the fullness of God" (Eph. 3:19). We must first know and experience Christ's love. When was the last time you ran to *Him* for your love? We *all* need love. Where do you get your love from when you're running on empty? Many times when we don't get the love we would like to have from our wives, we turn cold toward them or downright mean.

Men, don't blame your wife if she's not meeting your needs; you are most likely reaping what you have sown by your lack of love for her. Remember, you are to get your love from Christ and give that kind of love to your wife. Then she will respond by giving you the love you desire from her. **"Husbands, love your wives,** just as **Christ also loved the church** and gave Himself up for her . . ."** (Eph. 5:25). "For if you love those who love you, what reward have you? Do not even the tax-gatherers do the same?" (Matt. 5:46). "And if you love those who love you, what credit is that to you? For even sinners love those who love them" (Luke 6:32). Giving our wives love when they don't deserve it (loving the unlovable) is what Christ-like love is all about!

Unchanging love. "Who is a God like Thee . . . He [God] *delights* in **unchanging love**" (Mic. 7:18). Begin to demonstrate your unchanging love for your wife and children by showing, with your speech and actions, that you love them in all situations. Make sure they know that you will *always* love them.

How to *Really* Love Your Wife

Love her with your time. When we like someone, we enjoy spending time with him or her. Where is most of your time being spent? When you prioritize all that is important to you, where does your wife fit in? Most of us are guilty of wasting too much precious time on things that will mean absolutely nothing years from now. When you do spend time with her, where do you go or what do you do? Is it always *you* who decides where you will go or what you will do? Do you give your wife time to do the things she enjoys doing, or do you expect her to be the only one who cares for the children as she waits at home for you while you do your thing? Do you give her some of your time to fix, make, or move things, or is your "Honey Do List" more like a "My Husband Never Will Do" list. Show your wife you love her by giving her your time and attention.

Love her with your eyes. Even though our lives can be hurried, stressful, too full, and much too tiring, we must take the time to look lovingly into our wife's eyes. She needs to know that she is the apple of your eye! David desired this from the Lord in Psalm 17:8: "Keep me as the apple of [Thy] eye . . ." All the activities that seem to keep us so busy are usually temporary; therefore they have only temporal value. ". . . while we look not at the things which are seen, but at the things which are not seen; for the things which are seen are temporal, but the things which are not seen are **eternal**" (2 Cor. 4:18).

Put your paper or magazine down, turn away from the thing you are tinkering with, turn off the television, and give your wife some attention. Look her in the eyes and shock her by asking her something like, "How was your day today, sweetheart?" Then be prepared to show her your love by being patient and *listening*. Keep eye contact with her and respond by nodding your head and making short comments like, "That's great," "Did she really?" "I wish I could've seen that," etc. This may sound silly, but most of us have gotten so complacent with our wives, after years of marriage, that we need a basic lesson in communication! We often use proper communication skills with others, but we neglect them with our wives.

Love her with your touch. Touch is very important, as it is able to deliver both comfort and healing powers. What kind of touch do you give your wife? Do you only touch her when you want to be intimate? Do you make her feel cheap by grabbing her in embarrassing areas? What does your touch say to her? Do you comfort her by hugging her when she is crying, especially when you were the one who hurt her? Can she trust you enough to tell you what has hurt her, knowing you'll understand? Husbands, let's be honest. When our wives are giving us the "cold shoulder," it is almost always because they are reacting to our inappropriate behavior toward them. Most of us don't care to look at the uncaring seeds we have sown, and, if we do, we tend to pout or sulk about it instead of being man enough to sow good seed. Sow the "seed" of a loving touch and enjoy the harvest of a loving and affectionate wife.

Love her with your comfort. "Blessed be the God and Father of our Lord Jesus Christ, the Father of mercies and **God of all comfort,** *who comforts us in all our affliction* so that we may be able to **comfort** those who are in any affliction with the **comfort** with which we ourselves are **comforted** by God" (2 Cor. 1:3). Do you comfort your wife when she is hurt or when she cries? The truth is, we men are many times indifferent to our wives' tears. Maybe it's because we feel their tears have manipulated us in the past, and since we don't want to fall for that again, we remain cold. Men, don't miss an opportunity to comfort your wife. These are priceless moments that can be used to draw the two of you into the oneness that you desire. Your wife won't want to be intimate with you when she feels emotionally distant from you. Make it easy for her to love you by comforting her when she hurts.

Love her with honor. Honor is defined as "to regard highly." We are to regard our wives as worthy of honor—honor we should *already* be showing them. "You husbands likewise, live with your wives in an **understanding way,** as with a weaker vessel, since she is a woman; and *grant her* **honor** as a fellow heir of the grace of life, so that your prayers may not be hindered" (1 Pet. 3:7). Remember, by showing honor to our wives, we bring glory to God. When we don't give our wives this type of respect, we are dishonoring God and His Word. We are saying we are Christians but our deeds deny it. "They profess to know God, but by their deeds they deny Him, being detestable and disobedient, and worthless for any good deed" (Titus 1:16). Are you understanding of your wife? **"Good understanding** *produces favor,* but the way of the treacherous is hard" (Prov. 13:15). If you find that you can't understand your wife, maybe it is because you have lived with her in a treacherous way. Honor her from your heart. "This people **honors** me with their lips, but their *heart is far away from Me"* (Matt. 15:8). You must be humble: "And before **honor** comes humility" (Prov. 15:33). "But humility goes before **honor"** (Prov. 18:12). The result will be honor from your wife. "A man's pride will bring him low, but a humble spirit obtains **honor"** (Prov. 29:23).

Love her with your appreciation. Appreciation is defined as favorable recognition. To appreciate means to cherish, enjoy, value, understand, treasure (especially in the marriage vow), take loving care of, and keep alive (in emotion). We spoke earlier about doing things from the heart. If your wife is not one of your treasures, your heart is not with her. "For where your **treasure** is, there will be your *heart* also" (Matt. 6:21). Often when we lose something that we take for granted, we begin to realize how very important it is to us. Do you need to lose your wife before you'll begin to treasure her? If you think that could never happen to you because your wife is a Christian, think again. There are countless numbers of couples, many of whom you probably know, whose marriages have ended in divorce because the wife did not feel loved and treasured as she did when they were first married. Don't wait. Demonstrate your love for your wife now by showing her and telling her that you appreciate her.

Love her with your kind words. "A *soothing tongue* is a tree of life, but perversion in it **crushes the spirit"** (Prov. 15:4). If you have been speaking unkind words to your wife, then most likely her spirit toward you has been crushed. Have you been putting off doing things that you promised you would do for her? Then her heart may be sick toward you. **"Hope deferred** makes the *heart sick,* but desire fulfilled is a tree of life" (Prov. 13:12). How can we take care of our wives spiritually and keep their love alive for us emotionally? We need to consistently speak sweetly and kindly to our wives. This blessing then can be yours: "All the days of the afflicted are bad, but a **cheerful heart** has a *continual feast"* (Prov. 15:15).

Love her by taking your burdens to the Lord. When you have financial worries or job-related worries, take your troubles or worries to the Lord. "**Anxiety in the heart** of a man weighs it down, but a *good word* makes it glad" (Prov.12:25). Turn the pages of your "neglected-except-for-Sunday" Bible and find God's promises, so you can learn to lean on Him. Stop leaning on your wife when you have troubles; she was not designed to carry your burdens. "Trust in the Lord with all your heart, and do not **lean** on your own understanding" (Prov. 3:5). Once you have gone to the Lord with your problems and have grabbed a promise to stand on, you will be a new man when you get up from your chair! "A **joyful heart** is *good medicine,* but a *broken spirit* dries up the bones" (Prov. 17:22). Let your face show the joy that is in your heart. "A **joyful heart** makes a *cheerful face,* but when the heart is sad, the *spirit is broken"* (Prov. 15:13). Be truly thankful. "In *everything* **give thanks;** for this is God's will for you in Christ Jesus" (1 Thess. 5:18). Learn to be content in all situations. ". . . For I have *learned* to be **content** in **whatever circumstances** I am. I know how to get along with humble means . . . and in any and **every circumstance** I have **learned the secret** of being filled and going hungry, both of having abundance and suffering need" (Phil. 4:11–12). **Amen!**

Why Should You Love Her Like This?

You should love her because the Lord has been a witness. "And this is another thing you do: you cover the altar of the Lord with **tears,** with *weeping, and with groaning,* because He no longer regards the offering or accepts it with favor from your hand. Yet you say, 'For what reason?' Because **the Lord has been a witness** between you and the wife of your youth, against whom you have dealt treacherously, though she is your companion and your wife by covenant. But not one has done so who has a remnant of the Spirit" (Mal. 2:13–15). What is the definition of treacherous? Strong's Concordance defines this word as "to pillage, deal deceitfully or unfaithfully, to offend, to transgress, to depart." Have you ever done, or are you doing, any of the things in this definition? If so, you are living treacherously with your wife. Whether you want to acknowledge it or not, the Lord is very aware of how you treat her.

It was God who gave man the woman as a helper suitable for him. Let's not forget the love that the Lord feels for our wives. Is your wife crying out to the Lord because of the way you have been treating her? Are you neglecting her? Are the words you speak to her cutting and cruel? Maybe you've even knocked her around. Men, the beginning of wisdom is to fear the Lord. Do you fear God? Let us all remember a portion of the above Scripture and burn it into our minds and meditate on it: ". . . **The Lord has been a witness** between you and the wife of your youth, against whom you have dealt treacherously, though she is your companion and your wife by covenant. But not one has done so who has a *remnant* of the Spirit" (Mal. 2:15). You have not even a "remnant of His Spirit" in you if you have been unkind to the wife the Lord has given to you!

You should love her because it's never too late. You may be sitting there thinking that it's too late because you haven't been loving your wife properly for years. But the truth is, it's never too late to show your love for her. Begin with your words. Our wives need a kind word from us before they will accept our touch. A good place to start may be with a humble apology. Your words should be ones of deep conviction, sharing with her how wrong you've been, and then asking for her forgiveness. Be sure you don't forget to say, "I love you." Many a dying man has regretted not saying those three words more often to his wife and children.

You should love her in spite of your pride. Is your pride getting in the way? Maybe you would use the word self-esteem. Our world has taken God's command "to esteem others better than ourselves" and twisted it to try and deceive us into building up ourselves, rather than others. "Let nothing be done through strife or vain glory; but in lowliness of mind let each **esteem** others better than themselves. Do not look out for your own interests, but also for the interests of others. Have the attitude in yourselves which was also in Christ Jesus, who, although He existed in the form of God, did not regard equality with God a thing to be grasped, but emptied Himself, taking the form of a bond-servant, and being made in the likeness of men" (Phil 2:3–7, KJV; v. 4, NASB

What About Submission?

Kept entrusting. A woman called Restore Ministries and asked, "How far does God expect a woman to go in regards to submitting to her husband?" Why are women afraid or unwilling to submit to us as their husbands and leaders? God asks Christian husbands and wives to follow in Christ's steps: "For you have been called for this purpose, since Christ also suffered for you, leaving you an example for you to follow in His steps, . . . and while being reviled, He did not revile in return; while suffering, He uttered no threats, but **kept entrusting** Himself *to Him* who judges righteously" (1 Pet. 2:21-23).

Follow Him "in the same way." Jesus asks women specifically to follow Him and His example, as He immediately begins 1 Peter 3 with "In the same way." He tells our wives to submit to us as husbands as He submitted to His heavenly Father, the direct authority over Him. The second example God gives our wives is Sarah: "Thus Sarah obeyed Abraham, calling him lord, and you have become her children if you do what is right without being frightened by any fear" (1 Pet. 3:6). Our wives are to strive to obey us as their husbands like Sarah did. So why is this so difficult for them to do?

Frightened by any fear. "Thus Sarah obeyed Abraham, calling him lord, and you have become her children if you do what is right without being frightened by any fear" (1 Pet. 3:6). Is your wife afraid to obey you? What could she be fearful about? Well, what was Sarah asked to do by her husband Abraham that could have caused her to be fearful? In Genesis 12:11-13 and also in Genesis 20:2, we see that Abraham asked Sarah to lie! To sin! When Abraham told her to say that she was his sister, this caused her to fall into another sin, to be taken as another man's wife! Have you asked your wife to submit to (or go along with) something that she felt was wrong or sinful? So many women fear submission because they have been asked to sin by their husbands. If a wife cannot trust that her husband is following after the Lord, it makes her submission a burden of fear. Maybe you're saying to yourself, "Hey, I never asked her to be another man's wife!" First of all, to set the record straight, neither did Abraham. When he asked Sarah to say she was his sister, this was not only a "little lie," it was a "half lie" since she was his half sister. Nevertheless, this little "half lie" resulted in Sarah being taken twice as another man's wife!

The iniquity of the fathers to the third and the fourth generations. Did you know that Abraham passed this identical sin on to his son Isaac? "When the men of the place asked about his wife, he said, 'She is my sister,' for he was afraid to say, 'my wife,' thinking, 'the men of the place might kill me on account of Rebekah, for she is beautiful . . . Then Abimelech called Isaac and said, 'Behold, certainly she is your wife!

How then did you say, 'She is my sister'? And Isaac said to him, 'Because I said, 'Lest I die on account of her''" (Gen. 26:7). Isaac's sin was worse because Rebekah was not a half sister.

You may be unaware of the verses that remind us of the enormous consequences of a father's sin: ". . . visiting the iniquity of the **fathers** on the children, on the **third and the fourth generations** . . ." (Exod. 20:5). ". . . Yet He will by no means leave the guilty unpunished, visiting the iniquity of **fathers** on the children and on the grandchildren to the **third and fourth generations**" (Exod. 34:7). "The Lord is slow to anger and abundant in lovingkindness, forgiving iniquity and transgression; but He will by no means clear the guilty, visiting the **iniquity of the fathers on the children to the third and the fourth generations**" (Num. 14:18). "You shall not worship them or serve them; for I, the Lord your God, am a jealous God, visiting the iniquity of the **fathers** on the children, and on the **third and the fourth generations** . . ." (Deut. 5:9). Men, we would do well to keep this in mind when we even think of compromising the Truth!

You husbands likewise. The wife's section in 1 Peter is followed by the husband's verse that begins, "You husbands likewise . . ." (1 Pet. 3:7). How are we as husbands over our wives to behave? Let's read on: "You husbands likewise, live with your wives in an understanding way, as with a weaker vessel, since she is a woman; and grant her honor as a fellow heir of the grace of life, so that your prayers may not be hindered. To sum up, let all be harmonious, sympathetic, brotherly, kindhearted, and humble in spirit; not returning evil for evil, or insult for insult, but giving a blessing instead; for you were called for the very purpose that you might inherit a blessing. For, let him who means to love life and see good days refrain his tongue from evil and his lips from speaking guile. And let him turn away from evil and do good; let him seek peace and pursue it. For the eyes of the Lord are upon the righteous, and his ears attend to their prayer, but the face of the Lord is against those who do evil" (1 Pet. 3:9–12).

For the husband is the head of the wife. This portion of Scripture explains that our relationship with our wives is to mirror that of Christ and His church. "Wives, be subject to your own husband, as unto the Lord. For the husband is the head of the wife, as Christ also is the head of the church, He Himself being the Savior of the body. But as the church is subject to Christ, so also the wives ought to be to their husbands in everything" (Eph. 5:22–24). Isn't it sad that many churches don't submit to Christ and His teachings, just as so many women don't submit to their husbands? Probably a correlation here, don't you think?

Your companion and your wife by covenant. Why is it so important that we act according to God's Word? Because when we don't, our *actions* dishonor God and make a mockery of His Word. "Yet you say, 'For what reason?' Because the Lord has been a witness between you and the wife of your youth, against whom you have dealt treacherously, though she is your companion and your wife by covenant. But not one has done so who has a *remnant* of the Spirit. . . . So take heed to your spirit, that you do not deal treacherously. You have wearied the Lord with your words. Yet you say, 'How have we wearied Him?' In that you say, 'Everyone who does evil is good in the sight of the Lord, and He delights in them,' or, 'Where is the God of justice?'" (Mal. 2:14–17). As a Christian couple, our lives are supposed to reflect a picture of Christ and His church. When a husband loves, honors, and understands his wife and she doesn't submit and reverence her husband with a gentle and quiet spirit, then her husband is called a "wimp" or "henpecked." When a wife does submit and reverence her husband with a gentle and quiet spirit and her husband doesn't love, honor, and understand his wife, then she is told she is a doormat! Only when they are cleaved to each other and moving in the direction of the scriptural principles will God's Word be lifted up. (See Chapter 9, "Man Alone," for more knowledge.)

Now that we have searched the Scriptures, let us answer some questions with God's Wisdom . . .

Is submission applicable today? Some men who are kind or maybe just easygoing don't exercise authority over their wives because they feel that it's not applicable today. "Jesus Christ is the same yesterday and today, yes, and forever" (Heb. 13:8). In Matthew 5:18, Jesus says, "For truly I say to you, until heaven and earth pass away, not the smallest letter or stroke shall pass away from the Law, until all is accomplished." ". . . For there is no authority except from God, and *those which exist are established by God*" (Rom. 13:1). There is a false teaching that has permeated some churches. This teaching attempts to deceive men and women by saying that Jesus broke all bondage and therefore wives no longer must submit to their husbands. Well, there are a couple of big holes in this theory. First, Ephesians (where the topic of subjection is covered in great length) was written after Jesus' resurrection. And secondly, wives are not to be under their husbands in *bondage* but rather for their *protection*. If your wife doesn't feel protected but instead feels she is in bondage, you need to make a definite change in your actions and attitude toward her!

If our wives don't or won't submit to our authority, should we use "tough love"? In 1 Corinthians 13, it says that love is gentle and kind, not tough. In 1 Peter 2:23, Jesus uttered no threats when suffering and He says we are to follow in His steps! In 2 Timothy 4:4, it says that in the last days we will want to have our ears tickled and will turn to myths. Using "tough love" with our wives is a myth. And in 2 Timothy 4:3, it also says that we will accumulate teachers who go along with our own desires. It feels good to our flesh to give ultimatums and confront others. But, the Spirit and the flesh are in opposition to one another, "so that you may not do the things that you please" (Gal. 5:16).

Give a blessing instead. Instead of dishing out tough love, respond by ". . . not returning evil for evil, or insult for insult, but **giving a blessing instead**" (1 Pet. 3:9). ". . . And while being reviled, He did not revile in return; while suffering, He uttered no threats, but kept entrusting Himself to **Him** *who judges righteously* . . ." (1 Pet. 2:23). "Do not be overcome by evil, but overcome evil with good" (Rom. 12:21). "Hatred stirs up strife, but **love** *covers all transgressions*" (Prov. 10:12). "Above all, *keep fervent in your* **love** for one another, because **love** *covers a multitude of sins*" (1 Pet. 4:8). Again, we are to pattern our way of treating our wives after Christ's example of how He loves and treats His church.

How can we possibly do all that the Lord asks us to do as husbands in today's world? By grace! And how do we get grace? By humbling ourselves. In James 4:6 it says, "God hates the proud, but gives grace to the humble." And in 2 Corinthians 12:9 it says, "My grace is sufficient for you, for power is perfected in weakness." And yes, contrary to the world's foolish opinions, women are weaker than men. First Peter 3:7 says, "You husbands, likewise, live with your wives in an understanding way, as with a *weaker vessel,* since she is a woman . . ." We must **search for the Truth** in God's Word. We are to *protect* our wives, ". . . for among them are those who enter into households and captivate weak women weighed down with sins, led on by various impulses, always learning and never able to come to the knowledge of the Truth" (2 Tim. 3:6–7).

Personal commitment: To manage my own household. "Based on what I have learned from God's Word, I commit to walk in love with my wife. I will lead my family by my godly example. I promise to never ask my wife to sin, and I will protect her, so she will not fear submission."

Date: _____ Signed: _____

"Not that I have already obtained it, or have already become perfect, but I press on, in order that I may lay hold of that for which also I was laid hold of by Christ Jesus" (Phil. 3:12).

Homework

1. **3x5 cards.** Please use your 3x5 cards and write down the verses from *this* **chapter** that have spoken to your spirit. As stated before, please keep these cards with you and bring them out *regularly* as the Holy Spirit prompts you.

2. **Healing.** Have you noticed any change in the way you're thinking? Stay in His Word and renew your mind with the Truth. Seek out another man who manages his household well; you will know him by his fruits (a happy wife and well-behaved children). He may be hard to find!

3. Share the wisdom from *this* chapter with *one other man*. Remember, the more you boast about your weaknesses, the more the power of Christ will dwell in you—hallelujah!

Test Your Wisdom

1. When our wives insult us, what should we do? "Not returning _____ for _____ or _____ for _____!" (1 Pet. 3:9).

2. What about the idea of "tough love" with our wife? "Love is _____, love is _____ and is not jealous; love does not brag and is _____, _____, does not act unbecomingly; it does not seek its own, is _____ _____, does not take into account a wrong suffered, does not rejoice in unrighteousness, but rejoices with the truth; _____ all things, _____ all things, _____ all things, _____ all things. _____ never _____ . . ." (1 Cor. 13:4–8).

3. How did *our* example, Jesus, respond when He was reviled? _____, while suffering, _____ no _____ (1 Pet. 2:23).

4. Why do most women *not* follow their husbands in submission even though there are so many Scriptures pertaining to it? Because they are _____ (1 Pet. 3:6).

5. Have I ever asked my wife to sin? Yes / No (Does this jog your memory: "Just tell them I'm not home.") "If we say that we have no sin, we are deceiving _____, and the Truth is not in us" (1 John 1:8).

6. If your wife is not submissive to you, her husband, what is at stake? The Word of God will be _____ (Titus 2:5).

7. How can I possibly do all that the Lord asks me to do? By _____ (2 Cor.12:9).

8. How do I get grace? _____ _____ _____ (James 4:6).

*The answers to Homework questions are at the end of this workbook.

Chapter 9

Man Alone

*Then the Lord God said,
'It is not good for the man to be alone;
I will make him a helper suitable for him.'
—Genesis 2:18*

God designed a woman for a man: ". . . bone of my bones, flesh of my flesh" (Gen. 3:12). So why have we men stood back and allowed the feminist philosophies to dishonor the woman's role as wife, mother, and homemaker? Men have stood back because most men are unsure of what a woman was created and designed to do and to be. As we see in today's media-indoctrinated world, men are not men and women are no longer women. This has been part of the feminist movement's agenda for years—to try and *blend* the roles. We now have confusion and unhappiness in both of the sexes. The result? Homosexuality and lesbianism run rampant in our society!

Part 1
Uniquely Created

Created *for* the man. We must seek the knowledge found in God's Word to define **how** we were created and **why** we were created. "And the man gave names to all the cattle, and to the birds of the sky, and to every beast of the field, but for Adam there was not found a **helper suitable for him**" (Gen. 2:20). "For man does not originate from woman, but woman from man; for indeed man was not created for the woman's sake, but **woman for the man's sake**" (1 Cor. 11:8–9). As we begin to move into God's perfect plan for our lives, we then can live the abundant life God promises in His Word. Our lives will reflect God's Word, rather than deny it. Others will be drawn to Christ through the testimony of our lives.

Created male and female. "And God created man in His own image, in the image of God He created him; **male and female** He created them" (Gen. 1:27). "He created them **male and female,** and He blessed them and named them man in the day when they were created" (Gen. 5:2). "But from the beginning of creation, God made them **male and female"** (Mark 10:6). "And He answered and said, 'Have you not read, that He who created them from the beginning made them **male and female** . . .'" (Matt. 19:4). When a woman wears clothing or has a hairstyle that is unfeminine or downright masculine, she is denying that God created her differently.

Masculine. We were created to be men. Don't be duped by modern-day psychology into thinking you need to be more feminine. We need to learn the difference between a feminine man and a gentleman. Webster's Dictionary defines a gentleman as a man of high principles, honorable, and courteous—not ladylike! The disgusting truth is that our society is rampant with *effeminate* men! "Or do you not know that the unrighteous shall not inherit the kingdom of God? Do not be deceived; neither fornicators, nor idolaters, nor adulterers, nor **effeminate,** nor *homosexuals* . . . shall inherit the kingdom of God" (1 Cor. 6:9). If you try to change to be more like your wife, what example of a man will your sons have? Work toward being polite yet strong; learn to be a gentleman.

Man's clothing and woman's clothing. "A woman shall not wear **man's clothing,** nor shall a man put on a **woman's clothing;** for whoever does these things is an abomination to the Lord your God" (Deut. 22:5). We all know that the way people dress affects the way they act. When a little girl puts on a new dress, all her femininity bubbles up and she feels like twirling around and dancing. When a woman wears an apron, she feels more like sticking around the kitchen and baking for her family. When she's wearing a pretty dress, she feels elegant, beautiful, and even romantic. Clothes really do "make the person." Unfortunately, many women are dressing and looking more and more like their husbands by wearing jeans, athletic shoes, and very short hair. There are those women whose work uniform is really a man's clothing, complete with necktie. Their mannerisms usually reflect what they are wearing. Why is it that women are made to wear men's clothing and not the other way around? The reason is because men just wouldn't do it. Yet we allow ourselves as husbands and fathers to be manipulated into letting our wives and daughters look like fools because a bunch of unfeminine women tell us that we are chauvinist pigs if we protect them.

Men, it's time that we as Christians get hold of some of these concepts so we can begin to follow God's principles, teach them to our children, and not be ashamed to speak the Truth to our friends and family. If these principles from God's Word have not been followed because of ignorance or rebellion, now is the time to show ourselves approved. "Be diligent to present yourself approved to God as a workman who does not need to be ashamed, handling accurately the Word of Truth" (2 Tim. 2:15). Remember, many are perishing for a lack of knowledge. "My people are destroyed for lack of knowledge. Because you have rejected knowledge . . ." (Hos. 4:6).

Part 2
Become One Flesh

Leave his father and mother. "'For this cause a man shall **leave his father and mother,** and shall cleave to his wife; and the two shall become one flesh'" (Matt. 19:5). "Consequently, they are no longer two, but one flesh. What therefore God has joined together, let no man separate" (Matt. 19:6). Leaving physically is not exactly what these verses are talking about, since we know that in the days when the Old Testament was written, married sons would continue to live with their fathers after they were married. The Scriptures are talking about leaving spiritually and emotionally. It is a transfer of loyalty from a man's parents to his wife. It pertains to a man making his own decisions for the good of his own family, his wife, and his children. If you are making your decisions based on the likes and dislikes of your parents, you are missing the closeness God desires for your marriage. You must leave your parents (spiritually and emotionally) before you can properly cleave to your wife.

Cleave to wife. "For this cause a man shall leave his father and his mother, and shall cleave to his wife; and they shall become one flesh" (Gen. 2:24). Cleaving is defined as "a desperate holding onto." This is quite clearly not happening today, since so many men leave their wives. Are you still trying to please or find approval from the family that you should have left? "But," you may be saying, "doesn't the Bible say we are to honor our father and mother?" We are to honor our parents, even when we are adults. However, Scripture also states very clearly that we are to **honor** our wives. "You husbands likewise, live with your wives in an understanding way, as with a weaker vessel, since she is a woman; and grant her **honor** as a fellow heir of the grace of life, so that your prayers may not be hindered" (1 Pet. 3:7).

When we have a division between what our wife thinks or feels, and what our parents think or feel, what are we as men to do? Who should we honor? Jesus told us by quoting Genesis, "'For this cause, a man shall leave his father and mother, and shall cleave to his wife; and the two shall become one flesh'" (Matt. 19:5). He also said, "Consequently, they are no longer two, but one flesh. What therefore *God has joined together,* **let no man separate**" (Matt. 19:6). The reason why many men have not properly cleaved to their wife is that they have not "left" their mothers or fathers.

Do you and your wife argue about *your* family and *her* family? Do you defend your mother or father or even brother or sister when there is a dispute, instead of being on the side of your wife? If your family is getting between you, as a couple, then you have not cleaved—you are not one flesh with your wife.

Testimony: Amber's* husband had left her for another woman, but after about two years, praise the Lord, he returned home. However, there were still some troubles—all of which seemed to stem from his family. His parents refused to accept the way they, as a couple, raised their children. Among other things, they didn't accept the fact that they wanted to home school their children and they also couldn't understand why they wouldn't want to celebrate Halloween.

Amber's husband had tried for years to explain his strong Christian beliefs to his unsaved father and Christian mother, yet he found it impossible to reason with his parents. In addition, even though they lived states apart, there was a weekly phone call from his parents which would usually leave Amber's husband depressed. His parents continued to control, manipulate, and intimidate him even though he had been married for many years.

Amber was surprised and concerned when her husband told her that he was going to cut off all communication with his parents. She felt responsible, but her husband assured her that it was his decision and that he needed to do this so he could concentrate on his relationship with her.

After about seven months, Amber reported that she and her husband had come closer to a one-flesh union than they ever had been before. She has not questioned or pressured her husband to contact his parents, nor has she allowed false guilt to rob her of the blessing of her husband cleaving to and honoring her as his wife.

Men, do "whatever it takes" to show your wife that she is first in your life. When you do, you will realize a closeness with your wife that only comes when you become one with her.

One flesh. "So the Lord God caused a deep sleep to fall upon the man, and he slept; then He took **one of his ribs,** and closed up the flesh at that place. And the Lord God fashioned into a woman the rib, which He had taken from the man, and brought her to the man. And the man said, 'This is now bone of my bones, and **flesh of my flesh;** she shall be called woman, because she was **taken out of man**'" (Gen. 2:21). "And the two shall become **one flesh;** consequently, they are no longer two, but one flesh" (Mark 10:8). "Consequently, they are no longer two, but **one flesh.** What therefore God has joined together, let no man separate" (Matt. 19:6).

Being one flesh with our wives is certainly easy to comprehend during times of physical intimacy, but in addition to physical oneness, we need to be one with her emotionally, spiritually, and mentally. Do you and your wife have the same goals and directions? Are you allowing or encouraging division in your home? Have you encouraged or allowed your wife to pursue a degree or career that will eventually cause division?

God created woman to help and complete the man—not to be a second wage earner. Once a marriage takes place, they are "no longer two, but **one flesh.**" This means that they live their lives together as one, not as "roommates" where each has a life apart from the other. If your wife is the one pushing for division, pray. Satan is roaming around looking for marriages to devour. If yours becomes divided, it will no longer stand (Matt. 12:25, Mark 3:25, Luke 11:17).

It is an abomination. A physical "one flesh" can only be accomplished with a man and a woman. There is a void in a wife that was designed to be filled by her husband. God created us male and female to produce fruits (children) from our union. Homosexuality is sin. It is an abomination to the Lord. Since the media continuously tries to pervert our conception of the Truth, we need to renew our minds to line up with what is written in the Scriptures. "You shall not lie with a male as one lies with a female; **it is an abomination**" (Lev. 18:22).

We as Christians need to live our lives in an uncompromising way, so that we are not double-minded. "I hate those who are **double-minded, but I love Thy law**" (Ps. 119:113). ". . . being a **double-minded** man, unstable in all his ways" (James 1:8). "Draw near to God and He will draw near to you. Cleanse your hands, you sinners; and purify your hearts, you **double-minded**" (James 4:8). We cannot be lukewarm about something that is an abomination to God. Don't be afraid to speak the truth on this issue. (See Chapter 12, "Fruit of the Womb," for more knowledge.)

Man independent of woman. The one flesh union of a man and his wife brings about children as fruit, and yet we are also to have the fruit of our emotional and mental union: the blending of our hearts and our desires. God created women with certain needs and us men with certain needs; our spouses should fill the voids in our lives so that we function like a working gear as we move through life. If we fill our voids apart from our mates, the gear slips. The more we fill our voids apart from our spouses, the more our relationship slips. Soon we find there is nothing left to hang on to.

Many of us have believed the lie that it is not good to be dependent on each other. Being dependent is taunted as the "disease" of co-dependency from which we must be cured. "However, in the Lord, neither is woman independent of man, nor is **man independent of woman.** For as the woman originates from the man . . ." (1 Cor. 11:11–12). Remember, God created a void in each of us that only our spouses can (or should) fill. When we violate God's ways, we reap the consequences. We as men are to be the providers, the protectors, and the spiritual leaders for our wives and children. Our wives are to bear children (our heritage), nurture and teach our children, give comfort, provide meals for the family, and keep a clean, well-kept home.

In toil. "Then to Adam He said, 'Because you have listened to the voice of your wife, and have eaten from the tree about which I commanded you, saying, "You shall not eat from it"; cursed is the ground because of you; **in toil** you shall eat of it all the days of your life'" (Gen. 3:17). After the fall of man, the man and the woman were each given a punishment; the woman was given pain in childbirth, and the man would have to toil the ground (work). So why is *the man's* punishment often shared by both the man and the woman? When women earn their own money, they obviously want to make their own decisions on how it is to be spent. When wives have different careers than that of the home and children, it divides the couple's interests and makes them independent of each other.

Protector. When women protect themselves because they feel they can or need to "fight their own battles," they begin to feel they don't need our protection. Is it your wife who tells that salesperson off or gets rid of the guy at the door—probably with more gusto than you do? Have you forgotten how to handle these situations since you married your wife? Who really wears the pants in the family? If you tell your wife to take it easy or to slow down, does she tell you to mind your own business, or worse? It *is* our business to protect our wives and children. So what do we do when our wives continue to take charge or take over our position?

First, we must acknowledge that they have taken on this attitude because of our neglect. Either we didn't take on the challenges or we were absent because of our jobs, hobbies, or whatever. Once we can admit this, we can then confess it to our wives. Then, regardless of how she accepts the new arrangements, we must take on each challenge that comes against our family. We might say that we would attack anyone trying to harm a member of our family, but what about how we handle the bad service at the restaurant or the rude repairman? Do your teenage sons or daughters know that if they are ever disrespectful to their mother, they will suffer serious consequences from you?

Populate the earth abundantly. The Bible says that God is the one who opens the womb, but is there someone trying to control how many children you and your wife are going to have? Is it you, your parents, or your in-laws? How many times have you heard a man say that his wife doesn't want to have any more children? There was a time, in the not so distant past, when that could be used as a reason for a man to divorce his wife. But again, the feminist movement has changed all that. It is now legal to kill our "mistake" if our birth control fails.

Men, wake up! If you are not allowing God to determine the size of your family, then you are allowing your own heritage to be destroyed through ungodly, socialistic indoctrination! You are neglecting the primary reason God created the woman for the man—to be fruitful and multiply. "And as for you, be fruitful and multiply; **populate the earth abundantly** and multiply in it" (Gen. 9:7). If your wife is unwilling to have more children, you had better start praying that God will open her eyes to the Truth or send a godly woman who will influence her in the right way. And if you're the problem, you had better stop worshiping the Almighty Dollar or the Baal of Possessions, or else stop calling yourself a Christian because you're giving Christianity a bad name! (Again, see Chapter 12, "Fruit of the Womb," for more knowledge.)

Ask their own husbands at home. Brother, are you leading in spiritual matters? Does your wife come to you with her questions because you are her spiritual leader? Or, does she think, "Why would I go to him? What does he know? I'm the one who goes to all Bible studies and seminars!" "Her *husband* is known in the gates, when he sits among the elders of the land" (Prov. 31:23).

Men, we need to take an active role in leadership, both at home and in our churches. Don't leave your role as the spiritual leader to the pastor, the Sunday school teacher, or the Bible study teacher. Don't keep making excuses; begin now. "And if they desire to learn anything, *let them* **ask their own husbands at home;** for it is improper for a woman to speak in church" (1 Cor. 14:35). Guys, if you really want your wife to love you, become a mighty man of God. She will be drawn to you like steel to a magnet!

Father. As parents, many of us have been pushed out of our role or made to conform to the female type of parenting. Some of us have been criticized for the way we handle or treat the children so often that we have just stopped "interfering." Meanwhile, the media is trying to mold us into effeminate fathers, so that there will be no difference between mothering and fathering—thus, it becomes "parenting."

God purposely provided children with a mother and a father with distinctly different characteristics. Our children need both parents in order to grow up without a bunch of hang-ups or emotional troubles. If the roles are blended and blurred, who needs a *father?* "Honor your father **and** mother; and you shall love your neighbor as yourself" (Matt. 19:19).

An excellent wife, who can find? We husbands need a wife who can take care of our physical needs by cooking, laundering our clothes, caring for the home, and bearing, nurturing, teaching, and training our children. Have you and your wife declared yourselves "liberated" by rejecting the biblical husband and wife roles in your home? Or, are you following Christ and obeying God's Word? **"An excellent wife, who can find?** For her worth is far above jewels. The heart of her husband trusts in her, and he will have no lack of gain. She does him good and not evil all the days of her life. She looks for wool and flax, and works with her hands in delight. She is like merchant ships; she brings her food from afar. She rises also while it is still night, and gives food to her household . . . She is not afraid of the snow for her household, for all her household are clothed with scarlet" (Prov. 31:10–21).

"That's right," you're probably saying. "Who can find this excellent wife?" Men, you may be a bit disgusted right now as you think of the woman you married and consider how she has let you and your children down. But before you attack her, you must ask yourself this question: Who is ultimately responsible for everything that goes on in your household? You are. You are to be the proper husband, father, and leader of your family. Ask yourself if you have encouraged your wife to be a "keeper of the home," or have you instead let her be carried away by pursuing a college degree or her *own* career?

If you are in a situation that needs to be changed, don't go to your wife with new demands. Love her. Be patient with her. Listen to her. Understand her. If you truly love her and she feels it, she will do anything for you. Harshness will only result in hurts and/or rebellion.

Stop depriving one another. If you have gone along with the feminist way of thinking and your wife has been liberated from her duties as a wife and mother, more than likely you also have become "liberated" from your physical oneness. "But because of immoralities, let each man have his own wife, and let each woman have her own husband. Let the husband fulfill his duty to his wife, and likewise also the wife to her husband. The wife does not have authority over her own body, but the husband does; and likewise also the husband does not have authority over his own body, but the wife does. **Stop depriving one another,** except by agreement for a time, that you may devote yourselves to prayer, and come together again lest Satan tempt you because of your lack of self-control" (1 Cor. 7:2–5).

When there is lack of oneness in this area, we must get at the root of the problem—our roles are out of God's order. Many men, wanting to avoid any confrontation with their wives, allow the troubles at home to wear them down and eventually give in to weaknesses and temptations. "For the lips of an adulteress drip honey, and smoother than oil is her speech . . ." (Prov. 5:3). "With her many persuasions she entices him; with her flattering lips she seduces him. Suddenly he follows her, as an ox goes to the slaughter . . . So he does not know that it will cost him his life" (Prov. 7:21–23). Men, talking to your wife doesn't mean confronting her on the issue. If you lovingly share your heart and feelings with her, she won't be tempted to become defensive.

He who would restrain *her*. Don't fool yourself into thinking that you must "take control." It will only lead to an argument. Remember the contentious woman? "A constant dripping on a day of steady rain and a contentious woman are alike; **he who would restrain her** restrains the wind, and grasps oil with his right hand" (Prov. 27:15–16). Men, love your wife as the Bible says. "Husbands, love your wives, just as Christ also loved the church and gave Himself up for her . . ." (Eph. 5:25).

Part 3
Who Should Be the Spiritual Leader?

One question many women ask is "Who should be the spiritual leader since my husband won't or doesn't do it?" Or, many women will state, "I *have* to be the spiritual leader of our home because my husband is not even a Christian!" Why are so many men neglecting or forfeiting their position as the head of their family?

Her husband is known. True Christian women desire their husbands to be spiritual leaders. **"Her husband is known** in the gates, when he sits among the elders of the land" (Prov. 31: 23). However, some women have decided that they want to be the leaders. And since many of us have neglected our leadership duties, we have left our wives open to be deceived by the teachings of liberated pastors. Thus, many of our wives have been taken captive. "For among them are those who enter into households and captivate weak women weighed down with sins, led on by various impulses, always learning and never able to come to the knowledge of the Truth" (2 Tim. 3:6–7). Many churches are now overrun with weak men and strong-willed women. Our effectiveness as a church body has been greatly hindered because many men, Christian men, are not taking up their God-given roles of leadership! "You are the salt of the earth; but if the salt has become tasteless, how will it be made salty again? It is good for nothing anymore, except to be thrown out and trampled under foot by men" (Matt. 5:13).

Christ is the head of every man. Christ is the head of *every* man, not just every Christian man. "But I want you to understand that Christ is the head of **every** man, and the man is the head of woman, and God is the head of Christ" (1 Cor. 11:3).

Teach or exercise authority over a man. "But I do not allow a woman to **teach or exercise authority over a man,** but to remain quiet" (1 Tim. 2:12). "O My people! Their oppressors are children, and **women rule over them.** O My people! Those who guide you lead you astray, and **confuse** *the direction of your paths"* (Isa. 3:9). When a wife rules the home, there is nothing but trouble. If your mother or your wife's mother was in charge of her home, chances are that your home is following the same pattern. As a Christian man, you can't, in good conscience, allow this to continue. This doesn't mean going to your wife and demanding to take over. Remember, it was through your neglect that things got out of order. You must first make time for prayer, Bible reading, and meditation. This will take effort on your part, but God *will* lead you and direct your paths if you seek Him for answers. When your wife sees your spiritual strength demonstrated by your love for her, your children, and the Word of God, she will gladly give you the leadership position.

Be subject to your own husbands in everything. We as men cannot pick and choose when and if we want to lead our families. "Wives be subject to your own husbands, as to the Lord . . . to their husbands in *everything"* (Eph. 5:22–24). It is clear from the above Scriptures that God has put **all** husbands in the spiritual leadership role of the home.

No one can serve *two* masters. When things get out of order in our homes because we've neglected to lead our families and direct what goes on, our wives and children will begin to despise us. Remember, if you have turned over most of your authority to other people or institutions, confusion and rebellion will reign! "No one can serve *two* masters; for either he will **hate the one** and **love the other,** or he **will hold to one** and **despise the other**" (Matt.6:24). An example of this is when a child who listens and obeys his parents is sent off to school. After a couple of weeks, he begins to tell his parents that they are wrong and the teacher is right! (See Chapter 14, "Father's Instruction," for more knowledge on home schooling and what you should consider and pray about before sending your children to college.)

He will do it. Does your wife sometimes act as though she is your personal Holy Spirit? Why does she do this? Could it be because you have neglected to gain the spiritual wisdom and knowledge needed to effectively lead your family? Does your wife know her Bible better than you do? Or, are your children better versed in Scripture than you are? If you think that it's too late for you to learn or that you are too far behind to get ahead of your wife and children to properly lead them, you are wrong. Since God has called us to be the leaders of our homes, He will enable us. *We must confess our sin of neglect.* "Therefore, confess your sins to one another, and pray for one another, so that you may be healed. The effective prayer of a righteous man can accomplish much" (James 5:16). *Let's boast about our weaknesses.* "And He has said to me, 'My grace is sufficient for you, for power is perfected in weakness.' Most gladly, therefore, I will rather boast about my weaknesses, that the power of Christ may dwell in me" (2 Cor. 12:9). *And above all, trust the Lord.* "Commit your way to the Lord, trust also in Him, and **He will do it**" (Ps. 37:5).

Washing of water with the Word. Men, we need to understand that what we say to our wives, what we read to our wives, and what we permit or encourage our wives to see is extremely important. "Husbands, love your wives, just as Christ also loved the church and gave Himself up for her; that He might *sanctify her,* having *cleansed her* by the **washing of water with the Word,** that He might present to Himself the church in all her glory, having no spot or wrinkle or any such thing; but that she should be holy and blameless" (Eph. 5:25–27). Some of us complain that our wives nag us, lie to us, or start arguments with us. Yet, do we ever stop to consider what she is watching every day—possibly soap operas? Do you together watch the stupid evening sitcoms where the men are portrayed as buffoons and the women are all contentious comedians? What movies do you saturate your wife with? What movies do you saturate yourself with? The next time you and your wife or family sit down to watch *anything,* just think of what you're watching as a "training film," because the behavior *will* be learned and acted out!

The narrow gate. Men, enter through that **"narrow gate"** by turning off the television. And stop sending your weekly or monthly dues to the God-haters in Hollywood via the movie theater. "Enter by the **narrow gate;** for the gate is wide, and the way is broad that leads to destruction, and *many are those who enter by it"* (Matt. 7:13).

You will know them by their fruits. What kind of fruit are you producing as a Christian husband and father? **"You will know them by their fruits . . ."** (Matt. 7:16). If you are not leading your family daily in the Word, then you are most likely producing thorns, not fruit. Do you read your Bible daily; if so, for how long? Compare the time you spend reading the newspaper and magazines to the time you spend reading your Bible. If you're not spending enough time reading the Word, what are you going to do about it? Are you putting into practice what you have learned by reading this manual? Can anyone see any change in you? "For if anyone is a hearer of the Word and not a doer, he is like a man who looks at his natural face in a mirror; for once he has looked at himself and gone away, he has immediately forgotten what kind of person he was. But one who looks intently at the perfect law, the law of liberty, and **abides by it,** not having become a **forgetful hearer** but an **effectual doer,** this man shall be *blessed in what he does"* (James 1:23–25).

Part 4
The Husband and Wife Relationship

We men are to be the spiritual leaders of our homes. The Bible says that we are to have the same type of relationship with our wives as Jesus Christ has with His Church. Let's study His Word together and learn more about how we husbands are to be with our wives.

The head. "For the **husband** is the **head** of the **wife,** as **Christ** also is the **head** of the **church** . . ." (Eph. 5:23). "But I want you to understand that **Christ** is the **head** of **every man,** and the **man** is the **head** of **a woman,** and God is the head of Christ" (1 Cor. 11:3).

We learned in Chapter 8, "Manages His Own Household," about the relationship of authority in the home. We also learned about the benefits of our wives being subject to us, for their protection and our children's protection. The Scriptures compare Christ as the head of the church to us as the head of our wives. Just as good leadership is the key to a well-run company, so it is with our homes. We must lead! Don't miss this point— you must lead. Take control by coming up with solutions to the problems that arise in your home. Proper leadership means you walking the right way (through the narrow gate) and your wife and children following. Many men want to "tell" their wives and children what to do, yet they are unwilling to lead!

The savior. "For the **husband** is the head of the wife, as **Christ** *also* is the head of the church, He Himself being the **Savior** of the body" (Eph. 5:23). *The husband is the savior of the body.* Many of us act as though our wife is to be the savior of our family. An example of this would be when we allow, or more often encourage, our wives to go out and get a job when we are in financial crises. This only robs us of a blessing! You must fulfill your role as the head of your home and the savior of your family. Put your faith in God. He *will* direct you and guide you once you have become committed to leading your wife and children.

Created to carry the burdens. We men were created to carry the burdens for our families—just look at your broad and muscular shoulders compared to your wife's shoulders. Women have even tried to imitate those shoulders with shoulder pads! In addition to our physical strength, we are really designed to work best under pressure. Maybe you think you can't handle the pressures, because you've always had your wife as your safety net. But your wife was not created to bear up under extreme pressures from outside the areas where she is gifted. God made women with the ability to handle *many* things at once. They are able to run the home with all its maintenance, while managing children of various ages, personalities, and needs. They plan and prepare meals, clean and continuously tidy up, and keep everyone organized and on schedule. It seems as though women can do it all. But you must remember that your wife *is* the "weaker vessel." You've got to learn to protect her from excess pressure and stress. Don't dump all your problems on her or tell her how worried you are about this or that. Take your burdens to the Lord.

Are one. "For this cause a *man* shall leave his father and mother, and shall cleave to his *wife* and the two shall become **one flesh"** (Eph. 5:31). Also in Ephesians 5:28: "So *husbands* ought also to love their own *wives* as their **own bodies**. He who loves his own wife loves himself . . ." "Nevertheless, let each individual among you also love his own *wife* even **as himself"** (Eph. 5:33). We have heard the term "one flesh" so often without really understanding the meaning. We think only of reaching the "one flesh" as we consummate our marriage. Yet, we are falling short of the complete "oneness" if we don't also bond with our wives emotionally and spiritually.

Sanctify. Husbands, we play a big role in the sanctification of our wives, as we will see in the following Scriptures. **"Husbands,** *love* your wives, *just as* Christ also loved the church and gave Himself up for her; that He might **sanctify** her, having **cleansed** her by the *washing of water* with **the Word,** that He might *present to Himself* the church in all her glory, having no spot or wrinkle or any such thing; but that *she should be* **holy** and **blameless"** (Eph. 5:25). This is a very powerful biblical Truth that few will ever realize. We as husbands can sanctify (purify) our wives as we read and share Scripture with them. Do you read God's Word daily to your wife? How does the church keep the body cleansed from the sin that creeps into the church? It stays cleansed by the reading of *God's Word*. With wives, it's the same way. Men, how are you doing?

Love. **"Husbands, love** *your wives,* just as Christ also loved . . ." (Eph. 5:25). "So **husbands** ought also to **love** their *own wives* . . ." (Eph. 5:28). **"Husbands, love** *your wives,* and do not be embittered against them" (Col. 3:19). Since the feminist movement permeated the church with lies, there has been a "blending" of the roles and commandments given to men and women. We continue to hear others say that God commanded men and women to love their spouses. This "command" was only given to the husband. Actually, the only reference for a woman to love her husband is given in Titus. The older women are encouraged to *teach* the younger women to love their husbands and their children.

Deuteronomy 4:2 says, "You shall not add to the Word which I am commanding you . . ." Does that mean a wife isn't to love her husband? Emphatically no! ". . . And walk in love, just as Christ also loved you, and gave Himself up for us . . ." (Eph. 5:2). The wife's primary role is that of *respecting* and *submitting* to her husband—then love, genuine love, will follow. First John 4:19 says, "We love, because He *first* loved us." Our wives will love us when we first show our love for them.

A husband who shows true love for his wife, the way the Bible commands, will be protected from separation or divorce. Romans 8:35 says, "Who shall separate us from the **love of Christ?** Shall tribulation, or distress, or persecution, or famine, or nakedness, or peril, or sword?"

Your love for your wife will motivate her to do what you ask of her. "For the **love** of Christ **controls us** . . ." (2 Cor. 5:14).

Saying you love her is not enough; our actions must follow. ". . . And **walk in love,** just as Christ also loved you, and *gave Himself up for us . . .*" (Eph. 5:2).

Are subject. "But as the church is subject to Christ, so also the **wives** ought to be to their **husbands** in *everything"* (Eph. 5:24). **"Wives,** be **subject** to your **husbands,** *as is fitting in the Lord"* (Col. 3:18). "Wives, be **subject** to your own **husbands,** *as to the Lord"* (Eph. 5:22). Women are also to be ". . . pure, workers at home, kind, being **subject** to their *own husbands,* that the Word of God may not be dishonored" (Titus 2:5). We may delegate certain tasks, but our role is to be the head, and our wives are to be subject to us. We are not to allow our wives to be under another man's authority (i.e., a boss, a Sunday school teacher, or even a pastor). (Please see Chapter 13, "Provide for His Own," for more knowledge.) We are to be the final and ultimate authority here on earth for our wives and our children.

Gave Himself. "**Husbands,** love your wives, just as Christ *also* loved the church and **gave Himself** up for her . . ." (Eph. 5:25). Feminism has just about destroyed the "knight in shining armor" scenario. Yet, here in Scripture, we see that we *are* to be that gallant man who is willing to give all of himself for his wife and his family. Are you being "robbed of blessings" because your wife is the one who always "saves the day"? Men, get busy ruling your household. Be around more, not as a guest but as a working, ruling figure. Pay attention to what is happening around your house, so you can step in and make rulings during those "mini-crises" that go on constantly. This will allow your wife to be gentle, quiet, and feminine. She will then discover, or rediscover, you and begin to appreciate your strength and leadership. But you must do this humbly or she will resent you for taking over. Do it with a caring attitude. Let her know that you realize that you have left her with the entire burden for much too long.

Supply and provide. "But if anyone does not **provide** for his own, and especially for those of his household, he has denied the faith, and is worse than an unbeliever" (1 Tim. 5:8). If you are allowing (or encouraging) your wife to work outside your home, then Satan is using you to further his agenda to divide your home and steal blessings. Stop playing on his team. Renew your mind and take every thought captive to the obedience of Christ. This area is covered more in depth in Chapter 13, "Provide for His Own." Please understand that one of the foremost reasons why many women are so unhappy and frustrated is that they are trying to fill a role that they were not designed for—that of a provider. If both husband and wife are working, who is in the home? Men, the home that you and your wife work and slave for is sitting empty! Your "little blessings" are being cared for and taught by a poor imitation of your wife. Is it any wonder why you feel frustrated and your wife feels unfulfilled?

Feeds us. As men, we know that we are supposed to "bring home the bacon," but there is also spiritual food that our children and wives are literally starving for! ". . . For no one ever hated his own flesh, but nourishes and cherishes it, just as Christ also does the church . . ." (Eph. 5:29). This "feeding" must be from God's Word. Most of us feel inadequate in this area. Many don't know where to begin. Pray to the Lord for strength and guidance *daily!* Satan will surely attack you in this area because he knows how powerfully important it is to your family's spiritual growth. He will make you feel worthless, incapable, and downright stupid. He will try to use strife between you and your wife or children to stop your times of reading God's Word together. Are you man enough to fight back? Concentrate on winning one battle at a time, and you'll gain the momentum needed to become victorious in this area of your family's spiritual life. Don't just send them off to Bible studies, seminars, Sunday school, and vacation Bible school. To be an effective leader in your home, you must resist the temptation to give your authority over to others. If you feel you don't have enough time, pray that God will show you where you can cut back and make the time. Do it now—just a short prayer—then obey.

One wife. "An overseer, then, must be above reproach, the husband of one wife, temperate, prudent, respectable, hospitable, able to teach . . ." (1 Tim. 3:2). ". . . If any man be above reproach, the husband of **one wife,** having children who believe, not accused of dissipation or rebellion" (Titus 1:6). In this day of multiple marriages, let's remember that we as married Christians are to represent a picture of Christ and His church. Separation or divorce hurts our testimony to a lost and dying world. We need to show the lost world, through our example, that we are to be the husbands of one wife. Jesus said that two shall become one, not three or four become one. "Consequently, they are no longer two, but one flesh" (Matt. 19:6). Brothers, "Let your fountain be blessed, and **rejoice** *in the wife of your youth"* (Prov. 5:18).

REJOICE
in the
Wife of Your Youth!

Personal commitment: To become the spiritual leader of my family. "Based on what I have learned from God's Word, I commit to be the spiritual leader to my family, especially my wife. I commit to getting into the Word daily and washing my wife with the Word so that she will be without spot or blemish."

Date: _____ Signed: _____

"Not that I have already obtained it, or have already become perfect, but I press on, in order that I may lay hold of that for which also I was laid hold of by Christ Jesus" (Phil. 3:12).

Homework

His Word healed them. Once again, it is God's Word that will change and heal you. "He sent **His Word and healed them,** and delivered them from their destructions" (Ps. 107:20). Again, you must begin to renew your mind. Have you noticed a change in the way you're thinking? Are others noticing that you are not the same?

1. **3x5 cards.** Once more, gather your 3x5 cards and write down the verses from *this* chapter that have touched your heart. Are you keeping these cards with you and bringing them out *regularly* as the Holy Spirit prompts you? Is God prompting and reminding you to read them over?

2. **Healing.** Has God healed you in a particular area? If not, then it is important that you pray for the Lord to reveal what is blocking your healing. Have you sought the counsel of another (older) man? Did you have an opportunity to confess a weakness, a fear, or an unconfessed sin? If you did, then you can believe God for a breakthrough.

3. Share the wisdom from this chapter *with one other man* who unknowingly has given up, through default, his role as the leader of his home.

Test Your Wisdom

1. In 1 Corinthians 7:13–14, the Scriptures **do** teach us what to do with a non-believing wife. How will she be sanctified? Through her _____ _____.

2. Why should we remain with a non-believer? So that they will get _____ (1 Cor. 7:16).

3. What is the "first step" to encourage you to follow the Lord and leave your wife in the hands of the Lord?

Go into your inner room and _____ ____ _____ _____ (Matt. 6:6).

4. What is the promise God gives you concerning your family's salvation? "… You and your _____ will be saved (Acts 16:3).

5. What caution is given about reproving someone? They may _____ their neck and will suddenly be _____ beyond _____ (Prov. 29:1).

6. How can I be sure about God's Word? I can be sure because every Word of God is _____ (Prov. 30:5).

7. "Husbands, _____ your wives, and do not be _____ against them" (Col. 3:19).

The answers to Homework questions are at the end of this workbook.

Chapter 10

Various Trials

*Consider it all joy, my brethren,
when you encounter various trials,
knowing that the testing of your faith
produces endurance.
—James 1:2–3*

What is **God's** purpose for our tests, temptations, trials, and tribulations? Many Christians have no idea why God allows our sufferings. Without our understanding of this, is it any wonder that Christians today are so easily defeated? We will see that there are many **benefits** that come from our trials and tests, specifically the building of our faith and the endurance needed to finish the course set before us.

The most important thing that we need to realize during our trials, tribulations, tests, and temptations is that God **is** in control! It is *His* hand that allows these trials to touch us or not to touch us. When He does allow it, He sends His grace and mercy, which enable us to endure.

Temptations. The temptations that we experience, Scripture tells us, are common to man, yet God does provide a way of escape. "No temptation has overtaken you but that which is **common to man;** and God is faithful, who will not allow you to be tempted beyond what you are able, but with the **temptation** will provide **the way of escape** also, that you may be able to endure it" (1 Cor. 10:13).

Temptations are brought on by our *own* lusts. God cannot tempt us to do evil; it is our lusts that tempt us. "Let no one say when he is being tempted, 'I am being **tempted by God'**; for God cannot be tempted by evil, and He Himself does not tempt anyone. But each one is tempted when he is carried away and **enticed by his *own* lust**" (James 1:13). When we think of lust, we usually think of something sexual. However, the lust that the Bible refers to is greed for *all* things that feed our flesh; this includes getting our own way.

We are in His hand. "For I have taken all this to my heart and explain it that righteous men, wise men, and their deeds are **in the hand of God**" (Eccl. 9:1).

Permission for adversity. One of the most comforting things to know is that Satan cannot touch us without God's permission. "Then the Lord said to Satan, 'Behold, all that he has is in your power, only **do not put forth your hand on him**'" (Job 1:12). Satan not only needed permission, but he was also given specific instructions on how he could touch Job. Satan also asked for permission to sift Peter. "Simon, Simon, behold, Satan has demanded permission to sift you like wheat . . ." (Luke 22:31).

Repentance and salvation. "I now rejoice, not that you were made sorrowful, but that you were made sorrowful to the point of repentance; for you were made sorrowful according to the **will of God,** in order that you might not suffer loss in anything through us. For the sorrow that is according to the **will of God** produces a **repentance without regret,** leading to salvation; but the sorrow of the world produces death" (2 Cor. 7:9). God allows us to be sorrowful to bring us to repentance. *When we try to **make** our wives (or others) sorry for what they have done, it will not bring true and genuine repentance.*

We need grace. "And He has said to me, 'My **grace** is sufficient for you, for power is perfected in weakness.' Most gladly, therefore, I will rather boast about my weaknesses, that the power of Christ may dwell in me. Therefore, I am **well content** with **weaknesses,** with **insults,** with **distresses,** with **persecutions,** with **difficulties,** for Christ's sake; for when I am weak, then I am strong" (2 Cor. 12: 9–10). How do we get the grace we need? We gain grace through humility.

"God *hates the proud* but **gives grace** to the **humble**" (James 4:6).

"For everyone who *exalts himself* shall be **humbled,** but he who **humbles** himself shall be exalted" (Luke 18:14).

"Blessed are the **humble,** for they shall inherit the earth" (Matt. 5:5).

"A man's pride will bring him low, but a **humble spirit** will obtain honor" (Prov. 29:23).

Boasting about our weaknesses, confessing our faults, and being humble will enable the Holy Spirit to dwell in us. This is how we will learn to be content, no matter what our circumstances.

Learning contentment. We see that we must *learn* contentment through the difficult circumstances that God allows. "Not that I speak from want, for I have **learned** to be **content** in whatever circumstances I am. In every circumstance I have **learned the secret** of being filled and going hungry, both of having abundance and suffering need" (Phil. 4:11).

Learning obedience. Even Jesus learned obedience from His suffering. "Although He was a Son, He **learned obedience** from *the things* which He *suffered*" (Heb. 5:8).

He will perfect us. "For I am confident of this very thing, that He who **began a good work in you** will **perfect** it until the day of Christ Jesus" (Phil. 1:6). Once God has begun a good work in you, your wife, or your loved ones, *He* will complete it.

We are to be a comfort to others. We are not merely to accept God's comfort—we are commanded to give that comfort to others, no matter what their affliction! "The God of all comfort, who comforts us in all our affliction so that we may be able to **comfort** those who are in **any affliction** with the comfort with which we ourselves are comforted by God" (2 Cor. 1:3-4). Many men have difficulty comforting those who suffer. Some can't even comfort their wives or children (sometimes because they are the cause of the pain).

If we neglect our responsibility to comfort our loved ones, they will turn to others (which can be dangerous), and we will miss a blessing. The blessing is the chance to be closer to the person whom we comfort. Men, we need to comfort other men, especially those who are experiencing marital troubles. If we don't, they may turn to another woman (not their wife) for help. Be willing to humble yourself and share your weaknesses and failures so that your friend will feel able to share his with you. Take down the wall of pride; God will exalt you. Let yourself "boast" about *your* weaknesses as Paul did.

Our Father's discipline. Many times our suffering could be God's discipline for disobeying His Law. "My son, do not regard lightly the **discipline** of the Lord, nor faint when you are being reproved by Him; for those whom the Lord loves He **disciplines,** and He scourges *every son* whom He receives. It is for **discipline** that you **endure;** God deals with you as with sons. He *disciplines* us for our good, that we may *share His holiness"* (Heb. 12:5–11).

Discipline is a blessing. When we follow the example of the prophets of the Bible, we will be helping others to endure their adversity. "As an example, brethren, of suffering and patience, take the prophets who spoke in the name of the Lord. Behold, we count those **blessed** who **endured.** You have heard of the **endurance** of Job and have seen the outcome of the Lord's dealings, that the Lord is full of compassion and is merciful" (James 5:10). Men need to see other men enduring temptations and suffering, not compromising, but standing for what is right. Many of us are preoccupied with enduring things that have no eternal value, enduring things that are merely trivial.

Discipline may be sorrowful. Discipline is never joyful when you are in the midst of it. Yet, those who have been trained by His discipline know the rewards of righteousness—it brings peace. *"All* **discipline** for the moment seems not to be joyful, but sorrowful (painful); yet to those who have been **trained by it,** afterwards it yields the peaceful fruit of righteousness" (Heb.12:11). Those who are athletes take sports training seriously—what about faith training? How much more should we be "trained" (by suffering) to receive the peaceful fruit of righteousness!

To receive a blessing. When evil is done to us or insults are cast our way, we must endure, without returning evil, to receive our blessing. We need to remember that insults and evils are brought into our lives to give us an "opportunity" to receive a blessing. First Peter 3:9 says, "Not returning evil for evil, or insult for insult, but giving a **blessing** instead, for you were called for the very purpose that you may inherit a **blessing." "**But even if you should suffer for the sake of righteousness, you are **blessed"** (1 Pet. 3:14). How about you—are you able to resist the temptation to blast someone back, including your wife, when an insult is directed at you?

It begins with Christians. Why must suffering first begin with Christians? It begins with Christians because sinful, disobedient Christians will never draw others to the Lord. Again, it is the "will of God" that we be put though sufferings. We need to *allow* ourselves to suffer (usually at the hands of another) by entrusting ourselves to God. "For it is time for judgment to **begin** with the household of God; and if it **begins** with us first, what will be the outcome for those who do not obey the gospel of God? Therefore, let those also who **suffer** according to the **will of God** entrust their souls to a faithful Creator in doing what is right" (1 Pet. 4:17).

The power of our faith. It is faith that opens the door to miracles. You need to believe that He is able and not doubt it in your heart. "And Jesus answered saying to them, 'Have *faith* in God. Truly I say to you, whoever says to this mountain, be taken up and cast into the sea, and *does not doubt it in his heart,* but *believes* that what he says is going to happen, it shall be granted him. Therefore I say to you, all things for which you pray, they shall be granted unto you'" (Mark 11:22–24).

God in His Word has told us we *will* suffer. "For indeed when we were with you, we kept *telling you in advance* that we were going to *suffer affliction;* and so it came to pass, as you know. For this reason, when I could endure it no longer; I also sent to find out about your *faith,* for fear that the tempter might have tempted you, and our labor should be in vain" (1 Thess. 3:4–5). Don't give up! Don't let Satan steal the blessings that God has in store for you when you have endured and prevailed!

With God. "With men this is impossible, but with God *all things are possible"* (Mark 10:27). "Looking upon them, Jesus said, 'With men it is impossible, but not with God; for *all things are possible with God'"* (Matt. 19:26). Nothing (not a thing) is impossible with God. Work **with** God. And since He is not a respecter of persons, "What He's done for others, He's going to do for you!"

What you speak. ". . . Let us **hold fast our confession"** (Heb. 4:14). "But sanctify Christ as Lord in your hearts, **always being ready** to make a defense to everyone *who asks you* to give an account of the **hope that is in you,** yet with gentleness and reverence" (1 Pet. 3:15). "If it be so our God whom we serve is **able to deliver** us from the furnace of blazing fire; and He will deliver us out of your hand, O king. But **even if He does**

not . . ." (Dan. 3:17). We need to speak what God says in His Word, without wavering, with hope on our lips. But wait until you are asked to give an account. You *will* be asked, if you are filled with the joy of the Lord during the midst of your adversity! When you are asked to give an account, be sure that you answer the other person with reverence, respect, and gentleness. Never argue Scripture! "Blessed are the peacemakers, for they shall be called *sons of God*" (Matt. 5:9).

Gird your mind and stay fixed. "Therefore, **gird your minds** for action, keep *sober* in spirit, **fix your hope** completely on the **grace** to be brought to you at the revelation of Jesus Christ" (1 Pet. 1:13). (The word *sober* means clear thinking.) Be clear in your mind on how you stand to avoid the consequences of double-mindedness. Also, be assured that you cannot fight a spiritual battle if you are not physically sober. If you are a slave to alcohol, you are going to have trouble battling the evil thoughts and temptations that will eventually destroy you and your home.

Be joyful. We are to be joyful in our trials because we know they are producing endurance that will enable us to finish the course set before us. "Consider it all joy, my brethren, when you encounter **various trials,** knowing that the **testing of your faith** produces **endurance.** And let **endurance** have its perfect result, that you may be perfect and complete, lacking nothing. But if any of you lacks wisdom, let him ask of God, who gives it to all men without reproach, and it will be given to him. But let him ask **in faith, without any doubting,** for the one who doubts is like the surf of the sea driven and tossed by the wind" (James 1:2–6). We know our faith is being tested. Doubts and temptations come into everyone's minds; don't entertain them! Instead, think on **Truth** *only*. If you doubt, you will have trouble standing and it will be tougher to overcome the temptations. Certainly, we will have a variety of trials, some major and others mere irritations. Some of us seem to handle major trials better than the little irritations that plague us every day. What grade would your wife give you on the **test of your faith?** We need to endure our sufferings as Job did.

Rejoice. "**Rejoice** in the Lord always; again I say **rejoice! Let your forbearing spirit be known to all men,** the Lord is near! Be anxious for nothing, but in everything by prayer and supplication with **thanksgiving,** let your requests be made known to God. And the peace of God, which surpasses all comprehension, shall guard your hearts and your minds in

Christ Jesus. Finally, brethren, whatever is true, whatever is honorable, whatever is right, whatever is pure, whatever is lovely, whatever is of good report, if there is any excellence or **anything worthy of praise,** let your mind dwell on these things. The things you have learned and received and heard and seen in me, *practice* **these things;** and the God of peace shall be with you" (Phil. 4:6–9). Clearly most battles are won or lost in the mind. Follow the Lord's advice for peace in the midst of trials. Rejoice in what God is doing. Think on these things, speak of these things, and listen to only these things. You may be physically strong and in great shape, but how strong are you spiritually?

Faith is *not* seen. "For we walk by faith, **not by sight"** (2 Cor. 5:7). Others will want to know how things are going when they know you are experiencing trials in your life. They are looking for signs of improvement. We must remember that Scripture is very clear: faith is unseen! Answer their question with, "God is working!" "Therefore we do not lose heart, but though our outer man is decaying, yet our inner man is being renewed day by day. For our **momentary light affliction** is producing for us a far more eternal weight in glory far beyond comparison, while we look not at the things which are seen, but the things which are **not seen,** for the things which are seen are **temporal,** but the things which are **not seen are eternal"** (2 Cor. 4:16–18). Most people start believing when they begin to see something happening—this is not faith! "Now **faith** is the assurance of things hoped for, the conviction of things *not* **seen"** (Heb. 11:1).

Momentary. When we are experiencing what Paul calls "light affliction," it may still be crushing us. Let us remind ourselves of an important truth: these afflictions are only *momentary.* "For our **momentary light afflictions** . . . which are seen are **temporal!"** (2 Cor. 4:18). These same afflictions are not only temporary, but they are producing something wonderful for us in glory. Remember, the suffering is temporary and the benefits will last an eternity! We go "through" the valley of the shadow of death (Ps. 23). We go "through" the deserts (Isa. 48:21). God does not intend for us to live there, but only to *pass through!* "When you pass **through** the waters, I will be with you; and **through** the rivers, they will not overflow you. When you walk **through** the fire, you will not be scorched . . ." (Isa. 43:2).

Tied up, but not alone! Are you tied up and bound by sin? Another benefit to our passing through affliction is noted in the book of Daniel; the youths went in "tied up" but left "loosed," without any other outward appearances. "Then these men were **tied up** in their trousers, their coats, their caps, and their other clothes, and were cast into the midst of the furnace of blazing fire. For this reason, because the king's command was urgent, and the furnace had been **made extremely hot,** the flame of the fire slew those men who carried up Shadrach, Meshach, and Abed-nego. But these three men, Shadrach, Meshach, and Abed-nego, fell into the midst of the furnace of blazing fire *still* **tied up.** "Then Nebuchadnezzar the king was astounded and stood up in haste; he responded and said to his high officials, 'Was it not three men we cast bound into the midst of the fire?' They answered and said to the king, 'Certainly, O king.' He answered and said, 'Look! I see four men *loosed* and walking about in the midst of the fire *without harm,* and the appearance of **the fourth** is like a **son of the gods!'** Then Nebuchadnezzar came near to the door of the furnace of blazing fire; he responded and said, 'Shadrach, Meshach, and Abed-nego, come out, *you servants* of the Most High God, and come here!' Then Shadrach, Meshach, and Abed-nego came out of the midst of the fire. And the satraps, the prefects, the governors, and the king's high officials gathered around and saw in regard to these men that the fire had no effect on the bodies of these men nor was the hair of their head singed, nor were their trousers damaged, nor had the smell of fire even come upon them" (Dan. 3:21–27). What will your testimony be? Will you allow yourself to walk into the fiery furnace without kicking, screaming, or complaining?

Looking at our circumstances. When Peter looked at *his* circumstances, he sank—and you will too. "And He said 'Come!' And Peter got out of the boat, and walked on the water and came toward Jesus. But **seeing the wind,** he became frightened, and beginning to sink, he cried out, saying, 'Lord save me!' And immediately Jesus stretched out His hand and took hold of him, and said to him, 'O you of little faith, why did you doubt?'" (Matt. 14:29–31).

For our testing. "Consider it all joy, my brethren, when you encounter various trials, knowing that the **testing of your faith** produces endurance. And let **endurance** have its perfect result, that you may be perfect and complete, lacking nothing" (James 1:2).

10. Various Trials

More precious than gold. The *proof* of your faith is more precious than gold. "In this you greatly rejoice, even though for a little while, if necessary, you have been distressed by various trials, that the proof of your faith, being more precious than gold which is perishable, even though **tested by fire,** may be found to **result in praise** and **glory** and **honor** at the revelation of Jesus Christ" (1 Pet. 1:6–7). So many have failed their tests and have continued to walk in the desert as the people of Israel did. Don't be one of them.

Keep the faith. Do not turn in another direction when things get tough. Satan is known for bringing new (and wrong) solutions to our trials; this is a test of our faith. "I have fought the good fight, I have **finished my course,** I have **kept the faith;** henceforth there is laid up for me a crown of righteousness . . ." (2 Tim. 4:7). As the leader of your family, keeping a steady direction is a must!

Ask God for another man who will stand with you. Find another who will help you to stand and not to *bend* from your commitment. "Two are better than one for they have a good return for their labor. For if either of them falls, the one will lift up his companion. But woe to the one who falls when there is not another to lift him up. Furthermore, if two lie down together they keep warm, but how can one be warm alone? And if one can overpower him who is alone, two can resist him. *A cord of three is not easily broken"* (Eccl. 4:9–12). Since a cord of three is not easily broken, try to find two others who will stand, encourage you, and keep you firm in the direction of your faith. Here are some examples of "cords of three" found in the Scriptures:

Moses, Aaron, and Hur: "But Moses' hands were heavy. Then they took a stone and put it under him, and he sat on it; and Aaron and Hur supported his hands, one on one side and one on the other. Thus his hands were steady until the sun set" (Exod. 17:12).

Also **Shadrach, Meshach,** and **Abed-nego** in the book of Daniel, chapter 3.

Paul, Luke, and **Timothy.** When Paul was in prison, he had two men to help encourage him. When Demas left, Paul sent for Timothy. We are told that Demas left because the cares of the world choked the Word from him. The following verse tells us how: "And the one on whom seed was sown among the thorns, this is the man who hears the Word, and the **worry** of the world, and the deceitfulness of **riches** choke the Word and it becomes unfruitful" (Matt. 13:22). Scripture says specifically that we can become "unfruitful" because of worry and also because of riches. So let us be careful not to worry about our circumstances or get caught up in money matters or our possessions. We need to trust that "our God will supply all our needs" (Phil. 4:19), even when it doesn't "look like" there will be enough money. Many Christians have fallen from their faith because the Word was choked out as a result of financial problems.

Ask God for guidance through trials. "Trust in the Lord with all thine heart; and lean not unto thine own understanding. In all your ways acknowledge Him and He will direct thy paths" (Prov. 3:5–7). Let us call on *Him* for strength, draw close to *Him* in our time of need. Let us allow *Him* to discipline us, try us, and test us. Let us rejoice always in *all things,* not just the good things, but also in the troubles that come our way. Let us keep our hope close to our lips and stay steadfast in our minds. Let us always remember that it is *His will* that we face these hard times and that they are for our good!

And we know that God causes all things to work together for good to those who love God, to those who are called according to His purpose.
—Romans 8:28

Let us rejoice that He considers us worthy to suffer for His name!
—Acts 5:41

Here are Scripture verses to run to during your various trials:

God is in control, not man and not Satan.

1. Justice is from the *Lord* (Prov. 29:26).

2. An answer is from the *Lord* (Prov. 16:1).

3. The *Lord* turns the heart (Prov. 21:1).

4. Their deeds are in *God's* hand (Eccl. 9:1).

5. *Thou* (God) hast done it (Ps. 44:9–15).

6. *He* (God) raised the storm (Ps. 107:1–32).

7. *He* (God) removed lover and friend (Ps. 88:8, 18).

What do our trials do *for* us?

1. So the power of Christ will dwell in us (2 Cor. 12:9–10).

2. So we will learn to be content (Phil. 4:9).

3. So we will receive a reward (2 Tim. 4:7–8).

4. So we lack nothing (James 1:2–4).

5. To enable us to comfort others (2 Cor. 1:3–4).

6. To perfect what He started in us (Phil. 1:6–13).

7. To have our loved one back (Phlm. 1:15–16).

8. To receive mercy (Heb. 4:15).

9. To learn obedience (Heb. 5:7–8).

10. To produce endurance (James 1:2–4).

11. To receive the crown of life (James 1:12).

12. To prove our faith (1 Pet. 1:6–7).

13. To follow in His steps (1 Pet. 2:21).

14. To share in His sufferings (1 Pet. 3:13).

15. To be perfect, confirmed, strengthened, and established (1 Pet. 5:10).

Part 2

Temptations

*Now flee from youthful lusts,
and pursue righteousness, faith, love, and peace,
with those who call on the Lord from a pure heart.
—2 Timothy 2:22*

One of the strongest temptations that men face today is sexual immorality. There are many forms of sexual immorality, including, but are not limited to, adultery, pornography, and masturbation. We are going to focus primarily on Scriptures about "adultery," since this is the sin that I fell into. If it were not for God's divine mercy, and my precious wife demonstrating a love for me beyond what I thought was humanly possible, I would have completely destroyed my family.

These Scriptures from Proverbs speak to a son from his father. Please accept these verses from me as your Christian brother.

*My son, give attention to my wisdom,
Incline your ear to my understanding;
That you may observe discretion,
And your lips may reserve knowledge.
For the lips of an adulteress drip honey,
And smoother than oil is her speech;
But in the end she is bitter as wormwood,*

Sharp as a two-edged sword.
Her feet go down to death,

Her steps lay hold of Sheol.
She does not ponder the path of life;
Her ways are unstable, she does not know it.
Now then, my sons, listen to me,
And do not depart from the words of my mouth.
Keep your way far from her,
And do not go near the door of her house,
Lest you give your vigor to others,
And your years to the cruel one;
Lest strangers be filled with your strength,
And your hard-earned goods go to the house of an alien;
And you groan at your latter end,
When your flesh and your body are consumed;
And you say, 'How I have hated instruction!

And my heart spurned reproof!
And I have not listened to the voice of my teachers,
Nor inclined my ear to my instructors!
I was almost in utter ruin
In the midst of the assembly and congregation.'
Drink water from your own cistern [your own wife],
And fresh water from your own well.
Should your springs be dispersed abroad,
Streams of water in the streets?
Let them be yours alone,
And not for strangers with you.
Let your fountain be blessed,
And rejoice in the wife of your youth.
As a loving hind and a graceful doe,
Let her [your wife's] breasts satisfy you at all times;
Be exhilarated always with her love.
For why should you, my son, be exhilarated with an adulteress,
And embrace the bosom of a foreigner?

For the ways of a man are before the eyes of the Lord,
*And **He watches all** his paths.*
His own iniquities will capture the wicked,
And he will be held with the cords of his sin.
He will die for lack of instruction,
And in the greatness of his folly he will go astray.
—Proverbs 5:1–23

What can we learn from Scripture about the adulterer and the adulteress?

It is her words that will pull you into adultery. "For the lips of an adulteress drip honey, and smoother than oil is her speech; but in the end she is bitter as wormwood, sharp as a two-edged sword. Her feet go down to death, her steps lay hold of Sheol. She does not ponder the path of life; her ways are unstable, she does not know it" (Prov. 5:3–6). With this in mind, be very careful who you talk to. I would suggest not talking to other women, period! If you work with women, be extremely careful! This is where the majority of men fall into the pit of adultery, at their places of work! How do I know? That's where I fell! Also, Erin has counseled hundreds of women whose husbands have left them for other women, and she says nine out of ten times it was someone they met at work.

And men, don't get involved in "chat rooms" on the Internet! This is Satan's latest tool for destroying marriages and families. Don't be so stupid as to think it couldn't happen to you! We personally know of several men who began their adultery on the Internet. Men, sexual adultery begins with emotional adultery. Did you hear what I just said? **Sexual adultery begins with emotional adultery.** I have heard married Christian men and women say they use Internet chat rooms to witness. This is very naive and foolish thinking. Though they have the best of intentions, sin is crouching at the door. Don't be fooled—it's a trap!

Men, let me make this perfectly clear. **Do not be drawn into a conversation with any woman other than your wife!** If you ignore this warning, as I did, you most likely will live to regret it.

The adulterous woman will use her speech (how she talks to you and what she says to you) to pull you into adultery and into *spiritual death.* "With her many persuasions **she entices him;** with her **flattering lips she seduces him.** *Suddenly* he follows her as an ox goes to slaughter. So he does not know it will cost him his life" (Prov. 7:21–23). Many women whose husbands have fallen into the pit of adultery have reported that they warned their husbands, yet they never heeded their warnings. So many times we ignore our wives' warnings, to our own destruction. "And while he was sitting on the judgment seat, his (Pilate's) wife sent to him, saying, 'Have nothing to do with that righteous Man; for last night I suffered greatly in a dream because of Him'" (Matt. 27:19). Oh, if only *I* had heeded the cautions of *my* wife.

Once again, it is the words of the adulterous woman that will pull you into adultery. "That they may keep you from an adulteress, from the foreigner who **flatters with her words**" (Prov. 7:5). The adulteress flatters: "A man who flatters his neighbor is spreading a net for his steps" (Prov. 29:5). When someone flatters, the heart or motivation is to "get something."

Her smooth tongue. Again, it is her smooth speech that eventually will pull you into adultery and cause you to suffer financially also. "To keep you from the evil woman, from the **smooth tongue** of the adulteress. Do not desire her beauty in your heart, **do not let her catch you with her eyelids.** For on account of a harlot one is reduced to a loaf of bread, and an adulteress hunts for the precious life. Can a man take fire to his bosom, and his clothes not be burned? The one who commits adultery with a woman is lacking sense; he who would destroy himself does it. Wounds and disgrace he will find, and his reproach will not be blotted out" (Prov. 6:24–33). **"Do not let her catch you with her eyelids"** (Prov. 6:25).

Now do you understand why I have warned you not to talk to a woman other than your wife? If you ignore the Bible's warnings, you can expect a fall.

Keeping company with a harlot. God says that a man who keeps company with a harlot *will* suffer financially. "He who *keeps company* with harlots **wastes his wealth"** (Prov. 29:3). Several women have come to Erin over the years and told her that because their husbands were so successful in business, they didn't think this biblical principle could apply to them. But Erin knew that God's Word applies to all. *Every* one of these women later came to her and told of their husband's financial collapse. I, too, suffered financial collapse (and my family suffered right along with me). What a fool! *Men, I pray with all my heart that you are taking this all in.*

A slave of the one whom you obey. You must understand that the adulteress is basically, as they say, out to get you. But let me also say that many times this adulterous woman has no idea that she is being used by the devil to destroy a man and his family. "Do you not know that when you present yourselves to someone as slaves for obedience, **you are slaves of the one whom you obey,** either of sin resulting in death, or of obedience resulting in righteousness?" (Rom. 6:16). Often the adulterous woman is hurting. Perhaps she's hurting because her husband or boyfriend has left her, or she may be living in a troubled marriage. The trap is laid when she begins sharing her hurts with you, and you begin to sympathize with her and offer suggestions. Don't play with fire! If a woman begins to open up to you by sharing her hurts or feelings—flee! Don't worry about being rude. All you have to say is "I'm not the person you should be talking to about this—please excuse me." Then get away. Again, don't be concerned about hurting her feelings. Avoiding this trap for the sake of your wife and children is a million times more important!

A harlot is usually out of her home. "A woman comes to meet him, dressed as a harlot and cunning of heart, she is boisterous and rebellious; her feet do not remain at home" (Prov. 7:5). This could be the woman you work with, whom you sit next to on the airplane, or even the woman who is "out" on the Internet!

We *must* seek wisdom. **"*Wisdom*** shouts in the street, she lifts her voice in the square; at the head of the noisy streets she cries out; at the entrance of the gates in the city, she utters her sayings: 'How long, O naive ones, will you love simplicity? And scoffers delight themselves in scoffing, and fools hate knowledge? Turn to my reproof, behold, I will pour out my spirit on you; I will make my words known to you. Because I called, and you refused; I stretched out my hand, and no one paid attention; and you neglected all my counsel, and did not want my reproof; **I will even laugh at your calamity; I will mock when your dread comes,** when your dread comes like a storm, and your calamity comes on like a whirlwind, **when distress and anguish come on you.** Then they will call on me, but

I will not answer; they will seek me diligently, but they shall not find me, because they hated knowledge, and did not *choose the fear of the Lord.* They would not accept my counsel, they spurned all my reproof. So they shall eat of the fruit of their own way, and be satiated with their own devices. For the waywardness of the naive shall kill them, and the complacency of fools shall destroy them. But he who listens to me shall live securely, and shall be at ease from the dread of evil" (Prov. 1:20–33).

Men, please stay away from any woman who is not your wife! Friendly conversation can quickly move to intimate conversation, and you will be as an ox led to slaughter.

Personal commitment: To "consider it all joy" when I encounter various trials. "Based on what I have learned from God's Word, I commit to allow the **testing of my faith** to help produce my **endurance.** And I will **let** endurance have its perfect result, that I may be perfect and complete, lacking nothing."

Date: _____ Signed: _____

"Not that I have already obtained it, or have already become perfect, but I press on, in order that I may lay hold of that for which also I was laid hold of by Christ Jesus" (Phil. 3:12).

Homework

"Consider it all joy, my brethren, when you encounter various trials, knowing that the testing of your faith produces endurance" (James 1:2–3).

1. **3x5 cards.** It is extremely important that you write down the verses from *this* chapter. If you can go directly to His Word during a trial, test, or temptation, then you will certainly be an overcomer!

2. **Be an effectual doer.** "But one who looks intently at the perfect law, the law of liberty, and abides by it, not having become a forgetful hearer but an effectual doer, this man shall be **blessed** in what he does" (James 1:25).

3. Share this information with *one other man* who is currently going through trials in his life.

Test Your Wisdom

1. The _____ for adversity comes from God. "Simon, Simon, behold, Satan has demanded _____ to sift you like wheat" (Luke 22:31).

2. "A cord of _____ is not easily broken" (Eccl. 4:12).

3. "And we know that God causes _____ things to work together for good to those who _____ God, to those who are called according to _____ purpose" (Rom. 8:28).

4. What is one way to keep from the adulterous woman? ". . . Do not _____ her beauty in your _____, do not let her _____ _____ with her _____" (Prov. 6:24). In other words, don't look at any other women!

5. When we sin, especially adultery or divorce, we are passing on our sin to our children. ". . . He will by no means clear the guilty, visiting the _____ of the _____ on the _____ to the _____ and the _____ generations" (Num. 14:18).

6. It is the adulteress' words that will pull you into adultery. "For the lips of an adulteress drip _____ and then oil is her speech" (Prov. 5:3–6). "With her many _____ she entices him; with her _____ _____ she seduces him" (Prov. 7:21–23).

7. We know that we go through sufferings so that we can be a comfort to others. ". . . God of all comfort, who comforts us in _____ our affliction so that we may be able to comfort those who are in _____ affliction with the comfort with which we ourselves are comforted by _____" (2 Cor. 1:3–4).

The answers to Homework questions are at the end of this workbook.

Chapter 11

I Hate Divorce

*"For I hate divorce,"
says the Lord, the God of Israel.
—Malachi 2:16*

Why are so many marriages ending in divorce? We have all heard the statistics . . . 50 percent of first marriages end in divorce and 80 percent of second marriages end in divorce!

But why? "And the rain descended, and the floods came, and the winds blew, and burst against that house; and yet it did not fall, for it had been **founded upon the rock**" (Matt. 7:25). Most of our houses were not built on the Rock of God's Word.

Was your house built on the Rock? If not, then you, like me, were foolish. "And the rain descended, and the floods came, and the winds blew, and burst against that house; and it fell, and *great was its fall*" (Matt. 7:27).

The **Rock** that we need to build on is His Word. "Consequently, they are no longer two but one flesh. What therefore God has joined together, let no man separate" (Matt. 19:6). ". . . And the two shall become one flesh; consequently, they are no longer two, but one flesh" (Mark 10:8). ". . . But I say to you that everyone who divorces his wife, except for the cause of unchastity, makes her commit adultery; and whoever marries a divorced woman commits adultery" (Matt. 5:32). "And I say to you, whoever divorces his wife, except for immorality [fornication], and marries another woman commits adultery" (Matt. 19:9). "And He said to them, 'Whoever divorces his wife and marries another woman commits adultery against her'. . . ." (Mark 10:11). "Everyone who divorces his wife and marries another commits adultery; and he who marries one who is divorced from a husband commits adultery" (Luke 16:18).

"So then if, while her husband is living, she is joined to another man, she shall be called an adulteress; but if her husband dies, she is free from the law, so that she is not an adulteress, though she is joined to another man" (Rom. 7:3).

The Scriptures on marriage are very clear.

Commitment

Another reason for the high divorce rate is the lack of commitment. We are not committed to staying married. It's *out with the old; let's look for someone new*. The real shame is how many broken marriages are in the church, because the church accepts divorce as an option!

Accepting divorce as an option is another reason for the high divorce rate within the church. When we entertain a wrong thought or idea, God tells us that it is because ". . . each one is tempted when he is carried away and enticed by his own lust. (The definition of lust is a "longing" for what is forbidden.) Then when lust has conceived, it gives birth to sin; and when sin is accomplished, it brings forth death. Do not be deceived, my beloved brethren" (James 1:14–16).

Many will say that there is nothing wrong with divorce, especially in some circumstances; that's where the deception comes in.

The Deception

We must obey God rather than man. Everyone has his or her own opinion concerning marriage and what he or she "thinks" God tells us pertaining to marriage in His Word. The "gray area" is easiest for most Christians to stand on, but it is *not* grounded in Scripture. Divorce is very clearly a black and white issue. A firm stand is difficult and unpopular; that's why so many pastors don't want to take a strong stand against divorce. But, "We must **obey God** rather than man" (Acts 5:29).

He is our only hope for salvation. Don't look to follow what a person says. Instead, follow and obey God, for *He* is our only hope for salvation. Don't complicate His Word by trying to find "what you *think* He means." *He means exactly what He says!* Some of the more liberal or progressive churches have changed the miracles of Jesus into something quite different. We heard a woman pastor said in her sermon that the miracle of the loaves and fishes was nothing more than a lesson on "sharing." The little boy was the first to share his food; then others began to share what they had been hiding!

I am not ashamed of the gospel of Christ. Please stand by God's teachings regardless of what is popular or how many people in your church have divorced and remarried. "I am not ashamed of the gospel of Christ, for it is the power of God for salvation to everyone who believes" (Rom. 1:16). Please know that if marriages are to be saved, we must stand on Truth!

With gentleness, correcting those who are in opposition. Please do not debate the issue of divorce. Each person is only responsible to speak, teach, and live the Truth. The Holy Spirit will do the convicting and the Lord will turn the heart. "But refuse foolish and ignorant speculations, knowing that they produce quarrels. And the Lord's bond-servant must not be quarrelsome, but be kind to all, able to teach, patient when wronged, with **gentleness; correcting** those who are in opposition, if perhaps God may grant them repentance leading to the knowledge of the Truth, and they may come to their senses and escape from the snare of the devil, having been held captive by him to do his will" (2 Tim. 2:23–26).

The tree is known by its fruit. We can see the "fruits" of many of those in the church who have allowed loopholes and the widespread abuse of the exceptions for divorce. We have seen that it began with the loophole of "unfaithfulness or adultery" and led to divorce for practically any reason! It parallels what has happened with the abortion issue . . . rape, incest, and the health of the mother now account for less than 1 percent of all abortions performed—99 percent are for convenience's sake! "You will know them by their **fruits**" (Matt. 7:16). "Either make the tree good, and its fruit good; or make the tree bad, and its fruit bad; for the tree is known by its fruit" (Matt. 12:33). We can clearly see the bad fruit that has been produced—broken marriages and broken vows.

The Questions

Why must we understand and follow God's Law concerning marriage?

Because families are being destroyed, and, without the family, the foundation on which our country stands will have been removed and great will be our fall! We as Christians will be to blame. We cannot point the finger at others because of God's promise to us as believers: If "My people who are called by My name will humble themselves and pray and seek My face and turn from their wicked ways, then I will hear from heaven, will forgive their sin, and will *heal their land*" (2 Chron. 7:14).

Christian marriages are perishing at the same rate of destruction as those in the world. Why? "My people perish for a lack of knowledge" (Hos. 4:6). Christians have been deceived and are following the world's ways, rather than God's ways.

How can we know that we are being deceived about marriage and divorce?

We know we are deceived because we don't want to hear the Truth. "For the time will come when they will not endure sound doctrine; but wanting to have their ears tickled, they will accumulate for themselves teachers in accordance to their own desires and will turn away their ears from the Truth, and will turn aside to myths" (2 Tim. 4:3–4).

We know we are deceived because we are seeking worldly solutions for troubled or wounded marriages. "But you are a chosen generation, a royal priesthood, a holy nation, a *peculiar* people" (1 Pet. 2:9). We are not a "peculiar people" if we just follow the beaten path that leads to divorce court!

Because His Word is always consistent—God's Word is the opposite of the world's philosophies and sometimes difficult to understand and follow. "But a natural man does not accept the things of the Spirit of God; they are foolishness to him, and he cannot understand them, because they are spiritually appraised" (1 Cor. 2:14). "But I say, walk by the Spirit, and you will not carry out the desire of the flesh . . . so you may not do the things that you please" (Gal. 5:17).

Again, because we can easily see "the fruits" of all the Christian marriages that have been destroyed because they believed the lies. "You will know them by their fruits. Grapes are not gathered from thorn bushes, nor figs from thistles, are they? Even so, every good tree bears good fruit; but the bad tree bears bad fruit" (Matt. 7:15–17).

Scriptural Facts to Stand On

Let's search more Scriptures to see where God stands on marriage.

Wife by covenant. Marriage was to be a blood covenant. On the wedding night a blood covenant is made as the couple consummate their marriage. "This is the new covenant in My blood" (1 Cor. 1:25). "And this is another thing you do: you cover the altar of the Lord with tears, with weeping, and with groaning, because He no longer regards the offering or accepts it with favor from your hand. Yet you say, 'For what reason?' Because the Lord has been a witness between you and the wife of your youth, against whom you have dealt treacherously, though she is your companion and your **wife by covenant**" (Mal. 2:13–14). "My **covenant** I will not violate, nor will I alter the utterance of My lips" (Ps. 89:34). "All the paths of the Lord are lovingkindness and Truth to those who keep His covenant and His testimonies" (Ps. 25:10).

No longer two, but one flesh. Marriage is for life. We say the vows *until death do us part,* but do we mean it? "Consequently they are no longer two but one flesh. What therefore God has joined together, let no man separate" (Matt. 19:6). ". . . And the two shall become one flesh; consequently they are **no longer two, but one flesh**" (Mark 10:8).

For I hate divorce, says the Lord. God says that *He hates divorce!* First, He says, **"For I hate divorce, says the Lord"** (Mal. 2:16). And, He never changes. "Jesus Christ is the same yesterday and today, yes and forever" (Heb. 13:8). Not even for you, your friend, or your brother . . . "I most certainly understand that now God is not One to show partiality" (Acts 10:34).

The husband of one wife. We are to be the living example of Christ and His Church, the husband of one wife: ". . . the husband of one wife . . ." (1 Tim. 3:2). ". . . if any man be above reproach, the husband of one wife . . ." (Titus 1:6).

Commits adultery. Remarriage is not an "option"; it's "adultery"! ". . . But I say to you that everyone who divorces his wife, except for the cause of unchastity, makes her **commit adultery;** and whoever marries a divorced woman **commits adultery"** (Matt. 5:32). "And I say to you, whoever divorces his wife, except for immorality [fornication, KJV], and marries another woman **commits adultery"** (Matt. 19:9). "And He said to them, 'Whoever divorces his wife and marries another woman **commits adultery** against her . . .'" (Mark 10:11). "Everyone who divorces his wife and marries another commits adultery; and he who marries one who is divorced from a husband **commits adultery"** (Luke 16:18).

If you divorce, you are lacking sense! "The one who commits adultery with a woman is **lacking sense;** he who would destroy himself does it" (Prov. 6:32). "If there is a man who commits adultery with another man's wife, one who commits adultery with his friend's wife, the adulterer and the adulteress shall surely be put to death" (Lev. 20:10). "And I gave her time to repent; and she does not want to repent of her immorality. Behold, I will cast her upon a bed of sickness, and those who commit adultery with her into great tribulation, unless they repent of her deeds" (Rev. 2:21).

You'll be proved a liar. What about the *exception* clause? First of all, very few marriages in the church end because of adultery, even if that were the correct "exception." The verse says, ". . . but I say to you that everyone who divorces his wife, *except* **for the cause** of . . . *[adultery, fornication, moral impurity,* or *unchastity],* makes her commit adultery; and whoever marries a divorced woman commits adultery" (Matt. 5:32). In different Bible versions, the words *adultery, fornication, moral impurity,* and *unchastity* are used interchangeably as though they were the same word. They are not.

The "exception" Jesus is talking about is the word *fornication, moral impurity,* and *unchastity.* This is *porneia* (4202), *before* the marriage takes place. The word *adultery,* which refers to *after* marriage, is *moichao* (3429) in Strong's Concordance in the Greek or original language. Adultery or *moichao* (3429) and *porneia* (4202) are two separate and distinct sins. Therefore, you cannot divorce your spouse for the reason of adultery, moral impurity, or unchastity. Divorce was and is only allowed for the case of fornication when a woman was found not to be a virgin on her wedding night.

Another interesting notation is found in the definition of 4202. The author admits that he has added his own words. He states, "These words *have been added* to include 'adultery' and 'incest' for better understanding of fornication (*porneia*)." He is saying that adultery was added to the definition of the word *porneia*. But God's Word says, "Do *not add* to His Words lest He reprove you, and **you be proved a liar**" (Prov. 30:6).

Let me also quote Strong's note under *Signs Employed and Plan of the Book:* "Parenthesis . . . denotes a word given with the principal word to which it is annexed and a few words of explanation are ***added** to identify it.*" Again, one should never ". . . *add* to His Words lest He reprove you, and **you be proved a liar**" (Prov. 30:6).

Falsehoods and reckless boasting. Be careful what you say *God told you*. "Behold I am against those who use their tongues and declare 'The Lord declares.' Behold I am against those who have prophesied false dreams, declares the Lord, and related them and led my people astray by their **falsehoods and reckless boasting**" (Jer. 23:31–32). "For I hate divorce, says the Lord" (Mal. 2:16). God never tells us to go against His Word! He never changes.

Also, be careful what you say about divorce or remarriage; it could lead another to divorce or to remarry. "Woe to the world because of its stumbling blocks! For it is inevitable that stumbling blocks come; but woe to that man through whom the stumbling block comes! . . . It is better for him that a heavy millstone be hung around his neck, and that he be drowned in the depth of the sea" (Matt. 18:7, 6).

Great was its fall. If you believe that divorce is okay in some circumstances, you have been deceived. "And no wonder, for even Satan disguises himself as an angel of light" (2 Cor. 11:14). Whenever you feel led to say or do something, first make sure that it is consistent with Scripture. "Therefore everyone who hears these Words of Mine, and acts upon them, may be compared to a wise man, who built his house upon the rock. And the rain descended, and the floods came, and the winds blew, and burst against that house; and yet it did not fall, for it had been founded upon the rock. And everyone who hears these Words of Mine, and does not act upon them, will be like a foolish man, who built his house upon the sand. And the rain descended, and the floods came, and the winds blew and burst against that house; and it fell and **great was its fall**" (Matt. 7:26–27).

Spirit against the flesh. After you check Scripture, then check to see how driven you are about it. Fleshly desires feel good to the flesh. When you have urgency behind what you do, you need no grace to carry it out. "For the flesh sets its desire against the Spirit, and the **Spirit against the flesh;** for these are in opposition to one another, so that you may not do the things that you please" (Gal. 5:17).

What If

What if my wife is unfaithful and commits adultery, then am I allowed to divorce her?

No. His Word says that you can divorce for the reason of fornication only, which, as we saw previously, is intercourse prior to marriage. This was during the betrothal time. Fornication and adultery are not the same sin. If they were they would not both be listed in the same verse, as in this Scripture: ". . . neither *fornicators,* idolaters, nor *adulterers* . . ." (1 Cor. 6:9).

Divorce for the cause of fornication was allowed during the betrothal time, as with Mary and Joseph. "And Joseph, her husband . . . desired to divorce her secretly" (Matt. 1:19). The terms *fiancé* and *engaged* were not used during this period of history. Joseph was considered her husband because he had already committed to marrying Mary. He was allowed to *divorce her* because it was prior to their marriage, since divorce was allowed for the case of fornication. In the verse preceding this, it explains that the *divorce* was to take place *before* the marriage! ". . . When Mary had been betrothed to Joseph, *before* they came together she was found to be with child . . ." (Matt. 1:18). The latest a divorce could take place was the day after the wedding night, if the woman was found not to be a virgin.

What if my wife has died?

For those men who are widowed, it is important to know that if you meet a woman and you are considering marriage, she too must be widowed, or she must never have been married. Remember, Satan usually brings his best first—the Lord makes you *wait* and then brings His best! "Wait for the Lord, and keep His way" (Ps. 37:34).

"If either of you know any obstruction, why you may not be lawfully joined together in matrimony, you will now confess it. For be assured, that if any persons are joined together otherwise than as God's Word does allow, their marriage is not lawful" ("The Marriage Service," C.R. Gibson Co.).

What if I am already in a second or third marriage?

First, you must ask God's forgiveness, whether you were married before you were saved or not. You can't be effective in your Christian walk if you can't admit past sins. "He who covers his transgressions shall not prosper" (Prov. 28:13). "If we say that we have no sin, we are deceiving ourselves, and the Truth is not in us. If we confess our sins, He is *faithful and righteous* to **forgive us our sins** and to cleanse us from *all* unrighteousness" (1 John 1:8–9).

Time to repent. Remember Revelation 2:21, "And *I gave her time to repent;* and she does not want to repent of her immorality. Behold, I will cast her upon a bed of sickness, and those who commit adultery with her into great tribulation, unless they repent of her deeds." Have no fear of confessing, since *we are no longer under the law*. Praise God! "If there is a man who commits adultery with another man's wife, one who commits adultery with his friend's wife, the adulterer and the adulteress shall surely be put to death" (Lev. 20:10). "Therefore, confess your sins to one another, and pray for one another, so that you may be healed. The effective prayer of a righteous man can accomplish much" (James 5:16).

Not My will, but Thine be done. After you confess, you must lay *your will* aside and ask your heavenly Father for *His will* concerning what He would have you do. Many others who are in a second (or subsequent) marriage have faced this difficult task. Some had assurance that God intended them to stay in their present marriage and use their lives as a testimony against divorce. Others saw that their marriage was crumbling because they had been used by Satan when they destroyed their spouse's previous marriage. "The thief comes only to steal, and kill, and destroy; I came that they might have life, and might have it abundantly" (John 10:10).

Trust Him. You must trust Him. He wants to give you an abundant life, not a counterfeit.

Can Adultery Be Forgiven?

Yes. Jesus said to the woman caught in adultery: "Did no one condemn you? . . . Neither do I condemn you; go your way. From now on sin no more" (John 8:10–11). But you must confess your sins and not encourage others to sin as you did.

Actually, not only is **adultery** *not* grounds for divorce, it is **grounds for forgiveness** as shown by Christ in John 8:10 above. We also have an example in Hosea of a spouse forgiving adultery. "Then the Lord said to me, 'Go again, love a woman who is loved by her husband, yet an adulteress'" (Hos. 3:1).

Then in 1 Corinthians 6:9–11, when God refers to adulterers and fornicators, He says, "And such *were* some of you; but you were washed, but you were sanctified, but you were justified in the name of the Lord Jesus Christ, and in the Spirit of our God." We are washed in His blood of forgiveness.

Yet, many pastors say that adultery is grounds for divorce. "You have heard that it was said, 'You shall not commit adultery'; but I say to you that everyone who looks on a woman to lust for her has committed adultery with her already in his heart" (Matt. 5:27–28). If it is true that adultery is grounds for divorce, then most married women could divorce their husbands, since most men have lusted over pictures of women that they have seen on television or in magazines!

But *so many* churches and pastors say that divorce is right in some situations and that remarriage is okay if it's under the right circumstances. "Whoever then annuls one of the least of these commandments, and so teaches others, shall be called least in the kingdom of heaven; but whoever keeps and teaches them, he shall be called great in the kingdom of heaven" (Matt. 5:19).

How can I be sure that *this* teaching is right and what many of the churches are teaching is wrong? "Beware of the false prophets, who come to you in sheep's clothing, but inwardly are ravenous wolves. Many will say to Me on that day, 'Lord, Lord, did we not prophesy in Your name, and in Your name cast out demons, and in Your name perform many miracles?' And then I will declare to them, 'I never knew you; depart from Me, you who practice lawlessness'" (Matt. 7:15, 22–23). Aren't many of the families in your church crumbling and the marriages dissolving? These are the bad fruits of most "Christian marriage counselors."

Many pastors feel a "deep down" conviction about marriage, but don't want to "offend" anyone—especially all those "church members" who are in their second and third marriages. "Friendship with the world is hostility toward God. Therefore whoever wishes to be a friend of the world makes himself an enemy of God" (James 4:4).

If a pastor or church takes a stand against divorce and remarriage they are labeled "legalistic" or "judgmental." And those who want to "do their own thing" will go to another church to hear what they want to hear, to have their ears tickled. "For the time will come when they will not endure sound doctrine; but wanting to have their ears tickled, they will accumulate for themselves teachers in accordance to their own desires; and will turn away from the Truth, and will turn aside to myths" (2 Tim. 4:3–4).

Since I'm already divorced and "single again," couldn't I date or remarry and then ask God to forgive me?

First of all *you are not single!* Only someone who has *never* been married is single. "And He said to them, 'Whoever divorces his wife and marries another woman commits adultery against her . . .'" (Mark 10:11). "Everyone who divorces his wife and marries another commits adultery; and he who marries one who is divorced from a husband commits adultery" (Luke 16:18).

Secondly, you will reap what you have sown. "Do not be deceived, God is not mocked; for whatever a man sows, this he will reap also" (Gal. 6:7). You are willfully entering into sin. "Therefore to one who knows the right thing to do and does not do it, to him it is sin" (James 4:17).

God's vengeance. You'll set yourself up for God's vengeance. "For if we go on sinning willfully after receiving the knowledge of the Truth, there no longer remains a sacrifice for sins. How much severer punishment do you think he will deserve who has trampled under foot the Son of God? Vengeance is mine, I will repay. The Lord will judge His people. *It is a **terrifying thing** to fall into the hands of the living God*" (Heb. 10:26–31). "For if we go on sinning willfully after receiving the knowledge of the truth, there no longer remains a sacrifice for sins, but a certain terrifying expectation of judgment, and the fury of a fire which will consume the adversaries. Anyone who has set aside the Law of Moses dies without mercy on the testimony of two or three witnesses. How much severer punishment do you think he will deserve who has trampled under foot the Son of God, and has regarded as unclean the blood of the covenant by which he was sanctified, and has insulted the Spirit of grace? For we know Him who said, 'Vengeance is Mine, I will repay.' And again, 'The Lord will judge His people.' It is a terrifying thing to fall into the hands of the living God" (Heb. 10:26–31).

In closing a difficult topic, because of the magnitude of church sin, let us look at the firm statement Paul wrote to Timothy: "If anyone advocates a different doctrine and does not agree with sound Words, those of our Lord Jesus Christ, and with the doctrine conforming to godliness, he is conceited and understands nothing; but has a morbid interest in controversial questions and disputes about words, out of which arise envy, strife, abusive language, evil suspicions, and constant friction between men of truth" (1 Tim. 6:3–5). "If you love Me, you will keep My commandments" (John 14:15). If you choose to follow the world's beliefs, you have ultimately chosen to follow and be a slave to Satan. If you say you believe God, *then obey Him*. "And why do you call Me, 'Lord, Lord,' and do not do what I say?" (Luke 6:46). If you have decided to ask Jesus for your salvation but are not following His teachings, then He is *not* your Lord and Master. If He *is* your Lord, then be sure that you act like it by obeying His Word.

Let us make a personal commitment to

Remain Married

and encourage all men to do the same.

Personal commitment: To remain married and encourage others to do the same. "Based on what I have learned from God's Word, I recommit myself to my marriage. I will humble myself when necessary and strive to be a 'peacemaker' in my marriage. I will not cover my transgressions nor cause another to stumble. I will devote my lips to spreading God's Truth on marriage."

Date: _____ Signed: _____

"Not that I have already obtained it, or have already become perfect, but I press on, in order that I may lay hold of that for which also I was laid hold of by Christ Jesus" (Phil. 3:12).

Homework

". . . In reference to your former manner of life, you lay aside the old self, which is being corrupted in accordance with the **lusts of deceit,** and that you be **renewed** in the spirit of your **mind,** and put on the *new self,* which in the likeness of God has been created in righteousness and holiness of the Truth" (Eph. 4:24).

1. **3x5 cards.** Are you faithful to write down the verses from *each* chapter that has touched your heart? Continue to keep these cards with you, and bring them out *regularly* as the Holy Spirit prompts you.

2. **Are you just a hearer?** "But one who looks intently at the perfect law, the law of liberty, and abides by it, not having become a forgetful hearer but an effectual doer, this man shall be **blessed** in what he does" (James 1:25).

3. Share the Truth from *this* chapter with *one other man* who is planning, or speaking of, divorce.

Test Your Wisdom

1. Why are marriages "perishing" in the church at the same rate as those outside the church? (Hos. 4:6).

Marriages are perishing because the church is suffering from a lack of _____.

2. Why do many church members leave a church that takes a strong biblical stand on marriage? (2 Tim. 4:3–4). Because they want their _____.

3. How does God instruct us to check the error of our ways? "We will know them by their _____. Every good tree will _____ good fruit. Every tree that doesn't bear good fruit is _____ and thrown into the fire" (Matt. 7:16–19).

4. How does God view the man and woman once they have made the marriage covenant? They are no longer two but _____ (Matt. 19:6).

5. What did Jesus say about those who remarry? They commit _____ _____ (Matt. 5:32, Matt. 19:9, and Luke 16:18).

6. What does God say about divorce? "For I _____ _____," says the Lord, the God of Israel, "and him who covers his garment with _____," says the Lord of hosts. "So take heed to your _____, that you do not deal _____" (Mal. 2:16).

7. Why is it important that all of us as Christians teach others the Truth on marriage, divorce, and remarriage? Because we will be called _____ in the kingdom of heaven (Matt. 5:19).

The answers to Homework questions are at the end of this workbook.

Chapter 12

The Fruit of the Womb

*Behold, children are a gift of the Lord;
the fruit of the womb is a reward.*
—*Psalm 127:3*

As we look around at our society and see abortion, child abuse, and incest, we wonder when our country began to hate children. Scripture tells us that there are two foundations, one built on the rock and the other on sinking sand. Men, we are on sinking sand and now *great* is our fall (Matt. 7:26).

Who is the enemy?

Ultimately, it is Satan. This is who is behind the sin, and those who listen to his lies are *his* slaves. "Jesus answered them, 'Truly, truly, I say to you, everyone who commits sin is the slave of sin'" (John 8:34).

Fruit of the womb. We have many vocal spokesmen for the devil—at this time many are known as "feminists." One of their goals has been to pervert or eliminate God's plan for women to have and bear children. These mentally twisted women would find it a curse to ever bear a child or to allow "fruit" to be fertilized within them. "Behold, children are a gift of the Lord; the **fruit** of the womb is a reward" (Ps. 127:3). The women involved in the NOW organization literally hate men.

Many women have turned to lesbianism and to the government for the protection of their sin. These are the women who have deceived many of our wives into believing they don't want to bear children. These women say that you, the husband, have no rights in regard to your own children. These same women, who will never know or want to know a man, have convinced masses of women, along with their husbands (or boyfriends) as accomplices, to abort (murder) their own children as a sacrifice to the feminist god of "self." May God forgive us for listening and agreeing with their lies, "for they are of their father," the father of lies. (John 8:44).

Obey Him. If you choose to follow their beliefs, you have ultimately chosen to follow and be a slave to Satan. If you say you believe God, *then obey Him.* "Why do you call me Lord and not do what I say?" (Luke 6:46). If Jesus is Lord of your life, than you should act like it. If babies are a blessing, than act like it and trust God with your wife's fertility! If the feminists' deception and their continuous propaganda has fogged your thinking, let us "renew our minds" in Christ Jesus (Rom. 12:2).

What time did Jesus predict would be a more sorrowful time than even the crucifixion?

The time is now! When the Jewish women were mourning and lamenting over Jesus, He turned to them and said: "Daughters of Jerusalem, stop weeping for Me, but weep for yourselves and for your children. For behold the days are coming when they will say, '*Blessed are the barren, and the wombs that never bore, and the breasts that never nursed*'" (Luke 23:28–29). How many times have you heard women telling your pregnant wife, "Better you than me!" How many times have you heard men and women (even Christian men and women) say, "No way! I'm not having any more kids!"

Branding instead of beauty. Jesus was facing the lowest point in His life, yet He said there would be a time that would be worse! When we see the feminist movement and their push toward lesbianism and reduction or elimination of children, we can see we are in the midst of the times Jesus was talking about. "Now it will come about that instead of sweet perfume there will be putrefaction; instead of a belt, a rope; instead of well-set hair, a plucked-out scalp; instead of fine clothes, a donning of sackcloth; and branding instead of beauty" (Isa. 3:24).

How did the "anti-children" movement begin?

It began about 30 years ago when birth control became accessible, and we have been sinking ever since. Birth control means:

"I don't want children yet."

12. Fruit of the Womb

"I don't want too many children—one, two, three, or maybe four, but no more!"

"I don't want them too close together."

"If, and I say if, I want children, I want them *when* I want, *how often* I want. God is no longer in control; I am! I know what's best for me and what I can handle. I choose my own destiny!"

Why do you call me Lord? "Why do you call me Lord and not do what I say?" (Luke 6:46). To have Jesus as Lord of your life, you must follow His teachings and principles.

The Bible clearly says, "Be fruitful and multiply" (Gen. 1:28).

We must be willing to allow God to determine how many children we will have. "Unless the *Lord* builds the house, they *labor in vain* who build it" (Ps. 127:1). Allow Him to build your family, one child at a time.

God hates the lukewarm. Once we Christians started to tolerate the "gray areas," beginning with "natural family planning," then it was easy to slip into a darker gray, "the pill," and other forms of birth control. Now we have the black area—**abortion!** "So **because you are lukewarm** [using birth control], and neither cold [which is abortion] nor hot [trusting God entirely for your fertility], I will spit you out of My mouth" (Rev. 3:16).

How can we, *who hate abortion* (and maybe even work in the pro-life movement), convince a woman who is contemplating abortion that the child she carries is a blessing, when we are refusing a blessing ourselves?

In Mary Pride's book, *The Way Home,* she states: "Family planning is the 'mother of abortion.' Once couples look upon children as 'creatures of their own making,' all reverence for human life was lost. Children as God's gifts whom we humbly receive are one thing; children as articles of our own manufacturing are another. You can do anything you like with what you yourself have made. Hence, abortion, incest, child abuse."

God said, "Be fruitful and multiply and subdue the earth" in Genesis 1:22, Genesis 1:28, Genesis 8:17, Genesis 9:1, Genesis 9:7, Genesis 35:11, Genesis 48:4, Leviticus 26:9, Deuteronomy 7:13, Deuteronomy 8:1,

Deuteronomy 30:16, Jeremiah 30:19, Jeremiah 33:22, *and* Hebrews 6:14. **He told us 14 times!!**

But, haven't we already filled the earth?

Fill the earth. You may be saying, "Haven't we already filled the earth?" We continually hear about the dreaded "overpopulation problem," but two experts give us a different picture:

"We could put the entire world population in the state of Texas and each man, woman, and child could be allotted 2,000 square feet [the average home ranges between 1,400 and 1,800 square feet] and the whole rest of the world would be empty" (Mary Pride, *The Way Home,* pg. 62).

"Every person in the world could stand, without touching each other, within the city limits of Jacksonville, Florida" (Bill Gothard, *Institute of Basic Life Principles (IBLP) Publications).*

But I'm afraid that if we let God have control He would give us 20 children!

Do you believe that the Bible really is the infallible Word of God? If so, read this: "Behold, children are a gift of the Lord; the fruit of the womb is a reward" (Ps. 127:3). We Christians are picky about which blessings we will receive. Give us more cars, a bigger house, and a higher position in our job and the extra responsibility, trials, and work that go along with them. *But, for "heaven's sake," don't give us any more children!* God says that children are a *reward,* not a curse! We have been brainwashed by the feminists and by a worldly viewpoint! As a Christian, whom do you choose to believe, God or the feminists?

Opened her womb. Statistics show that in developed countries, the average woman without birth control will have five or six children, not twenty. Look at the Bible. Noah had just three, Sarah had only one, and both Rebekah and Rachel had only two. Gentleman, this was prior to birth control. Large families were the exception in the Bible, and also the most blessed.

Leah had six sons and a daughter, but Rachel had just two sons. "Now the Lord saw that Leah was unloved, and He opened her womb, but Rachel was barren" (Gen. 29:31). "Then God remembered Rachel, and

God gave heed to her and **opened her womb**" (Gen. 30:22). God gives exactly how many children He wants to give each woman. He gives them in exactly the perfect order and at God's perfect timing. In your desire to control your fertility, have you missed a blessing? "God also said to him, I am God Almighty; be fruitful and multiply; a nation and a company of nations shall come from you, and kings shall come forth from you" (Gen. 35:11).

Closed fast all the wombs. *Not* having children is God's *curse* or punishment. "They will play the harlot, but *not* increase" (Hos. 4:10). "For the *Lord closed fast all the wombs* of the household of Abimelech because of Sarah, Abraham's wife" (Gen. 20:18). This also shows us that it is *God* who opens and closes the womb. "For the Lord had **closed fast all the wombs** . . ." (Gen. 20:18). "And He opened her womb" (Gen. 29:31).

But what if I can't provide for any more children?

God shall supply all your needs. A lot of what we are lacking is faith. Claim this verse: "And my **God shall supply all your needs** according to His riches in glory in Christ Jesus" (Phil. 4:19). We need to reevaluate our priorities. Could the "needs" you think are needs actually be "wants"? "We are the richest people in history, yet are the most fearful about the costs of child-rearing" (Mary Pride, *The Way Home,* pg. 48). Let's be ". . . free from the **love of money"** (1 Tim. 3:3).

With these we shall be content. A lot of what you *want* to give your children is something that later will ruin them and lead to their destruction. Aren't the children who "have it all"—the toys, clothes, and their own room—the most spoiled, ungrateful, and miserable? Aren't these the same children who as teens are drawn into drugs, cults, or are often suicidal? Here is what Scripture says, "And if we have **food** and **covering, with these we shall be content.** But those who *want to get rich* fall into temptation, and a *snare,* and many foolish and harmful desires which plunge men into ruin and destruction" (1 Tim. 6:8–9).

Love of money. It seems that children today tend to be a financial burden for almost twice as long as they once were. The contribution from children to the family and society has now been delayed for years while they play and go to school. The young people in previous generations helped with preserving food, sewing clothing, and plowing and harvesting the fields, or they worked in apprentice positions to help the family financially. By the time they reached their teen years, they clearly became an asset instead of a liability. We all know many young people who are still living off their parents well into their twenties. This is even after their parents have paid out great sums of money for their college education. Ask yourself why you feel it is important to send your children to college; is it for godly character? "For the **love of money** is a root of all sorts of evil, and some by longing for it have wandered away from the faith, and pierced themselves with many a pang" (1 Tim. 6:10).

Fear. Instead of the *fear* of "having children" that the world keeps telling us about, let's talk about the fear of what they are *not telling us*. Not only do we miss blessings, but also we are living dangerously by what we use to stop God's blessings. Remember, "God is not mocked, what you **sow** this also you shall **reap**" (Gal. 6:7). Why do we want to sow a seed (by being intimate) and yet not reap the fruit of the womb (a baby)? With abortion, we actually rip the root right out of the soil! Men, how can you possibly trust God for your salvation, but not trust Him for the size of your family?

Multiply your seed. What are the dangers of stopping our fertility? "The Pill, an abortifacient, disturbs the lining of the uterus (endometrium), assuring that any baby who may have been conceived cannot implant himself correctly. Thus, the baby starves to death at about seven to nine days of age. The tiny infant is then cast out of the womb—a victim of abortion. The pill also causes hypertension, blood clotting, diabetes—hence the rise of maternal diabetes and a mandatory test is now recommended for all" *(from various IBLP publications)*. "Indeed, I will greatly bless you, and I will greatly **multiply your seed** as the stars of the heavens, and as the sand which is on the seashore; and your seed shall possess the gate of their enemies" (Gen. 22:17).

They labor in vain who build it. Many of us believed in Natural Family Planning. We believed that if we (and our wives) "planned" our family "naturally" we were working *with* God. Weren't we just being responsible? No. We were still saying we knew, *above God,* what was best for our families. Those of us who found the Truth and decided to trust God have experienced such freedom. Giving this responsibility over to God lifted such a burden. Some of us never had any more children and others had a few more. By trusting the Lord to build our house, we had the confidence that we had His best. "Unless the Lord builds the house, **they labor in vain who build it** . . ." (Ps. 127:1).

Wasted his seed. What about those contraception methods used by men? Not surprisingly, the Bible has covered them all, when the "seed was spilled" (Gen. 38:9). "And Onan . . . **wasted his seed** on the ground, in order not to give offspring to his brother. But *what he did was displeasing in the sight of the Lord;* so He took his life also" (Gen. 38:9–10).

Sterility. So many women are unable to become pregnant because of birth control, multiple partners, and damage from abortions. This has caused an obsession with some American women to have a child "at any cost." "Now the Lord saw that Leah was unloved, and He opened her womb, but Rachel **was barren"** (Gen. 29:31).

Abortion. We are told that it is wrong to allow "unwanted" children to be born. But the Truth is that those babies are definitely wanted. The long years of waiting for those wanting to adopt a baby are proof.

In vitro fertilization. Many see no wrong in test tube babies for a childless couple. But now we have been made aware of the many fertilized eggs that are disposed of in the Petri dish and also aborted from the womb. Since this method is so expensive, the doctor inserts several fertilized eggs, hoping that some will embed. Many times a "multiple pregnancy" results and the couple will have to choose "which and how many" will be spared and which will be aborted.

Surrogate mothers. These are women who are paid to carry a man's child for another woman. This is not new. Hagar is the first and most well-known surrogate mother. The hate that Sarah felt for her and the destitution of Ishmael and Hagar, not to mention the wars that have continued to this day, tell us the result of this sinful way of getting a child "at any cost"!

Homosexuality. "For this reason God gave them over to degrading passions; for their women exchanged the *natural function* for that which is *unnatural,* and in the same way also the men abandoned the natural function of the woman and burned in their desire toward one another, men with men committing indecent acts and receiving in their own persons the *due penalty of their error"* (Rom. 1:26–27). We have seen some of the "due penalty" of their error. AIDS is running rampant, especially among homosexuals. When women despise children, stop bearing the fruit of their wombs, and voluntarily sterilize themselves, this is unnatural!

Let's sum up what God has been telling us so far in His Word, since "all Scripture is inspired by God and profitable for **teaching,** for **reproof,** for **correction,** for **training** in righteousness . . ." (2 Tim. 3:16).

1. Children are **blessings.**

2. Our children are our **rewards.**

3. We should allow **God** to open and close the womb.

4. God commanded us to **multiply and fill** the earth.

5. The earth is not filled; we are **not overpopulated.**

6. We are not to give **wants** to our children, or it will lead to their destruction.

7. God supplies all our **needs;** we don't have to worry.

8. Not everyone will be blessed with a large family—some will only have one or two without even "helping God" with birth control or sterilization.

9. By using any form of birth control or sterilization, we are imposing a curse or punishment on our wives as God did on those in the Bible.

10. We can't really say we are pro-life if we use birth control—since it is the foundation of abortion.

What do you do if you want more children and your wife doesn't?

First, you need to pray and repent of anything that *you* may have done to encourage your wife not to trust God for her fertility. For example, do you rant and rave about the cost or burden of raising the children God has already given you? "Do all things without murmuring and complaining" (Phil.2:14).

Have you made your wife's job as "helpmeet" a miserable existence with all your demands on her when you arrive home from work? Maybe she's expected to bring home the bacon and cook it too—while you watch television! "When I was a child, I used to speak as a child, think as a child, reason as a child; when I became a man, I did away with childish things" (1 Cor. 13:11).

Are your children "pleasant to be around" or are they unruly and disrespectful? Do they rule your home, or do you? "Hear, my son, your father's instruction . . ." (Prov. 1:8).

Next, you need to pray. Ask the Lord to speak to your wife's heart concerning future children. "Behold, children are a gift of the Lord; the fruit of the womb is a reward" (Ps. 127:3). Ask God to restore your wife's heart to your children and toward future children. Share with her your heart change and this Scripture, Malachi 4:6: "And He will restore the hearts of the fathers to their children, and the hearts of the children to *their* fathers, lest I come and smite the land with a curse." Ask the Lord to turn your wife's heart. "The king's heart is like channels of water in the hand of the Lord; He turns it wherever He wishes" (Prov. 21:1).

If your wife continues to take the pill or watch for signs of her fertility, don't get upset with her; just pray. Trust that God will direct her. Your wife is responsible for obeying or rebelling against the authority God has placed over her. It is not your responsibility to make her submit.

What if I'm the one who has wanted to limit or space our children?

Examine your motives and your fears. Have you been motivated by selfishness, wanting more material things or more time for yourself? If selfishness has kept you from having more children, remember this Scripture: "But it is not so among you, but whoever wishes to become **great** among you shall be your servant; and whoever wishes to be first among you shall be **servant of all**" (Mark 10:43–44). Certainly a father who is solely providing for his family is a servant of all! This, my friend, is a real man.

Perhaps your wife has a fear of childbirth, and you don't want to put her through it again. Satan uses many varieties of fear with our wives. Some women who have had many children born naturally become fearful of the pain of childbirth.

On two different occasions when Erin was expecting one of our seven children, she became overwhelmed with fear as she was approaching her delivery date. This fear stemmed from the fact that she experiences very long, hard, and painful labors. "To the woman He said, 'I will greatly multiply your pain in childbirth, in pain you shall bring forth children; yet your desire shall be for your husband, and he shall rule over you.' Then to Adam He said, 'Because you have listened to the voice of your wife, and have [not filled the earth] which I commanded you, saying . . .""And as for you, be fruitful and multiply; populate the earth abundantly and multiply in it" (Gen. 9:7). Help your wife in any way you can if she experiences fear in bearing children; she needs your strength and assurance. Be there for her physically, mentally, spiritually, and her love for you will grow ever stronger.

Through one of our members, we recently discovered a wonderful new resource, **Supernatural Childbirth, by Jackie Mize!** A mother of 6 (who has a restored marriage and whose husband is a doctor) told me about it. She said that her first three she had naturally, the last three she had supernaturally—pain free!! We ordered the book and it was awesome and powerful! Now we are going to use this book, these principles, and Scriptures to prepare our three daughters for their future pregnancies (and us too, if the Lord has plans for us to have more children!). You can read testimonies on Amazon.com, but after reading my friend's testimonies and after reading the book, we are totally convinced it is not only possible, but it is God's plan for His own to give birth pain-free.

But, my wife and I feel overwhelmed with the children we already have.

If this is the way you're feeling, you need to check and see if you and your wife are following God's wisdom found in Proverbs concerning child training. (See Chapter 14, "Father's Instructions," for more wisdom.) Don't rely on Christian or secular child experts or authors; go to the Author and Creator of your children for the answers. "Blessed is the man who trusts the Lord . . ." (Jer. 17:5). "Cursed is the man who trusts in mankind and makes flesh his strength . . ." (Jer. 17:7).

Also, take the time to consider whether the things you do for your children (all "extra" curricular activities) have eternal worth. If not, trim back to an absolute bare minimum those that do not qualify. You can be sure that one of Satan's plans is to wear you and your wife out and cause you to feel overwhelmed, so he can achieve his goal of stopping any more Christian children from being born! Protect your wife and don't put too many demands on her. Sometimes it's the wife who feels her child needs to be in all the sports, music lessons, art classes, etc. Sometimes it's the child or teen who is pleading. Sometimes it's we fathers who remember our youth fondly and enjoy taking pride in our children at the games. Just keep in mind that we men are the protectors and we've been given the discernment. Use your discernment and pray about how God wants you to "train" the children He has given you.

When your wife works outside the home, the children you have, and any future babies, become a burden, not a blessing, since a lot of the paycheck goes to childcare. One woman sat down and figured her profit from working full time. She found that she only cleared $1.00 an hour after paying out childcare for her three children! A wife working outside the home will undoubtedly bring division to the home and family. Wives are "to be sensible, pure, **workers *at home*** . . ." (Titus 2:5). (See Chapter 13, "Provide for His Own," for "My people are destroyed for lack of knowledge. Because you have rejected knowledge . . ." [Hos. 4:6].)

Preserved through the bearing of children. God has a promise for those who trust God concerning the bearing of children. "But women shall be **preserved through the bearing of children** *if they continue* in faith and love and sanctity with self-restraint" (1 Tim. 2:15).

Here is another example of how you can help your wife. One woman's in-laws continuously harassed her husband to make her go back to work and earn her keep. Once her fourth child was born, her husband checked into childcare and found that they would actually lose money if his wife worked. His parents stopped pushing. She was "preserved" and able to stay in her home. Soon afterward her husband was given a substantial raise and they no longer needed additional income.

In Conclusion

Obey God. If you choose to follow the world's beliefs, you have ultimately chosen to follow and be a slave to Satan. If you say you believe God, *then obey Him.* "Why do you call me Lord and not do what I say?" (Luke 6:46). If Jesus Christ is your Lord and Savior, then act like it. If babies are a blessing, then act like it—by trusting God with your fertility!

**Your wife shall be like a fruitful vine
Within your house,
Your children like olive plants
Around your table.
—Psalm 128:3
May God Bless You!**

Personal commitment: To trust God in all areas of my life, including the number of children my wife and I have. "Based on what I have learned from God's Word and from observing the fruits of this generation's disobedience, I commit and surrender the size of my family to my God. If we are past childbearing years, or permanently unable to conceive, I commit to spreading *the Truth* and confessing *my faults* to others in order to discourage them from making the same mistakes."

Date: _____ Signed: _____

Homework

1. Make sure you stay faithful to writing down the verses on 3x5 cards from *each* of these chapters. Carry them with you at all times to counteract fear or anxiety over finances or anything else that causes you to reject the Word of God concerning childbearing.

2. Choose to renew your mind on the subject of childbearing. "But they refused to pay attention, and turned a stubborn shoulder and stopped their ears from hearing" (Zech. 7:11).

3. Share the Truth from *this* chapter with *one other man* who you know is planning to eliminate the opportunity of having any more children. "Cry loudly, do not hold back; raise your voice like a trumpet, and declare to My people their transgression, and . . . their sins" (Isa. 58:1).

Test Your Wisdom

1. When we "plan" our families, instead of trusting God's plan for us, what does Scripture say we are doing?

We _____ _____ _____ (Ps. 127:1).

2. What is the "curse" that Malachi 4:6 speaks of, which is happening to our land? Because our fathers' hearts are hardened toward children, God has _____ come _____ and _____our land with a _____.

3. How does the Bible say women will be preserved and protected? Through the _____of _____ (1 Tim. 2:15).

4. Many despise the thought of another child; however, their angels in heaven _____ behold the face of_____ _____ in heaven (Matt.18:10).

5. If we reject a child, whom are we really rejecting? The _____ (Matt. 18:5).

6. What will happen if we train our children to desire riches, by giving them all they ask for? They will fall into _____ and we will plunge them into _____and _____! (1 Tim. 6:8–9)

7. What does Hosea 4:10 mean, and how does it relate to our society today? We encourage our wives to play the _____, not wanting to _____ because we refuse more children (an increase).

The answers to Homework questions are at the end of this workbook.

Chapter 13

The Ministry of Reconciliation

*"Now all these things are from God,
who reconciled us to Himself through Christ,
and gave **us** the ministry of reconciliation . . ."*
—*2 Corinthians 5:18*

Everyone knows someone who is presently in a "bad" marriage or marital crisis. When your friend or family member shares the details, you feel hopeless, helpless, and very angry with the "other person." You pray for your friend or family member, you try to comfort them and offer some type of help, but what are you really supposed to do? Marital destruction is coming at us in epidemic proportions; what are we to do? *Are* we to help them? And if the answer is "yes," then **how** are we to minister to the broken, the angry, and/or the hurting?

God gave us the ministry of reconciliation. God gave **all** of us (those who claim the Lord Jesus Christ as Savior) the ministry of reconciliation, as 2 Corinthians 5:18–19 states: "Now all these things are from God, who reconciled us to Himself through Christ, and **gave *us* the ministry of reconciliation,** namely, that God was in Christ reconciling the world to Himself, not counting their trespasses against them, and He has committed to us the Word of reconciliation."

There are many verses that we will study in this lesson that confirm that we are to help those who come to us, but we must be very careful to help them within the guidelines of Scripture. When Erin was in the midst of the destruction and collapse of our marriage, everyone, and I mean everyone, had advice. It didn't take her long to find out that other people's advice could potentially cause further damage.

She found that well-meaning family members, who certainly cared for her, our children, and even me, gave her advice, which she followed and which ultimately continued to destroy our marriage. It was when she got fed up with the consequences of following other people's opinions (that they picked up from friends or shows like Oprah Winfrey) that she made up her mind to 1) not talk to others about our situation, and 2) make sure that what she was about to do lined up with God's Word. These are two of the core principles that are the foundation of our ministry.

Yet, even when God called her into ministry, she has told others time and again that she would have to honestly say she made too many mistakes as others came to her for help. It is one thing to seek the Lord for yourself, but an even bigger responsibility to help or guide another. It was early in her ministry when she made a commitment to every woman that she ministered to that she would only tell them what she has done or would do if faced with the same or a similar situation, and only if it lined up with Scripture.

Erin says that she counts it a privilege to have the opportunity in this chapter to share those mistakes with you, along with what the Lord has shown both of us, as we sought the Lord, which has brought much fruit during our ministry to those in marriage crises.

Many men and women who know about our ministry send their family and friends to us, and rightly so, but there are some people that only *you* will have contact with. Just as the pastor of your church is not the only one who is called to share the gospel to the lost, you, too, must be knowledgeable to lead others toward restoration.

We are ambassadors for Christ. Who do we work for when the Lord sends someone to us? We are ambassadors *for* Christ. "Therefore, we are ambassadors **for** Christ, as though God were entreating through us; we beg you on behalf of Christ, be reconciled to God" (2 Cor. 5:20). An ambassador is defined as "a diplomatic official of the highest rank sent as its long-term representative to another." We are to represent Christ in our dealings with this person whom the Lord has sent to us. This position is "long-term," meaning that we are called to see that person through to the victory of their marriage. However, as I have learned, our position cannot stand in the way of their personal relationship with Jesus as their

Savior, nor can we take the place of the Holy Spirit as we play "junior holy spirit," since this will inevitably stand in their way of restoration.

So the good news is that you are not alone in your endeavor, nor will you go unaided. The not-so-good news for some of you is that it will mean relying more on the Holy Spirit for guidance rather than relying on yourself. You will need to know God's principles rather than continuing to speak *your* thoughts and *your* ideas. "For My thoughts are not your thoughts, neither are your ways My ways, declares the Lord. For as the heavens are higher than the earth, so are My ways higher than your ways, and My thoughts than your thoughts" (Isa. 55:8–9).

To be effective in ministry, you will need to renew your mind with God's Word, with His ideas, and with His principles. You will need to refrain from telling others "what your friend did" or "what you heard on a talk show." Even some of the Christian books that you have read on marriage have probably filled your mind with ideas or techniques that will undoubtedly destroy their marriage rather than healing it. "He sent **His Word** and healed them, and delivered them from their destructions" (Ps. 107:20). What the Lord is asking you to do, as His ambassador, is to represent Him, His teachings, and His principles, in the spirit of His love and compassion, using His Word.

Though Erin has been blessed to have "walked the walk," having obtained a restored marriage, and has had over a decade of marriage crisis ministering, Erin says honestly that *she* has no earthly idea what to do when someone asks her for help for their failing or destroyed marriage. She has no idea how many times has she pleaded with the Lord to help her know what to do or not do and say or not say to a hurting and desperate woman.

Therefore, unless you, too, are totally dependent on the Holy Spirit in humility of mind, knowing that you are incapable of helping a person in marital crisis without His working through you, you will inevitably cause the person whom you are trying to help to stumble in the midst of the enemy's attack in their life and marriage. In Luke 17:1–2, Jesus warned, "It is inevitable that stumbling blocks should come, but **woe** to him through whom they come! It would be better for him if a millstone were hung around his neck and he were thrown into the sea." So take heed to the counsel you offer or the sympathy you give when you are not in total and complete servanthood to the Lord.

A stumbling block to Me. Matthew 16:23 says, "But He [Jesus] turned and said to Peter, 'Get behind Me, Satan! You are a stumbling block to Me; for you are not setting your mind on God's interests, but man's.'" One of the greatest ways to destroy your friend or family member is to fail to understand the reason or reasons behind the marital destruction and/or to take sides in the matter. Let's first talk about the reasons behind the destruction of every marriage.

What Caused the Marriage to Be Destroyed?

When you read the book *How God Can and Will Restore Your Marriage* (which, by the way, is required reading for this lesson), you will notice right away that it begins with comfort. That comfort is based on the fact that God has allowed this situation for *their* good, so that He can draw them closer to Him. And as an ambassador, you will need to help them find the way to—or the way back to—Him. It is not your place to take His place, but to point them to Him for comfort. For some this is a very hard thing to do. You may have been given the gift of mercy, but if this gift is not being controlled by the Holy Spirit, it can inadvertently injure those you are trying to help.

We are to comfort, but "with the comfort which we ourselves are comforted by God," not apart from or instead of God. Second Corinthians 1:3–5 says it this way: "Blessed be the God and Father of our Lord Jesus Christ, the Father of mercies and God of all comfort; who comforts us in all our affliction so that we may be able to comfort those who are *in any affliction* with the comfort with which we ourselves are comforted by God. For just as the sufferings of Christ are ours in abundance, so also our comfort is abundant *through* Christ."

So the first, main, and most important reason this trial has occurred is that the Lord wants to use this crisis as a means to draw the person *to* **Him** or *back to* **Him.** This must be in the forefront of your mind and this goal must take precedence in any and all contact with those who are seeking your help. It is not for you to become closer (though often this occurs) and it is not even for them to draw closer to their spouse (though this, too, usually occurs as they are transformed more into the Lord's image), but it is for the sole purpose of gaining a deep and lasting relationship with the Lord *through* this painful, and often long, trial. If you miss this most important reason, you will get in the way of the Lord's working. You may do all you can to try to "fix" the problems and to find solutions for them; however, you must resist this temptation and instead help them to seek the Lord for His solution, His comfort, and His guidance.

Destroyed for lack of knowledge. The second reason this trouble has occurred is found in Hosea 4:6. It says, "My people are destroyed for lack of knowledge." Most of us entered marriage and stumble through marriage without knowing or understanding the principles of marriage. Therefore, we are destroyed for that lack of knowledge. To take this principle further, if we are unaware or lack the knowledge of what to do or what not to do when a crisis hits in marriage, then we will further damage the marriage.

For you to help someone else, you will need to know the principles yourself. Do you? Have you studied to show yourself "approved unto God, a workman that need not be ashamed, rightly dividing the Word of Truth"? (2 Tim. 2:15, KJV). Well then, "Be diligent to present yourself approved to God as a workman who does not need to be ashamed, handling accurately the Word of Truth" (2 Tim. 2:15). This manual, along with the *Restore Your Marriage* book, will help you. However, if you do use any other material, once again, be careful that it is *founded on* and not just *quoting* Scripture.

Many authors love to quote Scripture in order to "prove" their point; however, the principle must be founded on Scripture so that it will remain standing when the trials come against it. "Therefore everyone who hears these words of Mine, and acts upon them, may be compared to a wise man, who built his house upon the rock. And the rain descended, and the floods came, and the winds blew, and burst against that house; and yet it did not fall, for it had been founded upon the rock" (Matt. 7:24–25).

The authors also must prove themselves by fruits. Whether you want to believe it or not, there are many false prophets in the world today. And many have a large following, perhaps including even you. Jesus warned us in Matthew 7:15–20, "Beware of the false prophets, who come to you in sheep's clothing, but inwardly are ravenous wolves. *You will know them by their fruits*. Grapes are not gathered from thorn bushes, nor figs from thistles, are they? Even so, every good tree bears good fruit; but the bad tree bears bad fruit. A good tree cannot produce bad fruit, nor can a bad tree produce good fruit. Every tree that does not bear good fruit is cut down and thrown into the fire. So then, *you will know them by their fruits*."

However, if you don't know the Word yourself, you could easily be deceived. The more I know of the Word, the more I am able to discern error in authors. I have read some authors who have later gotten off track, but if I had not had a firm knowledge of the Word, I would have taken it as Truth. My all-time favorite authors use a lot of Scriptures. Learn to know the Word of God well enough to discern error in what you read and in what you believe. Then use the Word frequently when ministering to others. Why? Because . . .

"The law of the Lord is perfect, restoring the soul;

The testimony of the Lord is sure, making wise the simple.

The precepts of the Lord are right, rejoicing the heart;

The commandment of the Lord is pure, enlightening the eyes.

The fear of the Lord is clean, enduring forever;

The judgments of the Lord are true; they are righteous altogether.

They are more desirable than gold, yes, than much fine gold;

Sweeter also than honey and the drippings of the honeycomb.

Moreover, by them Thy servant is warned;

In keeping them there is great reward.

Who can discern his errors?

Acquit me of hidden faults.

Also keep back Thy servant from presumptuous sins;

[Let this be your prayer]

Let them not rule over me; then I shall be blameless,

And I shall be acquitted of great transgression.

Let the words of my mouth and the meditation of my heart

Be acceptable in Thy sight, O Lord, my Rock and my Redeemer" (Ps. 19:7–14).

Taking Sides

When you listen to something that has occurred between two individuals, it is only natural to take the side of the one from whom you have heard the story. However, Proverbs warns us, "The first to plead his case *seems* just, until another comes and examines him" (Prov. 18:17). Trust me, everything you hear is not all there is to the matter. In all the years of our ministry, we have never seen a one-sided situation even if it "appeared" that way in the beginning. Whether there is infidelity or abuse, alcohol or drugs on the wife's side, we have never seen that the husband is innocent of fault, which ultimately helped to destroy the marriage.

At this point it seems logical to go and listen to the other side of the story. Counselors do this by bringing in both parties to "fight" it out in their presence as they act as referee. This method we do not advise, and, to tell you the truth, we refuse to be a party to it. Erin once was put in this predicament when she was called to meet a woman who was in jail. When she arrived, the woman's husband was there. This woman was in her glory as she erroneously assumed Erin would be there to judge who was right or wrong. Erin simply left. She did this on scriptural grounds. "For God did not send the Son into the world to judge the world, but that the world should be saved through Him" (John 3:17). If God didn't send Jesus to judge the world, we're sure He did not send us (or you) either!

Don't allow yourself to get in the middle of a situation trying to *judge* who has done what. It is not what you or I have been called to do. Rather, we are to minister Truth and comfort as we seek the Lord to lead us. This leads me to one of the many lessons I have learned in the area of ministering.

- **NEVER listen to anger, but comfort and listen to those who are expressing their pain and hurt.**

When someone writes or I am called on to minister in my own church, I refuse to listen to anger or "venting," as it is called today. It is not only futile to try to minister to someone in this state of emotion, but also it is catching! Proverbs 22:24–25 warns, "Do not associate with a man given to anger; or go with a hot-tempered man, lest you learn his ways, and find a snare for yourself."

- **NEVER listen to slander. We refuse to listen to what a spouse has done or is doing.**

In addition to not listening to someone's anger, I also refuse to hear much in the way of *details,* for several reasons: first, to save the person sharing the details from destruction. Psalm 101:5 warns, "Whoever secretly *slanders* his neighbor, **him I will destroy;** no one who has a haughty look and an arrogant heart will I endure." When we allow someone to go on and on sharing slanderous details about their spouse, we are setting them up for destruction. We have laid a net for their feet.

This is probably so hard for you to comprehend since this is the way most counseling sessions are conducted, and besides, we are curious and we love to hear the details. Isn't that why even Christians watch all those terrible shows where each person is slandering his family and friends for the world to witness? It's the stuff we are never to listen to for many reasons. Here are just a couple of them:

We shouldn't listen because it is disgraceful even to speak of the things that are done by them in secret. Ephesians 5:7–13 says, "Therefore do not be partakers with them; for you were formerly darkness, but now you are light in the Lord; walk as children of light (for the fruit of the light consists in all goodness and righteousness and Truth), trying to learn what is pleasing to the Lord. And do not participate in the unfruitful deeds of darkness, but instead even expose them; for it is disgraceful even to speak of the things which are done by them in secret. But all things become visible when they are exposed by the light, for everything that becomes visible is light." Therefore, do not be partakers with them when they attempt to tell you details of what has happened or is happening in their marriage.

We shouldn't listen because it will separate you from the other party in the marriage. "A perverse man spreads strife, and a slanderer **separates intimate friends**" (Prov. 16:28). "He who covers a transgression seeks love, but he who repeats a matter **separates intimate friends**" (Prov. 17:9). I cannot tell you how often Erin or I have heard, before we have had a chance to stop someone in our church, things about someone's spouse who was one of our pastors, an elder, or a close friend of Erin's and mine. Each and every time we both have had a really hard time looking at this friend of ours in the same way. We have trouble not thinking of that person in the negative light that their own spouse shared with us. And it seems that we always feel that our facial expression shows that "we know *all* about you!"

That's why, when we pair men with men or women with women as ePartners in our ministry, we warn them about sharing details, for the very reasons stated above. However, there is an antidote for the feelings that will arise when ministering to a couple. If you are ever caught in this trap of the enemy, first stop the person who is trying to share, and secondly, be faithful to *pray* for their spouse. There is no better way of curing hateful feelings, which is what you get when you hear some of these reports, than to pray for your new enemy. Matthew 5:44–46 tells us, "But I say to you, **love your enemies**, and *pray* for those who persecute you [or someone you love] . . . For if you love those who love you, what reward have you? Do not even the tax-gatherers do the same?"

You will do your friend or family member no good if you take up offenses against their spouse. Don't allow the enemy to pull you in to do his dirty work and help that man tear down his own house! When you listen to details, you can't help becoming bitter against the offender. "See to it that no one comes short of the grace of God; that no root of **bitterness** springing up causes trouble, and by it *many be defiled*" (Heb. 12:15). It was once said in a Bill Gothard seminar that God gives His grace only to the person in the midst of the evil, not the one who witnesses it or the one who later hears about the injustice. We must be very careful not to judge a situation even when we witness it. We are not capable of looking at the heart of either person, or the circumstances leading up to the event.

With all this in mind, then how can we help?

Listen to the **hurts.**

Comfort them in their pain.

Quiet their spirit and tongue.

Pray for and with them.

Encourage them to share *their own* shortcomings.

Point them to **Truth** from the Word, and introduce them to the principles from the *Restore Your Marriage* and *Wise Man* books.

Walk with them, side by side, toward restoration—**first** their restoration *with* **God,** then, as a result, their restoration with their spouse.

Listen to the hurts. "'Comfort, O **comfort** My people,' says your God" (Isa. 40:1). If God has *ever* comforted you in anything, then you are capable of comforting your friend or family member in *anything* that they are going through right now. For it is He "who comforts us in all our affliction so that we may be able to comfort those who are in *any affliction* with the comfort with which we ourselves are comforted by God" (2 Cor. 1:4). That was part of why you went through what you went through, to have the compassion to comfort others who need to find the Lord in the midst of their pain. You don't necessarily need to identify with the cause of their pain, but you can certainly identify with the agony of their pain.

Quiet their spirit and tongue. Once you have allowed them to share their hurt and pain (not their anger through venting), then quiet them with love. Isn't this the way the Lord deals with you? Oh, the love of the Lord—knowing He cares for us! Tell them you love them and remind them (or tell them for the first time) that the Lord loves them. Once they have shared their hurts once, that is when to stop them. Don't allow them to go round and round again stirring up more pain. Often on the second "go-round" it stirs up anger. It's time for you to do the talking. So once you tell them that you love them, and that God loves them, then stop and pray for them (and for wisdom to guide them).

If you are physically with them, and not ministering over the telephone, make sure you hug them and/or put an arm on their shoulder. You know that they are feeling unloved and alone. Touch is a powerful tool for reaching out to the hurting and drawing them to their Savior. Jesus did a lot of touching, especially of those who felt unclean. If you are not a "touchy" person, then ask the Lord to enable you to be His ambassador and bless you with this ability.

When Erin began this ministry back in 1990, she was not a person who enjoyed hugging or touching people outside of her family; it was not the way she was brought up, nor was it her nature. Maybe this is you too. But God has a way of getting around the way we were brought up and giving us *His* nature. Not only has she had the privilege of hugging and holding those who were broken and even dirty or smelly, but also just recently she was given the "mantle" of a sisterly kiss. It happened quite unexpectedly when a very influential and well-known woman in our country hugged her, kissed her cheek, and told her she loved her.

Soon afterward, Erin met a brokenhearted woman at the altar who came down for prayer. She hugged her, kissed her, and told her that she loved her, all before she realized what she was doing! Whatever wall was up inside her—fear, self-consciousness, or lack of compassion—the kiss of this influential woman who was willing to embrace and love her was like Elijah's mantle being thrown upon Elisha's shoulders. We pray that the Lord would grant you, too, a precious mantle that cannot be worked up or made up, but instead is the very arms of the One for whom you and I are ambassadors—the King of kings!

Pray

I have put My words in your mouth. A man who has a call to be a "minister of reconciliation" must be a man of prayer. You must not just pray *for* the men you are ministering to, but also that the Lord will speak *through* you. How dangerous and arrogant to believe for one minute that we have any wisdom in ourselves. Even if we are well versed in our knowledge of the Bible as it relates to a marriage ministry, how do we really know what is going on behind the scenes in a man's life?

Deuteronomy 18:18 says, "I will raise up a prophet from among their countrymen like you, and **I will put My words in his mouth,** and he shall speak to them all that I command him."

"And **I have put My words in your mouth,** and have covered you with the shadow of My hand, to establish the heavens, to found the earth, and to say to Zion, 'You are My people'" (Isa. 51:16).

"Then the Lord stretched out His hand and touched my mouth, and the Lord said to me, 'Behold, **I have put My words in your mouth**'" (Jer. 1:9).

With a total and complete dependence on God for how and what we are to speak to the man in marriage troubles, we can allow God to speak through us; thus we are not on our own, but merely messengers of the One who sent us.

Pray *with* them. It may surprise you, but there are many men, even in the church, who are not comfortable praying out loud. Some don't know how to pray at all. This is part of your ministry to teach others how to pray. However, if you are not a praying person then you will have trouble leading others. Make sure that when you pray with them you are careful not to be too flowery or too spiritual. This will cause them to feel that they will never be able to pray "good enough."

We like to pray a short and simple prayer first, then stop and ask them to pray. If they hesitate, we encourage them by telling them that praying is just talking to God or the Lord; that is, it's just like the way they have been talking to us. Most will hesitate for a time (some for a very long time) but we try to keep silent long enough to let them take that first step. Once they get going their heart opens up and they are on their way to a special and intimate walk with the Lord. Our favorite blessings come when we are able to encourage those who have never prayed before; these new believers will pray the kindest, most child-like prayers that often can bring us to tears.

"Therefore, confess your sins to one another, and pray for one another, so that you may be healed. The **effective prayer of a righteous man can accomplish much**" (James 5:16).

Pray *for* them. So often we neglect to pray. We say we will pray for someone, but too often we completely forget. The best remedy is to right there, right then, pray for your friend, your family member, your coworker, or the man at church. There is nothing that touches another person's heart more than to hear someone calling out to God or touching heaven on their behalf. When Erin is approached in the foyer of our church by someone asking her to pray for them or someone else, she has gotten into the habit of taking their hands and saying, "Let's pray." She doesn't care who is around or what others think! (This is something that I am trying to incorporate too.)

Later, the Lord usually will bring a person to mind that you have said that you would pray for, but just in case, keep a little spiral-bound notebook (or your palm pilot) handy and jot down who you have promised to pray for so that you can add them to your prayer cards later.

We have not ceased to pray for you. Being "led" by the Spirit is wonderful when He faithfully puts a man on your heart to pray for, but we must be diligent and faithful to pray for him every day. Our family has 3x5 cards where we put the people's names to pray for, for at least a month, so that we are faithful in our commitment to pray for others. Some people like to keep a prayer notebook. Whatever the method, make sure that you do not neglect to pray for those whom God sends to you.

"For this reason also, *since the day we heard of it*, we have **not ceased to pray for you** and to ask that you may be filled with the knowledge of His will in all spiritual wisdom and understanding, so that you may walk in a manner worthy of the Lord, to please Him in all respects, bearing fruit in every good work and increasing in the knowledge of God; strengthened with all power, according to His glorious might, for the attaining of all steadfastness and patience; joyously giving thanks to the Father, who has qualified us to share in the inheritance of the saints in light" (Col. 1:9–12).

Walk in a Manner Worthy

The verse you just read in Colossians is a marvelous outline of how you can pray for each man God has sent to you. Let's take a good, close look at this verse to glean some wonderful insights about what God wants to accomplish in his life as you gently guide him along his walk toward restoration.

To ask that you:

May be *filled* with the **knowledge** of ***His will*** in all spiritual **wisdom** and **understanding** . . .

So that you may *walk* in a **manner worthy of the Lord**, to *please **Him*** in all respects, *bearing fruit* in every *good work* and *increasing* in the **knowledge of God** . . .

Strengthened with ***all* power,** according to ***His** glorious might*, for the attaining of all **steadfastness** and **patience** . . .

Joyously **giving thanks to the Father,** who has *qualified us* to share in the inheritance of the saints in light" (Col. 1:9-12).

It's interesting that the first line, "may be *filled* with the **knowledge** of ***His will*** in all spiritual **wisdom** and **understanding**," contains the same components of building a house in Proverbs: "By **wisdom** a house is built, and by **understanding** it is established; and by **knowledge** the rooms are filled with all precious and pleasant riches" (Prov. 24:3–4).

Teaching Sound Doctrine

Clearly you must encourage the man to whom you are ministering to begin to renew his mind in the ways and precepts of God. There would be no better way than to meet with him regularly and go through this series with him once he has gotten through the "crisis." (This is what the *Restore Your Marriage* book is designed to do: get the marriage out of crisis.) If you are careful to make **prayer** and **teaching** your main goals for your meetings, this will eliminate so much slander, self-pity, debating, and/or controversy. Take charge of your get-togethers by initiating prayer and getting down to the ministry of teaching. You will see that there will be little time left for empty chatter, murmuring, complaining, and slandering.

"But as for you, speak the things which are fitting for sound doctrine. Older men are to be temperate, dignified, sensible, sound in faith, in love, in perseverance…urge the young men to be sensible; in all things show yourself to be an example of good deeds, with purity in doctrine, dignified, sound in speech which is beyond reproach, so that the opponent will be put to shame, having nothing bad to say about us" (Titus 2:2, 6–8).

It is a big job to teach or encourage a man in all that we are called to, but now it's as easy as inviting your friend to your house, fixing coffee, and reading the *Wise Man* book. Many men feel inadequate to lead a man to the Lord or to lead him to become a godly man; however, any man is capable of opening up his home and inviting another man to spend a couple of hours with him once a week. (For more knowledge about how to teach, see Lesson 16, "Men, Encourage the Younger Men.")

If you are uncomfortable meeting with him alone (or you know he is uncomfortable meeting alone with you), then pray about getting a few of your friends or his friends together once a week. It can be planned around food, which always brings people out. Just use the book to do the lesson. Many men who lead a group find that it is so refreshing because they are not the "bad guy" or the "spiritual one" speaking the Truth. It's our ministry that they can become angry with. And if they do become angry, remember to agree with them. Try to understand where they are coming from. Get on their side. This is scriptural and may be the only way to keep them coming back.

Matthew 5:25 (KJV) says, **"Agree** with thine adversary quickly, whiles thou art in the way with him; lest at any time the adversary deliver thee to the judge, and the judge deliver thee to the officer, and thou be cast into prison."

Proverbs 18:19 says, "A brother **offended** is *harder to be won* than a strong city, and contentions are like the bars of a castle."

And finally, Proverbs 16:21 tells us, "The **wise in heart** will be called *discerning*, and **sweetness of speech increases persuasiveness."**

If you are "wise in heart," you will be discerning. Usually the men who oppose the Truth are believers living in rebellion or are not true born-again believers at all. It takes the working of the Holy Spirit to help you discern whether to agree and be kind or to boldly state the Truth. Since you are on God's mission, He will be faithful as long as you trust Him to guide you. Just be careful that you "do not lean on your own understanding. In all your ways acknowledge Him, and He will make your paths straight" (Prov. 3:5).

However, we all make mistakes. It is unrealistic to believe that you will not do the wrong thing and rebuke when you should have agreed or vice versa. It's what you do *when* you make a mistake that will reveal whether you have the character of a godly man, or if you are just going through the motions. "For a **righteous** man falls *seven times*, and rises again . . ." (Prov. 24:16). At your earliest opportunity, go to him or call him and humble yourself by admitting your mistake. Don't wait for the enemy to come in and use your arrogance to capture someone who is weak in spirit. Matthew 5:23 tells us how important it is: "If therefore you are presenting your offering at the altar, and there remember that your brother has something against you, leave your offering there before the altar, and go your way; first be reconciled to your brother, and then come and present your offering."

Proverbs 28:13 warns us about the danger of covering up our mistakes and gives a promise to the one who is faithful to confess when he or she has made a mistake. "He who **conceals** his transgressions will not prosper, but he who confesses and forsakes them will find compassion."

After you go to him privately, if there were others who witnessed your mistake, then it is proper to make sure you tell them as well. Since we learned the enormous blessing of "boasting about my weaknesses," we actually *try* to find opportunities to tell others about our mistakes. "But He gives a greater grace. Therefore it says, 'God is opposed to the proud, but gives grace to the humble'" (James 4:6). "And He has said to me, 'My grace is sufficient for you, for **power is perfected** in weakness.' Most gladly, therefore, I will rather *boast about my weaknesses,* that the **power of Christ** *may dwell in me*" (2 Cor. 12:9).

The devil will work through our pride. Instead of encouraging us to share our faults and weaknesses, he will prompt us to share our "victories" with others who in turn will *flatter* us for a job "well done." Proverbs 29:5 warns us, "A man who *flatters* his neighbor is spreading a net for his steps." We all love people to admire us; unfortunately, it is nothing but a trap. Therefore, when you share a victory with anyone, make sure that it is what the Lord has done! If you must boast, boast in Him! Second Corinthians 10:17 tells us, "But he who boasts, let him boast in the Lord." We are merely the vessels that He has chosen. How can *we,* the piano, boast of the music that is being played when it is the Pianist, the Lord, who is the true Musician?

You must be utterly and completely dependent on the Lord for every move you make, for every step you take. As a leader and a teacher, you will be accountable for all those whom the Lord has given you. "Your leaders ... keep watch over your souls, *as those who will give an account*" (Heb. 13:17).

Reconciling the World to Himself

Let's once again read our opening verse, 2 Corinthians 5:18–19: " Now all these things are from God, who reconciled us to Himself through Christ, and gave us the ministry of reconciliation, namely, that God was in Christ **reconciling the world to Himself,** not counting their trespasses against them, and He has committed to us the word of reconciliation."

Your main focus with your "ministry of reconciliation" must be to lead your friend or group of men to reconcile with the Lord. After a decade of ministering in marital crises, there is one thing that we are convinced of and that is that a marital problem is nothing more than a spiritual problem manifesting itself in a marriage. Therefore, our goal, yours and mine, as "ministers of reconciliation," needs to be to get to the root of the problem: to look at the source of their destruction, which is their desperate need for a close and intimate relationship with the Lord. We begin by allowing God to work *through us* as He entreats the broken and desperate man to find Him in a new, deep, and wonderful way. "Therefore, we are ambassadors for Christ, as though *God were **entreating** through us;* we beg you on behalf of Christ, be reconciled to God" (2 Cor. 5:20).

The word *entreat* means to "beg somebody repeatedly." The verse goes on to say it a second time: "We *beg* you on behalf of Christ . . ." Though the man you are ministering to might think that it is his wife who needs to be reconciled to God, the truth is that He first wants **him!**

Brokenness

A man who is in a marital crisis will either be angry or broken. Sometimes you see both of these emotions, which often means that the anger is being broken but is not yet complete. After trying for years to help men and women in both categories, we have concluded that we will **not** minister to a man or woman who has **not** come to the place of brokenness, for three reasons:

There really is no point. No matter what we say, or how we share with them, even sharing our past hurts and becoming transparent about our own sins or shortcomings, they cannot hear us. Our words are not able to penetrate a heart of stone that shows itself through anger. "If anyone has an ear, let him hear" (Rev. 13:9). He simply is not interested in hearing what we are saying.

At this point they are simply attempting to get someone to hear their side and side with them. "For the time will come when they will not endure sound doctrine; but wanting to have their ears tickled, they will accumulate for themselves teachers in accordance to their own desires . . ." (2 Tim. 4:3).

If we take our time and effort to attempt to minister to the hardhearted man or woman who is angry at his or her spouse, angry at God for allowing this to happen, and now angry at us for trying to help in a way that he or she doesn't want to be helped, then we will be worn out and not available to minister to the person who *is* broken and willing to be healed. "Behold, I say to you, lift up your eyes, and look on the fields, that they are *white for harvest*" (John 4:35). There are plenty of hearts that are *white for harvest;* don't make the mistake of trying to reap a soul before it is ripe.

Also, our rebuke or reproof will eventually result in a person becoming even angrier. Proverbs 29:1 warns us, "A man who **hardens** his neck *after much reproof* will suddenly be **broken** beyond remedy." This is the same reason why we tell men not to continue to appeal to their wives— because it will inevitably result in a complete break in their relationship. The same goes for your relationship with your friend, family member, or coworker. God is the only one who can take a heart of stone and turn it to a heart of flesh. "And *I shall* give them one heart, and shall put a new spirit within them. And *I shall* take the *heart of stone* out of their flesh and give them a *heart of flesh* . . ." (Ezek. 11:19).

Schemes of the devil. "Put on the full armor of God, that you may be able to stand firm against the *schemes* of the devil" (Eph. 6:11). A scheme is defined as "a secret and cunning plan, especially one designed to cause damage or harm; a systematic plan of action." It is a scheme of the devil to make you feel you must do more (more talking, more persuading) to turn your friend around. No amount of talking will break him. That is the job for the Lord. He will allow a new turn of events, more of the situation to be revealed, or an even greater crisis in order to bring him to a place where he knows he needs God. Don't get in His way.

More highly of himself. In addition, do not let the devil try to convince you that your call as a minister is more than it is. "For through the grace given to me I say to every man among you not to think *more highly of himself* than he ought to think; but to think so as to have sound judgment, as God has allotted to each a measure of faith" (Rom. 12:3). We are the Lord's ambassadors, nothing more and nothing less. It is ridiculous for a U.S. or other government ambassador to begin to act on his own behalf rather than on the behalf of the president or ruler of the country he represents.

An ambassador is the "go between" who uses his or her skill to reconcile two parties who are "at odds" with one another. "Therefore, *we are ambassadors for Christ,* as though God were *entreating through us;* we beg you on behalf of Christ, be reconciled to God" (2 Cor. 5:20).

Healing

"And they have **healed the brokenness** of My people *superficially,* saying, 'Peace, peace,' but there is no peace" (Jer. 6:14).

Superficial healing. Anytime we try to take the place of the great Physician or administer a healing balm apart from the Word of God, we will heal others superficially. It will "appear" as if they are healed, but deep down the cancer will still be growing. Jeremiah 8:22 asks us, "Is there no balm in Gilead? Is there no physician there? Why then has not the health of the daughter of my people been restored?" There is a healing balm in the Word of God; there is a Physician, so why is the spiritual health of God's people, the Christians, in such a devastating condition? Because we have turned to the philosophies of mankind, turned our focus to the mind of man, the psyche, rather than to his spirit. Though it is true that the psyche is the center of thought and behavior, and maybe even the soul of a man, it is the spirit that will remain. The spirit is the center of our existence and need for God and His Word, which feeds and heals our spirit.

Jesus "answered and said, 'It is written, "man shall not live on bread alone, but on every Word that proceeds out of the mouth of God"'" (Matt. 4:4).

To omit or limit the Word of God from the man who is broken is to starve his soul from the nourishment that he is desperate for. And just like when a person is starving in body, the water or food is given slowly but consistently until they are able to feed themselves. First liquids, then later meat: "Like newborn babes, long for the pure milk of the Word, that by it you may grow in respect to salvation" (1 Pet. 2:2).

His Word healed them. Psalm 107:20 says that "He sent **His Word** and healed them, and delivered them from their destructions." You must use His Word when attempting to heal the hurting and brokenhearted. Nothing short of this will do. Nothing but the pure, unaltered Word of God will do. Don't water it down; it must be given in its full strength to bring about the miraculous cures that only He is able to accomplish. This is why so many men write to us about the incredible transformation our restoration book (or another book of ours) has brought about in their lives. It is because all of our resources are mostly Scripture; it is healing them deep in their spirit, which is what is bringing about their transformation. When coupled with the *By the Word of Their Testimony*, it is a powerful double punch that rids them of the attacks of the evil one as it calms and soothes their souls.

Forsaken

A man forsaken and rejected needs love, understanding, and often our time. However, our goal must be, once again, to introduce or reintroduce him to the One who "will never leave him nor forsake him" (Heb. 13:5). We cannot always be there for him, nor should we try. If we cause him to become dependent on us, rather than on the Lord, we have done more damage than good.

When he truly finds the "lover of his soul," he will need no other—not you and not his wife either, for "my God shall supply all [his] needs according to His riches in glory in Christ Jesus" (Phil. 4:19). When the "neediness" is gone from a man who was once "grieved in spirit," his wife's heart will be turned back to him: "You have removed my acquaintances far from me; You have made me an object of loathing to them" (Ps. 88:8). "The ... heart is like channels of water in the hand of the Lord; **He turns it** wherever *He* wishes" (Prov. 21:1).

Not Counting Their Trespasses Against Them

"For God did not send the Son into the world to **judge** the world, but that the world should be saved through Him" (John 3:17).

"Do not **judge** lest you be judged. For in the way you judge, you will be judged; and by your standard of measure, it will be measured to you" (Matt. 7:1–2).

"And do not **judge** and you will not be judged; and do not condemn, and you will not be condemned; pardon, and you will be pardoned" (Luke 6:37).

With a ministry of reconciliation, you must be rid of all and every kind of judgment. You may have compassion for the man you are ministering to, but if you stop there and judge his wife, you have missed the purpose of your calling. It may be your job to listen to his hurts, but you must not pass judgment on either of them. Believe me, it is almost impossible to do. The only way for you to accomplish this is to have "the mind of Christ," who was "moved with compassion." Jesus saw beyond their sins, their tears, and their afflictions. Only through Him, as His Spirit abides in us, will we find and fulfill the great commission.

It is not our place to determine who is more in the wrong. Instead we are instructed to minister the Word of God in such a way as to lead the man to the One who can heal, transform, and restore him.

And finally, before concluding this chapter, let me share one note of **caution.** Make sure that you minister to men only. The only woman to whom you can safely minister must be blood-related: your daughter, your sister, or your mother. None of these should be "step," either. The devil is very clever. I have seen men caught in adultery and unfaithfulness when they attempted to help a close friend or family member who was not blood-related. And don't pride yourself that it would "never happen."

None of us are above anything. It is only by the grace of God that you (or Erin) have not succumbed to unfaithfulness, since apart from God we can do nothing!

In a situation when a woman approaches you, it is wise to send them to your wife or give them a woman's *Restore Your Marriage* book. If they return to talk about it, then kindly, but firmly, send them to our ministry's fellowship for support and encouragement. Or, if you know about another woman who is in a similar situation, encourage them to meet together as encouragement partners.

In Conclusion

We are ambassadors of Him who sent us. We are the saving link between the man in distress and destruction. We pray "standing in the gap" so that God will find someone there. We are to reach out to them, bringing them to, or back to, their Savior. We are to nurture them in the ways and admonition of the Lord, teaching them what is good and right.

We are not to judge them or their wives. We are not to take the place of the One who sent us. We are not to heal them superficially by giving them philosophies of men or by watering down the Truth and power of His Word. We are not to attempt to minister to the man who is still angry and not broken, but leave room for God to finish the work He started.

It is a high calling to be an ambassador of Christ in the ministry of reconciliation. It is difficult and painful but so very rewarding. When you choose to be sent into the battlefields of marriage destruction, you will put yourself in the place of seeing miracles firsthand. It is a job we highly recommend.

> *"Then I heard the voice of the Lord saying,*
> *'Whom shall I send,*
> *and who will go for Us?'*
> *Then I said,*
> *'Here am I. Send me!'"*
> *—Isaiah 6:8*

13. The Ministry of Reconciliation

Personal commitment: To acknowledge and accept the ministry of reconciliation. "Based on what I have learned from God's Word and from observing the epidemic of separation and divorce occurring in the world today, I commit and surrender my will to the Lord's desire that I should be *His* ambassador. I will be faithful to offer hope through a tract or 'Hope card' and also be willing to invest my time to lead them to the One who can heal and restore."

Date: _____ Signed: _____

Homework

1. Make sure you stay faithful to write down the verses on 3x5 cards from *each* of these lessons. Carry them with you at all times since you never know when you may run into someone in the grocery store who tells you that his wife has just left him.

2. Be prepared by having some "At Last There's Hope" tracts or "Hope Cards" from our ministry. It may be that all the Lord is calling you to do is to make someone aware of our ministry and we will take it from there.

3. Share the Truth from *this* lesson with *one other man* who you know is planning to divorce or separate from his wife.

Write his name on this line. _____ _____

Test Your Wisdom

1. Who has God called for the ministry of reconciliation? "Now all these things are from God, who reconciled us to Himself through Christ, and gave _____ the ministry of reconciliation . . ." (2 Cor. 5:18–19).

2. Who are we ambassadors for? "Therefore, we are ambassadors _____ _____, as though God were entreating through us; we beg you on behalf of Christ, be reconciled to God" (2 Cor. 5:20).

3. Marriages are crumbling because "My people are destroyed for _____ _____ _____" (Hos. 4:6).

4. Why should we never take sides? "The first to plead his case _____ just, until another comes and examines him" (Prov. 18:17).

5. What must we be committed to when ministering to the man who has been rejected in his marriage?
"For this reason also, *since the day we heard of it*, we have not _____ _____ _____ for you" (Col. 1:9–12).

6. When you give any counsel other than the Word of God, what kind of healing will take place? "And they have **healed the brokenness** of My people _____, saying, 'Peace, peace,' but there is no peace" (Jer. 6:14).

7. Why should we refrain from judging the man or his wife? "For God _____ _____ _____ the Son into the world to judge the world, but that the world should be saved through Him" (John 3:17).

The answers to Homework questions are at the end of this workbook.

Chapter 14

Provide for His Own

*But if anyone does not provide for his own,
and especially for those of his household,
he has denied the faith,
and is worse than an unbeliever.*
—*1 Timothy 5:8*

An extremely important role of a husband and father is that of the provider. The "Proverbs 31 Woman" did have "earnings" and her worth was far above jewels. Does that mean that having a *"working wife"* is what God intended? We must be careful in teaching this concept; we must neither add to nor take away from His Word. We must look at all the Scriptures that refer to women, wives, and especially mothers before making a decision to have our wives work outside the home. We must also examine the "fruits" of women who do work. Let's begin searching His Word for the Truth that we can follow and share with others.

Many Christian men use the example of the "Proverbs woman" to justify their wives working outside the home. The key to looking at the "Proverbs woman" is to note that she *bought a field and planted a vineyard*. In today's world we would call that being a farmer. As a farmer, she was not out of the home, away from her children or in the work force as most of the working women are today. She was under the authority of her own husband and therefore under the Lord. Since all travel was very slow, her field was most likely next to, or surely within walking distance from, her home, so she could still oversee the needs of her household.

Wives are to be under their *own* husbands. Your wife is not to be under another man's or woman's authority. "Wives, be subject to *your own* **husbands,** as unto the Lord" (Eph. 5:22). ". . . You wives be submissive to *your own* **husbands** . . ." (1 Pet. 3:1). "Wives, be subject to *your* **husbands,** as is fitting to the Lord" (Col. 3:18). "It is not good for the man to be alone; I will make a **helper** suitable *for him"* (Gen. 2:18). Is your wife a helper for another "him" (or her) at her job?

Wives are to work *at home*. ". . . (Women) be sensible, pure, **workers at home** . . ." (Titus 2:5). The harlot, we are told, "is boisterous and rebellious; her feet *do not* **remain at home**" (Prov. 7:11). Here we are told about just one of the rewards of having your wife remain at home: "And she who **remains at home** will *divide the spoil"* (Ps. 68:12). It is important to be honest here. When your wife works outside the home, she can't help but neglect many of her duties at home. We will get more specific later in this chapter. Many times working women miss out on savings because they cannot shop for "sales" due to the lack of time. Also, those wives who stay at home are able to cook meals from scratch and do away with a lot of the expensive prepared foods.

A working wife cannot give the same time and attention to her children. We know that *no one* can take a mother's place when it comes to love, sacrifice, and patience with her children. *"Quality* time" is a lie and it violates the following Scripture: "And you shall teach them diligently to your children and shall talk of them when you sit in your house, and when you walk by the way, and when you lie down, and when you rise up" (Deut. 6:7). In other words, *all day long*. Unfortunately, we have seen the fruits of the children who have been left on their own or given over to the care of someone else. Despite what others may say, the fact is that only a mother can give children the love and nurturing they so desperately need. That's not to say that we fathers don't have a role to play, but as someone once said, there is nothing like a mother's love.

Your working wife eventually will feel dissatisfied with her life. Special interest groups and the media have encouraged women to **copy men's role** in society. They have tried to "blur" the differences between men and women and make us, especially our wives, unhappy in our "God-given" and specially created roles. God tells us in Genesis that a wife is to be her husband's "helper." The feminists (and some of us) push or encourage our wives to get out and work—leaving behind their children, their homes, and us. And as our roles have become "blurred," it has had a devastating effect on our children, our homes, our families, and our nation. Children look to their peers for guidance and approval. A wife now has her "own life" in her job and with her coworkers. This often causes a division in the husband/wife relationship that far too often results in divorce.

Having a working wife will damage your marriage. When your wife works outside the home, it creates an *independence from you as her husband*. In one issue of *Business Week* magazine, they looked at divorce from a financial standpoint. This study showed that "when a woman can provide for herself, she no longer feels the need to be married." We know that she also begins to believe she doesn't need to submit to her husband concerning what and when to buy, because she has "her own money." "But as the church is subject to Christ, so also the wives ought to be subject to their husbands in everything" (Eph. 5:24). When our wives are bringing in part of the family income, we tend to be careful not to touch the subject of money. This "authoritative equality" weakens the strength and effectiveness of our home and eventually our family's future. Yet, many husbands encourage their wives to help out by going back to work. They never realize the ill effects this decision will have on the entire family. "He that is greedy of gain will trouble his own house" (Prov. 15:27).

Do not weary yourself to gain wealth. Proverbs 23:4 says, **"Do not weary yourself to gain wealth,** cease from your consideration of it. When you set your eyes on it, it is gone. For wealth certainly makes itself wings, like an eagle that flies toward the heavens." The question is, do you believe God's Word? "And *my God* shall supply all your needs, according to His riches in glory by Christ Jesus" (Phil. 4:19). His ways are perfect. Will you trust Him? Or do you think He needs your wife to abandon your home and work to supply all that you need?

A working wife must divide her affections and her priorities. Here's some food for thought. If your wife works outside your home, she will actually display, toward her boss, those attitudes and characteristics of an ideal wife! "But He knew their thoughts, and said to them, 'Any kingdom divided against itself is laid waste; and a house divided against itself falls'" (Luke 11:17). When your wife is employed, she must fulfill and respond to all *her boss's* needs and desires in order to keep her job. She may be asked to give up her time with her family: working late, coming in early, or working weekends. She will show gratitude when her boss compliments her on her appearance or her job performance. He may even take her out to lunch or give her a bonus or a gift.

Your wife will find herself in two competing worlds; each world has a different set of demands and rewards. Scripture tells us that we cannot serve two masters. *"No one* can serve **two masters;** for either he will hate the one and love the other or he will hold to one and despise the other" (Matt. 6:24). Men, wake up! Do you want your wife out there with the wolves? Don't be naive; it's not just men running off with their secretaries or coworkers anymore. There has been an incredible increase in the number of women leaving their husbands for other men they met through their jobs!

A working wife will experience many destructive pressures. Working with others, especially non-Christians, will take its toll. Many feel that they are the "light" in their place of work. Consider Scripture that tells us to "leave the presence of a fool or you will not discern words of knowledge" (Prov. 14:7). "Do not be deceived: Bad company corrupts good morals" (1 Cor. 15:33). Another common pastime of women in the workplace is gossip. Proverbs 20:19 says, "He who goes about as a slanderer reveals secrets, therefore *do not associate with a gossip."* Your wife will listen to other women who are dissatisfied or downright disgusted with their husbands and this will begin to breed the same attitude in your wife toward you.

Having a working wife sets a bad example to others. A working wife usually puts her husband's needs on the back burner. Her husband must fend for himself when it comes to meals or having his clothes cleaned and pressed. Even his wife's listening and sympathetic ear is gone, as she hurries in the evening to get ready for the next workday. Since we men typically don't confide in other men, we may eventually find that "listening and sympathetic ear" in a woman from our workplace. "But each one is tempted when he is carried away and enticed by his own lust. Then when lust has conceived, it gives birth to sin; and when sin is accomplished, it brings forth death" (James 1:14–15). This can result in spiritual death and the death of our marriage.

Also, if your wife is working, she probably won't be home when your children come home from school. Many women think that the "right time" to go to work (or go back to school) is when their children are all in school. This is why we have so many "latchkey kids" spending hours in front of the television watching immoral shows. Men, *do not allow this to happen.* If you do, you will be putting your children in a place of temptation. Consider Luke 17:2: "It would be better for him if a millstone were hung around his neck and he were thrown into the sea, than that *he should cause one of these little ones to stumble.*" Shocking studies have revealed that the parents' own bed is the site of most premarital sex— while the parents are both out working. "Let marriage be held in honor among all, and let the marriage bed be undefiled; for fornicators and adulterers God will judge" (Heb. 13:4).

Also, many of us are expected to be "helpers" to our wives, doing the grocery shopping, picking up the children, etc. We are expected to do "our share" of the household chores, all for the "love of money." Studies have confirmed, however, that we men rarely help out. Instead we allow our wives to exhaust themselves trying to do it all.

God tells us that "having it all" is vanity. "It is vain for you to rise up early, to retire late, to eat the bread of painful labors; for He *gives* to His beloved even in his sleep" (Ps. 127:2). When was the last time your wife was at the door to lovingly greet you when you came home from work? Many men find that being married to a working woman is like living as a bachelor without the benefits of the peace and quiet.

Having a working wife is financially unwise. Many husbands feel that their wives must work outside the home in order to make ends meet. Your combined gross income may be more, but you will also spend a lot more and pay more in income taxes. When both husband and wife are working, most families will acquire or upgrade their second car. They will spend more on clothing, dry cleaning, eating out, and of course childcare.

Your working wife will have no time to be an older Titus woman. "Older women . . . teaching what is good, that they may encourage the young women to *love their husbands,* to love their children, to be sensible, pure, *workers at home,* kind, being subject to their own husbands, that the Word of God may not be dishonored" (Titus 2:3–5). If your wife has stayed at home with your children when they were young, you may think that now is the "ideal time" for her to go back to work or enter the work force. If this were the case then your wife will be joining so many other older women who are now spending time at their jobs. These older women are no longer available to teach the younger women how to be godly wives and how to discipline and train their children properly. These women are totally ineffective in regard to spiritual guidance since they have chosen to surround themselves with the foolish talk and ideas of the world. They have decided to follow the ways of the world rather than God's ways. "Older women . . . teach what is good!" (Titus 2:3). If you allow your wife to follow this path, she will undoubtedly begin to absorb these worldly ways, bring them back to your home, and pass them down to your children and grandchildren.

Stewardship

Debt. *Surely the biggest reason for us wanting our wives to work is that we are in debt.* Rather than waiting for the things that we want, we buy on credit. Instead of living within our means, we live above our means. **"Owe nothing to anyone** except to love one another; for he who loves his neighbor has fulfilled the law" (Rom. 13:8). "The rich ruleth over the poor, and the borrower is servant to the lender" (Prov. 22:7).

Getting out of debt. We must pray and work with God to get out of debt. This must be our heart's (and prayers') desire. You as the leader must set the example by not using your charge card and making sure each purchase is absolutely necessary. Consider fixing the things you feel you must replace. The key is to learn to wait! "The thief comes only to steal, and kill, and destroy; I came that they might have life, and might have it abundantly" (John 10:10). Satan's plan is to steal your children (to daycare), to divide your home (two careers), and to ultimately destroy your family (divorce).

Does your wife overspend? Many men blame their financial troubles on their wives' overspending. And often this may be true. But you as the head of your home must take the authority given to you by God and put a stop to a pattern that could eventually destroy your home. "But I want you to understand that Christ is the head of every man, and the man is the head of a woman, and God is the head of Christ" (1 Cor. 11:3). But, before you point your finger at her, you must make sure that there isn't a log in your eye! Are *you* also overspending?

Stop buying. One way to break the spending mode is to de-junk your house. I recommend you read the book *Clutter's Last Stand* about de-junking your life by Don Aslett. As you begin to perceive many of your possessions as junk, you **stop buying** a lot of unneeded stuff. *It worked for us.*

Contentment. "Not that I speak from want; for I have *learned to be content* in whatever circumstances I am" (Phil. 4:11). "And if we have food and covering, with these we shall *be content*" (1 Tim. 6:8). We husbands must fulfill the following verse: "But if anyone does not provide for his own, and especially for those of his household, he has denied the faith, and is worse than an unbeliever" (1 Tim. 5:8). Discontentment stems from coveting others' possessions. Teach this precept to your family. But again, your example, not merely your words, will have the most influence on your wife and children.

Faith. We men need to have faith that God will provide for our families' needs (and so often our wants, too!) if we just learn to wait! "Wait for the Lord; be strong, and let your heart take courage; yes, wait for the Lord" (Ps. 27:14).

Love of money. It isn't money that is evil, but the "love" of money that destroys us. "For the *love* of **money** is a root of all sorts of evil, and some by longing for it have wandered away from the faith, and pierced themselves with many a pang" (1 Tim. 6:10). "Let your character be free from the *love* of **money,** being content with what you have . . ." (Heb. 13:5).

Getting deeper into debt. Once a man gets a second job or sends his wife out to work, rather than getting out of debt, the couple will likely get into deeper debt. They inevitably will buy more and thus raise their standard of living to a higher level they must work to maintain. "Do not weary yourself to gain wealth, cease from your consideration of it. When you set your eyes on it, it is gone. For wealth certainly makes itself wings, like an eagle that flies toward the heavens" (Prov. 23:4).

Out of order. Pray that you alone will be able and willing to support your family. One of the reasons you may be having a hard time financially supporting your family could be that **your wife handles the finances.** A man is ripped of his manliness when his wife pays the bills. Men, you need to be aware of not only how much money is coming in, but also where it is being spent. Be prepared for opposition, however. Many wives have a hard time giving up the "purse strings." There is too much submission involved for their liking. Most women don't want their husbands to know how much money they spend or where they spend it. They would rather "control" the money.

Men, allowing your wife to control the money is a big mistake. Many will make excuses and say that their wives are better with numbers, have more time, or are more responsible. Your wife needs to be under your authority in *all things*. "But as the church is subject to Christ, so also the wives ought to be to their husbands in *everything*" (Eph. 5:24). More arguments between husbands and wives are over money issues than anything else. Take back your authority in this area; do it today! Your family needs your protection and discernment in this area. If you need help, look around in your church for other men who control the finances in their homes and ask them for advice. Just be sure that their suggestions line up with Scripture before you begin to follow them.

Let us pray Psalm 37:4–9: "Delight yourself in the Lord; and He will give you the desires of your heart. Commit your way to the Lord, trust also in Him, and *He* will do it. And He will bring forth your righteousness as the light. Rest in the Lord and wait patiently for Him; do not fret because of him who prospers in his way. Do not fret, it leads only to evil doing. But those who wait for the Lord, they will inherit the land."

May God Keep the Christian Wife at Home!

Personal commitment: To obey God's command, to provide for my own, and allow my wife to be a worker at home. "Based on what I have learned from God's Word, I commit to praying to be the sole provider for my family. I will commit to keep my wife in our home or require that she return home. I will appreciate the wife, home, and children God has given me. I will share the Truth about working wives with other men and pray that they too will want their wives to return home."

Date: _____ Signed: _____

"Not that I have already obtained it, or have already become perfect, but I press on, in order that I may lay hold of that for which also I was laid hold of by Christ Jesus" (Phil. 3:12).

Practical Application

If your wife is one of the few women who are privileged to be at home:

Encourage her to do all she can to reduce her spending and make sure each purchase is necessary. Encourage her to spend her time wisely, to keep your house in order, to keep up with all her responsibilities. Encourage your wife to learn the tasks that you are now paying for, like cutting your family's hair, sewing and mending rather than throwing out, planting a garden, making crafts for gifts or to decorate your home, baking bread and other things from scratch. Encourage your wife to find an older Titus woman to help her. One way to increase the productivity of your home is to home school your children—pray about it!

Mothers who teach their children rather than sending them to school are mothers who, for the most part, are utilizing their talents and time at home for the good of the family. Encourage her to cut the amount of time she spends talking on the phone. "Let your foot rarely be in your neighbor's house" (Prov. 25:17). Remove the television. "I will set (TV set) no worthless thing before my eyes" (Ps. 101:3). "She does not eat the bread of idleness" (Prov. 13:27). Be sure to encourage and support your wife. You must also use your discernment to see the areas that are wearing out your wife and help her to rid herself of such burdens. This is a very delicate situation and we must be bathed in much prayer before we speak, act, or enforce a decision. Lastly, give your wife a kiss every night when you return home and thank her for caring for you, your children, and your home!

Obey Him

If you say you believe God, ***then obey Him.*** "And why do you call Me, 'Lord, Lord,' and do not do what I say?" (Luke 6:46). If Jesus is your Lord of your life, then why don't you act like it? Provide for your family and encourage your wife to remain at home to care for the family.

We must *not* **debate Scripture** with our pastors or with other men but "be ready to make a defense to *everyone* who asks you to give an account for the hope that is within you, yet with gentleness and reverence" (1 Pet. 3:15). Also remember to "keep a good conscience so that in the thing in which you are slandered, those who revile your good behavior in Christ may be put to shame. For it is better that if God should will it so, that you suffer for doing what is right rather than for doing what is wrong" (1 Pet. 3:16–17).

If others teach or tell you something **contrary to Scripture,** remember, "If anyone advocates a different doctrine, and does not agree with sound words, those of our Lord Jesus Christ, and with the doctrine conforming to godliness, he is conceited and understands nothing; but he has a morbid interest in controversial questions and disputes about words" (1 Tim. 6:3–6).

All of us must be careful to **obey God's Word,** and by our example, teach others what He commands. "Whoever then annuls one of the least of these commandments, and so teaches others, shall be called **least** in the kingdom of heaven; but whoever keeps and teaches them, he shall be called **great** in the kingdom of heaven. For I say to you, that unless your righteousness surpasses that of the scribes and Pharisees, you shall not enter the kingdom of heaven" (Matt. 5:19–20). This includes teaching not only your sons and daughters, but also your sons-in-law, daughters-in-law, brothers, sisters, and friends.

Remember, you can easily find someone who will tell you **what you want to hear,** "For the time will come when they will not endure sound doctrine; but wanting to have their ears tickled, they will accumulate for themselves teachers in accordance to their own desires; and will turn away their ears from the Truth, and will turn aside to myths" (2 Tim. 4:2–3). You must commit to following God's ways!

Homework

1. Please, write down the verses from *this* chapter on your 3x5 cards.

2. Men, turn your wife's heart towards your home! "For where your treasure is, there will your heart be also" (Luke 12:34). Erin's and my heart's desire is to see Christian women free from needing to make money so they will be available to minister to their husbands, children, other (younger) women, the poor, and the widows. (See Proverbs 31 and Titus 2.)

3. Share this information with *one other man* whose wife is currently working outside the home.

Test Your Wisdom

1. Your wife should not be under another man's or woman's authority. "Wives, be subject to _____ _____ **husband,** as unto the Lord" (Eph. 5:22). ". . . You wives be submissive to _____ _____ **husbands** . . ." (1 Pet. 3:1). "Wives, be subject to _____ **husbands,** as is fitting to the Lord" (Col. 3:18).

2. God's Word tells us where our wives are to be: ". . . Be sensible, pure, **workers at** _____ . . ." (Titus 2:5). The harlot, we are told, ". . . is boisterous and rebellious; her feet *do not* **remain** _____ _____" (Prov. 7:1).

3. We must have our hearts steadfast on being the sole providers for our families. "For the eyes of the Lord move to and fro throughout the whole earth that He may _____ _____ those whose _____ is completely His . . ." (2 Chron. 16:9).

4. We need to live within the means that we provide for our families. "Not that I speak from want; for I have _____ _____ _____ _____ in whatever circumstances I am" (Phil. 4:11). "And if we have food and covering, with these we shall _____ _____" (1 Tim. 6:8).

5. Once men send (or allow) their wives to enter the work force, most will get into deeper debt. "Do not _____ yourself to gain wealth; cease from your _____ of it. When you set your eyes on it, it is gone. For wealth certainly makes itself _____, like an eagle that flies toward the heavens" (Prov. 23:4).

6. We, as the heads of our homes, must control the finances and checkbook, since God's Word says, "But as the church is subject to Christ, so also the _____ ought to be to their husbands in _____" (Eph. 5:24).

7. One of the biggest pitfalls is the "_____ ___ _____." "For the _____ ___ _____ is a root of all sorts of evil, and some by longing for it have wandered away from the faith, and pierced themselves with many a pang" (1 Tim. 6:10). "Let your character be free from the _____ ___ _____, being content with what you have . . ." (Heb. 13:5).

The answers to Homework questions are at the end of this workbook.

Chapter 15

Father's Instructions

*Hear, my son, your father's instruction . . .
Indeed, they are a graceful wreath to your head,
And ornaments about your neck.
—Proverbs 1:8*

Today there is *a lot* of talk about discipline and very little about training or love. What method should I use? Certainly, one that works—one that brings about bountiful fruits! God said that anything that is not founded on *His Word* is on sinking sand. How can we discern whether the method we follow is based on Scripture? We must know what God's Word says concerning love, discipline, and child training. Let's search the Scriptures and seek the Truth.

Part 1
We Must Love Our Children

We love, because He first loved us. The foundation of love is found in 1 John 4:19: "We love, because He first loved us." His example toward us is what we should follow. "For you have been called for this purpose . . . leaving you an example for you to follow in His steps" (1 Pet. 2:21). A child cannot give love without being loved first. When I give my love first, only then will my child learn to love. Love motivates obedience. As we grow more in love with our Lord, we are motivated to righteous living.

Have you ever wondered why children of godly parents, ones that without a doubt followed God's Word on discipline, still went astray? Could it have to do with an inadequate expression of love? Of course, most parents love their children, but does it show up in the way they look at their children, their loving words, their loving touch, the happy times they spend with their children? How much time do you spend with your child?

Do you express loving words? The bottom line is: does your child *feel* he or she is loved?

Blessing or curse? In Chapter 12, "Fruit of the Womb," we learned from God's Word that children are a blessing, even though our society tells us differently. But what do *you* believe in your heart? You cannot give the deepest heartfelt love to your children if you think of children as a curse.

What do you say in front of them? What do you say behind their backs? What does your attitude toward your children convey to them? Do you say one thing to your children, say something else to others, and, at the same time, dread the thought of any more children? "For let not that man expect that he will receive anything from the Lord, being a *double-minded* man, unstable in all his ways" (James 1:7–8).

What then is *love*? We are told about love in our books, our movies, and our media. Everyone tells us what *they* think love is. But shouldn't we go to the Author of love for the true description? "And if I have the gift of prophecy, and know all mysteries and all knowledge; and if I have all faith, so as to remove mountains, but do not have **love,** *I am nothing*. And if I give all my possessions to feed the poor, and if I deliver my body to be burned, but do not have **love,** *it profits me nothing*. Love is **patient,** love is **kind,** and is **not jealous;** love does not brag and is not arrogant, does **not act unbecomingly;** it does not **seek its own,** is **not provoked,** does not take into account a wrong suffered, does not rejoice in unrighteousness, but rejoices with the Truth; **bears all things, believes all things, hopes all things, endures all things. Love never fails"** (1 Cor. 13:2–8). It is quite clear that love is more than just a feeling, as we have been told. Love is an action or reaction we make toward others. Let's look deeper into the words that are in bold in the preceding Scripture.

Patient. Patience is a reaction. Patience is definitely more than a necessity when dealing with children. We only need to look at the parents we see in public with their children to see that patience is in very low supply today. If these parents are this fed up with their children in public, how do they act in private? The following verse is a perfect prescription for a father to use with his children: "And we urge you, brethren, *admonish the unruly, encourage the fainthearted, help the weak,* be *patient with all* men" (1 Thess. 5:14). "And the Lord's bond-servant must not be quarrelsome, but be *kind to all, able to teach, **patient** when wronged . . ."* (2 Tim. 2:24).

Kind. Kindness goes a long way when dealing with children. Sometimes, however, we seem to forget. "And the Lord's bondservant must not be quarrelsome, but be **kind** to all, able to teach, patient when wronged . . ." (2 Tim. 2:24). We must speak kindly and gently with our children. When training your children, it is important to get their attention first by calling their name. Then take the time to look at them in the eyes and speak kindly to them. This does not mean that we are trying to plead or beg for their obedience; it is merely the difference between speaking gentle words and barking out commands.

Not jealous. We should be keenly aware that favoritism will cause jealousy between siblings. If one child exhibits unfavorable habits, mannerisms, or the like, it may cause you to favor his sibling(s). Instead, love your troubled child enough to work with them on their weaknesses. Or have you forgotten the discord in Joseph's family caused by favoritism? It resulted in a notorious jealousy! "And his brothers were **jealous** of him, but his father . . ." (Gen. 37:11).

Not act unbecomingly. Acting unbecomingly has become commonplace in too many of our homes, as well as in public. Major "scenes" or "ranting and ravings" go on all too often. Love your children enough to control *your* spirit. Then *control theirs* until you can teach them to control their own. "Like a city that is broken into and without walls is a man who has **no control over his spirit**" (Prov. 25:28).

Seek its own. We men are bombarded every day with encouragement to "just do it" and to have "our own life." Only a few years ago we would have called that attitude "selfish and self-centered." Regardless of the popularity of this new concept, selfishness will reap only sorrow and regrets. God's Word says, "Do nothing from selfishness or empty conceit, but with humility of mind let each of you regard one another as **more important than himself** . . ." (Phil. 2:3).

Not provoked. How short is your fuse? Are you quick to fly off the handle? Is most of what you say in a raised voice? "A hot-tempered man stirs up strife, but the **slow to anger** pacifies contention" (Prov. 15:18). "He who is **slow to anger** is better than the mighty, and he who rules his spirit, than he who captures a city" (Prov. 16:32). "A man's *discretion* makes him **slow to anger,** and it is his glory to overlook a transgression" (Prov. 19:11).

We must learn to be discreet when we are offended or disappointed. Royalty is taught to control their feelings in public. Men, we are children of Christ the King; we should therefore act accordingly in the presence of all others and teach our children to do the same.

Bears all things. God expects us to bear burdens with His help. The burdens of a father can sometimes seem unbearable; don't be too proud to run to Him. "Blessed be the Lord, who daily **bears our burden,** the God who is our salvation. Selah" (Ps. 68:19). "For this finds favor, if for the sake of conscience toward God a *man* **bears up under sorrows** when *suffering unjustly"* (1 Pet. 2:19).

Believes all things. To follow Scripture when training and disciplining our children will take faith. But, praise God! We have His promise that we will not be disappointed! ". . . for *with the heart* man **believes**, resulting in righteousness, and with the mouth he confesses, resulting in salvation" (Rom. 10:10). For the Scripture says, "Whoever believes in *Him* will not be *disappointed"* (Rom. 10:11). Authors and manufacturers tell us that following their directions or buying their products will change our life. Trust our Creator and the Author of life to receive *His* promises!

Hopes all things. Our hope for our children needs to be in Him. As you follow Him in obedience to His Word and have faith that He will complete what He began in you, your wife, and your children—*know* that He will complete it. This is our hope! "The **hope** of the righteous is gladness, but the expectation of the wicked perishes" (Prov. 10:28). "Know that wisdom is thus for your soul; if you find it, then there will be a future, and your **hope** will not be cut off" (Prov. 24:14).

Endures all things. When we feel we are at the end of our rope, God encourages us to hang on to Him. "But the one who **endures to the end,** he shall be saved" (Matt. 24:13). "And you will be hated by all on account of My name, but the one who **endures to the end,** he shall be saved" (Mark 13:13).

Love never fails. This is our greatest promise: His love for us and our love for one another, especially our children, will never fail! "Hatred stirs up strife, but **love** covers all transgressions" (Prov. 10:12).

Show your children that you love them. "Better is *open rebuke* than love that is concealed" (Prov. 27:5).

Unchanging love. "Who is a God like Thee . . . He (God) *delights* in **unchanging love**" (Mic. 7:18). Be sure your children know that you will always love them.

How then can I convey love to my children?

Many fathers give their children material possessions. Children need something else. They need you!

Your time. The most important thing you can give to your child is your time. When we like someone, or love someone, we want to spend our time with that person. Where is your time being spent most? Where does your child fall in the level of importance to you? If you wait for there to be time for your children, they may not be children anymore! Then they will show their gratitude to you by having little or no time to spend with *you*. What could possibly be more important than that little boy or girl? We know we waste so much precious time on things that will mean absolutely nothing years from now. There is such a great reward in spending our time with our children. It is the greatest investment you could ever make. You will be investing in their future and your future too.

Make eye contact. "I will instruct you and teach you in the way which you should go; I will counsel you with My **eye** upon you" (Ps. 32:8). We need to teach and instruct our children with our eyes. But how can we do that when we are continually dropping our children off at a multitude of activities? Even if we do stay to watch, many times we become involved in a conversation with another father instead of paying attention to our children.

If our children are never around because of school, sports, music lessons, and other activities, how can we possibly instruct or guide them? We must make the time to look into their eyes, to show our love for them, and to instruct them. They must know that they are the apple of our eyes! "Keep me as the apple of the eye . . ." (Ps. 17:8). All the activities that seem to keep us so busy are usually temporary; therefore, they have only temporal value. ". . . while we look not at the things which are seen, but at the things which are not seen; for the things which are seen are temporal, but the things which are not seen are eternal" (2 Cor. 4:18).

Your touch. Touch is very important. It has healing and comforting powers. Consider these verses:

"And they were bringing even their *babies to Him* so that He might **touch** them . . ." (Luke 18:15).

"And they were bringing *children to Him* so that He might **touch** them . . ." (Mark 10:13).

" And they brought a blind man to Him, and entreated Him to **touch** him" (Mark 8:22).

"And all the multitude were trying to **touch** Him, for *power was coming from Him and healing them all*" (Luke 6:19).

"But Jesus said, 'Someone did **touch** Me, for I was aware that *power had gone out of Me'*" (Luke 8:46).

Your child's first touch. The decision to breast-feed is an important decision. It is important that you as the husband and father understand that it is not only for food but also for your baby's first touch. The formula companies are now required by law to tell the truth in their ads that breast milk is best for the baby. As fathers, we should want the best for our children and thus encourage, not discourage, our wives to breast-feed. Pray that an older woman will encourage your wife "to love her children" (Titus 2:4). "Older women . . . that they may **encourage** the young women to love their husbands, to love their children . . ." (Titus 2:3–4). Let's look a bit further into this issue.

God made the perfect food. Babies long to be close to their mother— for her milk. They are born with this strong desire. Doctors tell us it is a reflex and a basic need for survival. Scripture says, ". . . like newborn babes, *long* **for the pure milk** of the Word, that by it you may grow in respect to salvation . . ." (1 Pet. 2:2).

Are we to comfort or not? "Blessed be the God and Father of our Lord Jesus Christ, the Father of mercies, and **God of all comfort** *who comforts us in all our affliction* so that we may be able to **comfort** those who are in any affliction with the **comfort** with which we ourselves are **comforted** by God" (2 Cor. 1:3). The natural response of a mother whose baby or child is crying is to comfort. Experts come and go, along with their recommendations on whether to respond to a crying child. We are presently being told to teach our children to comfort themselves, to help them to become independent.

Children comfort themselves by hugging a stuffed animal, rocking themselves, sucking their thumbs or their fingers, or taking a pacifier. Children whose needs have been thwarted seem never to "wean" completely or at the proper time. This causes those who have been given a "substitute" for God's provision to become insecure. These children are sucking longer and longer. If you take the time to look around, you will notice that it is not just babies sucking their thumbs, but children of elementary school age and older! This is now commonplace and accepted in today's schools! This should be a warning to us that something has deviated from God's perfect plan and design. God's ways are always perfect.

Are we to hear and respond to their cries or not? Do *we* plead with God, asking Him to hear us, comfort us, and help us? Then let us not ignore our children's cries for us. Even if nothing works when you try to comfort your child, your child can still *feel* your love. *We* want understanding and comfort. "Hear, O Lord, when I **cry** with my voice, and be gracious to me and answer me" (Ps. 27:7). "Hear... when I cry to Thee for help . . ." (Ps. 28:2). ". . . Give ear to my cry; do not be silent at my tears . . ." (Ps. 39:12).

Parenting techniques come and go. Throughout your lifetime different psychologists and child "experts" will tell you different things in regard to raising children. Let's hold all things up to the "light" of Scripture to clearly see the Truth. Then we will be founded on the Rock.

Loving discipline. We must also express our love for our children with loving discipline. "Those whom I love, I reprove and discipline; be zealous therefore, and repent" (Rev. 3:19). Our children need our discipline so that others can love them as well. We have heard the saying

He is a son only a mother could love. A child who is undisciplined, unruly, and lacking in self, or parental, control has been done a great disservice by his parents. It is especially shameful to the mother. "The rod and reproof give wisdom, but a child who gets his own way brings **shame to his mother**" (Prov. 29:15). Our children need us to train them so they can become responsible adults. This all takes time, patience, and kindness. You will need to bear many things, believe many things, hope many things, and endure many things, but that kind of **love** will never fail! Men, do not expect your wife to do all of the disciplining or training of the children when you are at home—you take the lead.

They are too big. No one is too big to need affection and a gentle touch. If they are in their teen years, begin with a pat on the back, a loving squeeze on their arm, or a quick hug. Give them a smile with your eyes and praise them for something. Ask God to set up the perfect opportunity for you to say something kind, loving, and sincere.

They are grown. You may be reading this and thinking that it's too late because your children are grown. No, it is never too late to show love. Begin now to love your grown children. Begin with your words. Are they loving, accepting, and caring? Lay the groundwork with a loving hug and an "I love you," no matter what their age.

Regrets. Have you made mistakes, or do you have regrets about your parenting? Have you shared these regrets with your grown child? It's humbling, but rewarding. "A man's pride will bring him low, but a humble spirit will obtain honor" (Prov. 29:23). If your family needs healing, there is a Scriptural recipe. "Therefore, confess your sins to one another, and pray for one another, so that you may be healed. The effective prayer of a righteous man can accomplish much" (James 5:16).

Pray for an opportunity, for the right words to say and for the heart of your grown child to be receptive to hear. Be prepared to hear their hurts. God tells us, "A brother offended is harder to be won than a strong city, and contentions are like the bars of a castle" (Prov. 18:19). But do not lose heart. Proverbs 10:12 says, "Hatred stirs up strife, but love covers all transgressions." And 1 Peter 4:8 says, "Above all, keep fervent in your love for one another, because love covers a multitude of sins." Make sure that you accept all responsibility.

Part 2: Discipline
Our Foundation Must Be His Word

For teaching, for reproof, for correction, for training. Discipline is referred to 90 times in the Old Testament when God disciplines His children and when God's children discipline their own children. Discipline is found 36 times in Proverbs, almost always referring to the parent-child relationship. If we want to be well versed in child training, we should read and mark these verses in Proverbs as our foundation for training our children. "All Scripture is inspired by God and *profitable* **for teaching, for reproof, for correction, for training** in righteousness; that the man of God may be adequate, equipped for every good work" (2 Tim. 3:16–17). As we will see in the following verses, discipline is a tool for *restoration* rather than condemnation, to bring a person back to his rightful place *spiritually*.

To know what was in his heart. Discipline does not always denote the infliction of pain or disappointment. As fathers, *we* must live disciplined lives in order to properly discipline our children. We must be determined to win every conflict with *our* self-control and not "give-in" or overlook the behavior or attitude. ". . . The fruit of the Spirit is love, joy, peace, patience, kindness, goodness, faithfulness, gentleness, **self-control;** against such things there is no law" (Gal. 5:22). Have you been negligent in your disciplining because you really don't want to be bothered? "God left him to test him, that He might **know all that was in his heart**" (2 Chron. 32:31).

What has kept us from following God's Word?

Not knowing the Scriptures. It is our responsibility to know Scripture well enough to not be deceived. "Be diligent to present yourself approved to God as a workman who does not need to be ashamed, **handling accurately the Word of Truth**" (2 Tim. 2:15).

He will go astray. The lack of proper instruction from God's Word in our Sunday school classes or from the pulpit has resulted in the repercussion of masses of rebellious children. "He will die for lack of instruction, and in the greatness of his folly **he will go astray**" (Prov. 5:23).

Lack of knowledge. We lack the biblical knowledge to correctly train and discipline our children. Therefore, "My people are destroyed for **lack of knowledge**" (Hos. 4:6).

Turned aside to fruitless discussion. Many Christians follow the most popular "experts" of their day. However, we are told in Scripture that we are not to pay any attention to them. ". . . Instruct certain men not to teach strange doctrines, nor to pay attention to myths and endless genealogies, which give rise to mere speculation . . . For some men, straying from these things, have **turned aside to fruitless discussion** . . ." (1 Tim. 1:3).

Myths. We are told that we will look for what we "want" to hear. "For the time will come when they will not endure sound doctrine; but wanting to have their ears tickled, they will accumulate for themselves teachers in accordance to their own desires; and will turn away their ears from the Truth, and will turn aside to **myths**" (2 Tim. 4:3–4). What are some of the more popular myths that are prevalent in some Christian books and are accepted *theories* among Christians on discipline?

The "strong-willed" child. When searching Scripture, you will find that God makes *no distinction* between personality types such as strong-willed, melancholy, lion, etc. when disciplining, training, or teaching children. Certainly, a child who does not bend when switched should be dealt with carefully lest we neglect the Word of God. We must be very careful to resist adding to God's Word. "You shall not add to the Word which I am commanding you, nor take away from it, that you may keep the commandments of the Lord your God which I command you" (Deut. 4:2).

Another thing we are erroneously told is not to break the "spirit" of the child. But, the purpose of punishment is to *destroy* the "spirit" of rebellion. If you tell the child not to do something and they do it, you must punish the *rebellion*. Threatening will not destroy a "spirit" of rebellion. As a matter of fact, constant threatening will only intensify the spirit of rebellion. You must punish with the rod. Never "threaten." You must always mean what you say and carry out the punishment after you have warned. If you don't, you are lying to your child! "A youngster's heart is filled with **rebellion,** but punishment will **drive it out of him**" (Prov. 22:15, KJV).

Deliberate defiance. Another misconception found in popular books on discipline is that we must only discipline for "deliberate defiance." Yet, we clearly find in Scripture that this is not the Truth. "Foolishness" is also a call for punishment—for example, when a child forgets to do things that he is told to do. **"Foolishness is bound up in the heart of a child; the rod of discipline** will remove it far from him" (Prov. 22:15). But why would we embrace something that is false and not found in Scripture? Could it be that we *want* to hear something untrue about child discipline? Could it be our fear?

Fear of man brings a snare. But if we do discipline the way Scripture tells us to, well, what about the HRS and child abuse? Again, let's look at Scripture for the Truth. "The **fear of man brings a snare,** but he who trusts in the Lord will be exalted" (Prov. 29:25).

Do not fear the reproach of man. What might other people (family or friends) say? "Listen to Me, you who know righteousness, a people in whose heart is My law; **do not fear the reproach of man,** neither be dismayed at their **reviling"** (Isa. 51:7). (Reviling is defined as verbal attacks. Reproach is defined as blame, disgrace, or discredit.) We are then not to be worried about verbal attacks or people trying to disgrace or discredit us. "And you, son of man, neither fear them nor fear their words, though thistles and thorns are with you and you sit on scorpions; neither fear their words nor be dismayed at their presence, for they are a rebellious house" (Ezek. 2:6).

Do not add to His Words. Shun the "theories" and correction "techniques" of today's world—i.e., "time out," "grounding," or removing privileges, etc.—in lieu of using the rod. **"Do not add to His Words** lest He reprove you, and you be *proved* a liar" (Prov. 30:6).

His way. Make a covenant with God that you will follow **His way** regardless of what the world says.

The Truth on Discipline

Let's look at specific references in Scripture for wisdom:

When you punish a child it proves to him that you love him. "He who spares his rod *hates* his son, but he who **loves** him takes care to chastise him" (Prov. 13:24). I have explained to my children that I don't discipline other children, only my own. This is because I love them in the same way as our heavenly Father loves us and He only disciplines those who are His. "For those whom the Lord loves He disciplines, and he scourges every son whom He receives" (Heb. 12:6).

The time to punish is from the beginning. Don't wait to turn your child from his wrong ways. "Discipline your child **early** while there is still hope" (Prov. 19:18). The Living Bible adds, "If you don't you will ruin his life." This means both early in age and early in their disobedience. So many think that you can't or shouldn't train a baby to do the right thing. However, you'd be amazed what a very young child is able to understand. The hardest thing to *break* is a toddler's or older child's behavior (or attitude) that they have been allowed to enjoy. Stop and punish the bad behavior the first time they do it.

Fools despise wisdom and instruction. We can see that we must not just break the "will" of the child, but we must break the "spirit" of rebellion. But how can we tell if it's the will or the spirit that has yielded? If the child exhibits any type of anger, resentment, or sarcasm after the punishment, it means the spirit of rebellion is still there! "The fear of the Lord is the beginning of knowledge; **fools despise wisdom and instruction**" (Prov. 1:7). Rebellion opposes authority and thus opposes God.

He will not die. *Temporary pain* is profitable for *permanent character change*. Who is stronger and more determined, you or your child? "Do not withhold discipline from a child. If you punish him with a rod, **he will not die**" (Prov. 23:13). In life we must face pain "for a season" to enjoy what God wants to give us for a lifetime.

What are the benefits of properly disciplining our children? The real benefits of punishment are spiritual. "Punish him with a rod and you'll save his **soul from Sheol**." The Living Bible says, "They won't die if you use a stick on them; punishment will keep them **out of hell**" (Prov. 23:14).

Again, when you punish a child, it proves to him that you love him. "He who spares his rod *hates* his son, but he who **loves** him takes care to chastise him" (Prov. 13:24).

The purpose of punishment is to redirect the life. "Guide a horse with a whip, a donkey with a bridle, and a rebel with a rod to his back" (Prov. 26:3). Don't use a whip since your child is not a horse, nor a belt since your child is not a donkey. To follow Scripture we must use a rod that is "wooden" on the backside. We have used a switch that has brought about true repentance. "The rod and reproof give wisdom, but a child who gets his own way brings shame to his mother" (Prov. 29:15). Avoiding punishment will eventually bring shame to the mother. All the Scriptures are clear about punishment: the rod is the only "cure" for rebellion. Other "techniques" can be used after the rod, but they are rarely needed and should be used sparingly and cautiously.

The ministry of reconciliation. "You're grounded!" Many parents believe in and practice the method of grounding. During a designated period of time the child is to be "in the dog house," so to speak. But this is not Scriptural. We must apply physical punishment (the rod) and then train our children to ask for forgiveness. Then we should forgive! "Now all these things are from God, who reconciled us to Himself through Christ, and gave us the ministry of reconciliation, namely, that God was in Christ reconciling the world to Himself, not counting their trespasses against them, and He has committed to us the Word of reconciliation" (2 Cor. 5:18–19).

Forgive and comfort him. Show your love for them afterwards: ". . . forgive and comfort him, lest somehow such a one be overwhelmed by *excessive sorrow*. Wherefore I urge you to reaffirm your love for him" (2 Cor. 2:6).

Applying the Rod

He who loves him disciplines him. Do you love your child enough to apply the rod? "Discipline your son while there is hope, and do not desire his death" (Prov. 19:18). "He who spares his rod hates his son, but **he who loves him disciplines him** diligently" (Prov. 13:24). And, "Those whom I love, I reprove and discipline; be zealous therefore, and repent" (Rev. 3:19).

Many parents let their children get away with disobedience because they fail to tell them what is expected of them and don't believe it's "fair" to apply the rod. Instead they warn, warn, and warn. When you tell your children they are to do or not to do something, see if there is a reference for your teaching in the Bible. If there is a specific Scripture that applies, then open up the Bible and have them (or you) read it out loud. Fathers, this is a good reason to know the Word!

Your goal in using a rod (a switch) is for the child to associate sin with pain. What is most important is that the child knows, through your actions, that you are not angry with him, but rather you hate the sin. Isn't this following the same pattern our heavenly Father uses with us? God will discipline us but He never stops loving us.

When you call a child to come, and he chooses not to comply, simply walking over and switching the back of his little leg will encourage him to move. When a child is told not to call out for a drink or anything else after she has been put to bed, it is as simple as walking in, pulling back the covers and applying a little switch. Then bend down, kiss her again and tell her *kindly* and *lovingly* not to call again. When two children have been told not to fight, it is as simple as walking over to them and giving each a quick switch. There is no need to yell, be angry or *explain!*

If they seem shocked, you may explain *after you have already applied the rod*. There are too many parents who spend time debating with their children. Fathers, your family is not a democracy. God in His infinite wisdom created a line of authority for a purpose. Don't undermine your authority with verbal debates with your children. **And don't wait until you are angry.** "A joyful heart is good medicine, but a broken spirit dries up the bones" (Prov. 17:22). If you wait, hoping they will come, obey, or stop what they are doing, then there is a good chance that you will become angry. If, instead, you apply the rod (a switch) that brings about a sting without delay, you can keep your countenance joyful.

You were made sorrowful to the point of repentance. The use of the rod is to bring about compliance and repentance. "I now rejoice, not that you were made sorrowful, but that **you were made sorrowful to the point of repentance;** for you were made sorrowful according to the will of God, in order that you might not suffer loss in anything through us" (2 Cor. 7:9). "You shall beat him with the rod, and deliver his soul from Sheol" (Prov. 23:14). If at this point you want to tell me that your children won't respond to a switch or any other physical correction—hen you are not applying enough of them or they are not hard enough! You simply must make sure it hurts.

Many parents are afraid of permanent damage, or they are afraid that they may become abusive. All a child ever needs is to feel the "full effects" of a rod *one time* for them to always respect the switch and their parents. Abuse stems from anger. If you "nip it in the bud" each and every time, instead of ignoring improper behavior, then you will never reach the point of abuse. Abuse is on the increase because parents have stopped using corporal punishment with their children. By the time the child has totally exhausted the parent's patience (because all the other methods simply don't work), then the frazzled parent responds by losing control.

Speaks from that which fills his heart. It is sometimes important to ask for an "I'm sorry, please forgive me for . . ." since "the heart of the wise teaches his mouth, and adds persuasiveness to his lips" (Prov. 16:23). "The good man out of the good treasure of his heart brings forth what is good; and the evil man out of the evil treasure brings forth what is evil; for his mouth **speaks from that which fills his heart"** (Luke 6:45). This should be sincere without any resentment, anger, or coaxing. If the child again rebels against your authority by refusing to comply to your request with the right heart, then repeat the switches until they feel the "full effects."

A countenance that is lifted up. You must *see* true repentance. ". . . So Cain became very angry and his countenance fell. Then the Lord said to Cain, 'Why are you angry? And why has your countenance fallen? If you do well, will not **your countenance be lifted up?** And if you do not do well, **sin is crouching at the door;** and its desire is for you, but you must master it'" (Gen. 4:5–7). If you are too frightened to follow through, and you allow their covert anger towards you as the authority, you will someday find that their bitterness towards you will destroy your relationship.

Forgive and comfort him. Once you have a child whose rebellious spirit is broken, then reaffirm your love for him, verbally and physically. Hug him or hold him in your lap, if he is not too old or too heavy. "Wherefore I urge you to reaffirm your love for him" (2 Cor. 2:8). "Sufficient for such a one is this punishment which was inflicted by the majority, so that on the contrary you should rather **forgive and comfort him,** lest somehow such a one be overwhelmed by excessive sorrow" (2 Cor. 2:6–7). At this point, there should be no need for you to "ground them," "send them to their room," "take away their privileges," or use any other means of punishment.

Reaffirm your love for him. After using the rod on your child, make sure that you show your love for him. "Wherefore I urge you to **reaffirm your love for him"** (2 Cor. 2:8). Never correct or administer the "rod" in front of those outside the immediate family. We should never shame our children while embarrassing the onlookers in the process. "Let all that you do be done in love" (1 Cor. 16:14). "The wise in heart will be called discerning, and sweetness of speech increases persuasiveness" (Prov. 16:21). Love is an important foundation for you to show to your child. "But the goal of our instruction is **love from a pure heart** and a good conscience and a sincere faith" (1 Tim. 1:5). *Make sure that your attitude toward them confirms that all is forgiven and forgotten.*

Warning: If your wife has done what she should, by going through the proper steps of correction, then there should be no need to punish them a second time—"when their father gets home." If your wife wants to make you aware of a problem that has transpired during the day, then do it privately. Even our court system does not allow anyone to be tried twice for the same crime!

Happiness and peace of mind. God's Word is true. Do you trust Him, or do you trust the world's advice or the world's warnings? "Discipline your son and he will give you **happiness and peace of mind**" (Prov. 29:17).

Make a Commitment

Don't wait too long. Begin to train and discipline your children when they are young. Don't wait to correct bad behavior. Move into action as soon as he *starts* the disobedience or the disagreeable attitude.

Author of rebellion. Remember that the **author of rebellion** is Satan. God is the author of discipline and authority. Whom will you serve? Whom will your child serve?

Breed respect. Discipline **breeds respect** for you and for all authority. Moreover, the lack of proper correction **breeds disrespect** for you and for all authority.

Confess your sins. Parental correction is only temporary; you only have a few years! So begin early while the clay is soft. If you wait until they're teens, you will need a sledgehammer to chip away at concrete. If your children are grown and you didn't discipline and train them biblically, then you probably have had much heartache and many sleepless nights. Your comfort is in prayer! God is a God of miracles. Confess your lack of obedience to His Words and His ways to your adult child. "Therefore, **confess your sins** to one another, and pray for one another, so that you may be healed. The effective prayer of a righteous man can accomplish much" (James 5:16).

Energy and commitment. It will take **energy and commitment** on your part, but the results are worth it! Pay now or pray later!

Part 3: Training

Raising a child to be a godly adult takes more than discipline—it takes training. "Train up a child in the way he should go, even when he is old he will not depart from it" (Prov. 22:6). This verse says to train him in the way he should go, not *shouldn't* go. Many times we spend all of our time telling the child "no" or what *not to do,* instead of using the time to train. By following God's Word, you will prevent the need for a lot of discipline. Train your children what *to do!*

Lack of knowledge. Scripture tells us, "My people perish for a **lack of knowledge**" (Hos.. 4:6). Are your children perishing because they lack the knowledge of what they *should* do?

Whatever a man sows. We send our children to school or to Sunday school for them to get knowledge, but God gave them to us. Are they learning what *we* would teach them, if we took the time? Let's remember, "Do not be deceived, God is not mocked; for **whatever a man sows,** this he will also reap" (Gal. 6:7).

He *should* go. If we don't train them and discipline them, can we honestly claim: "Train up a child in the way **he should go,** even when he is old he will not depart from it" (Prov. 22:6).

I did away with childish things. Therefore, if we want to claim the promise of Proverbs 22:6, we must teach and train our children. Help them to do away with childish things as they grow to adulthood. "When I was a child, I used to speak as a child, think as a child, reason as a child; when I became a man, **I did away with childish things"** (1 Cor. 13:11). But this can only be accomplished if we, as the head of our homes, have done away with childish things. So many women complain that **they** are the only adult in the home. Does your wife feel this way?

Diligence

Teach them to work with diligence. Diligence is enthusiasm, enjoyment, excitement, delight, devotion, and fervor. Help your child to learn good **work** ethics. Give them tasks that they must do every day. Parents who only have one or two children many times do not require their children to help with the housework or yard work. By not teaching them to do "their" part, you will greatly compromise your children's future.

Wanted and needed. When you require a child's help it shows the child that he is wanted and **needed.** There is a chapter in *Workers at Home: Making the Most of Your Time* that will help your wife (with your support) to implement a system with your children that has kept our home in running order for years!

Responsibility! Work teaches them to appreciate what they have and in turn teaches them **responsibility!** If they *earn* what they have, they will care for it and be appreciative of all God gives them in the future. We require our children to pay for sport uniforms or sign-up fees, orthodontic retainers, and most of their own clothes.

Gainfully Employed

Jobs. Employ your children by making jobs available for them to *earn* money. These should be above and beyond their normal duties.

When they are young. Begin by first looking around the house for things they are able to do. You must not wait until they are too old; begin when they are young. We pay our younger children with treats or privileges or a mere quarter for good labor.

Outside. Next, as they grow, they can begin to work around the yard, in the garage, or on the car. Outside is the next step after they have mastered the inside responsibilities.

The neighborhood. Finally, after they have graduated from inside to outside and they work well, they are then ready to work around the neighborhood. They can wash cars, do yard work, feed animals, bring trashcans out to the street, and help older women with their chores. As their parent, look around for the needs in your neighborhood.

Note: Make sure that helping you or a neighbor is not always for money—they are to be helpful to you, to widows, and to the poor.

Money they've earned. What do they do with the money *they've* earned? It is important that you don't stop the instructional process once they've earned money. You must instruct them on how to spend wisely the money they've earned.

Children's wants. The worst thing you can do is provide for all your children's wants. Also, do not replace the things that they have lost or damaged, or that have been stolen—if it was caused by *their* irresponsibility.

Carried over to their adult life. Whatever you teach them to do with the money they've earned now will be carried over to their adult life. Do you want them to rely on *you* once they're out *supposedly* on their own?

God supplies all our needs. First tithe! Teach your children that God supplies all our needs. God only asks us to give Him 10 percent and we get to keep 90 percent! Require your children to tithe from all money that is earned.

Save 10 percent. Save! Teach the child to save the next 10 percent.

Future needs. Next they need to pay for needs. Look ahead to their future needs as stated above (dues, equipment, or clothing) or possibly a birthday gift, Mother's Day gift, etc.

Teach wise buying. Lastly, the child may spend on his "wants." The caution here is to teach wise buying.

His *own* money. Don't allow toys, games, or books that have a bad influence on your child, just because he is using his "own money." Also, don't allow them to buy rebellious clothing (things you wouldn't buy for them), just because it's *their* money.

Organization

Teach them organization. You must **train a child to be organized,** but you can't teach what you haven't learned yourself! Erin's mother, God bless her, was the most disorganized person you could ever meet. When Erin and I got married, she had no clue how to get our home organized and running smoothly. If your wife has trouble in this area, there is hope. Erin wrote down most of her methods for keeping our house and family (of nine) running smoothly—while homeschooling, writing, and helping me with my business. Pick up a copy of *Workers at Home: Making the Most of Your Time* for your wife.

Any way they like. Be diligent about your children keeping their rooms in good order. Many parents think that because this is "their room" they can keep it any way they like, as long as the door is shut. I don't think you'll be too popular with your daughter-in-law when your son keeps his home as he was allowed to keep his room!

Caution: Be careful not to let your children acquire "territorial attitudes" about **their room** and **their things.** You need to teach and exhibit to your children that "we own nothing." We are stewards over all that **God** has entrusted to us.

How *to* do it. Teach them how to do all the tasks and chores they are asked to do.

Done right. Work together with your child at first. Later, when they've mastered the skill, periodically check their work to make sure it was done right.

Everything is wonderful. Many experts tell us that we will damage our child's self-esteem if we don't tell them "everything is wonderful" (then after they are safely gone out of the room we can "fix" what they missed or did wrong). Children want and *need* the truth from us. Don't be afraid to correct them. Just make sure it is motivated by love, not a desire to prove them a failure.

Prepare ahead. Teach them how to prepare ahead by laying out clothes for the next day, packing their sporting bags after the clothes are clean and dried, and placing things by the door to collect when they're going out the door. You'll find some tips on this in *Workers at Home: Making the Most of Your Time*.

Housework

Many men think their sons should not have to do housework or even make their beds! Shun this notion and allow your wife to use them to ease her load. This will teach your children to take orders and carry them out. In the military, men make up their own bunks, shine their own shoes, scrub decks, do K.P., etc., etc. The home is their first training ground, to learn to take care of themselves and those with whom they share their lodgings.

Lower your expectations. When working with children, patience is needed the most, along with lower expectations than we might have for ourselves.

Investment in the future. It may be easier now to do everything yourself, but, by training your children, you are making an investment in the future—yours and theirs.

Don't just pick up after them. Teach them to keep your home clean and tidy. Call them (into the room or into the house) when they have left something out of place. Don't just pick up after them!

Children in the kitchen. Having them assist your wife in the kitchen can be helpful also. Caution: Don't send the children to the kitchen when dinner is late or you're expecting guests—it will be difficult for your wife to be patient!

Train your young men. Train boys to do the laundry. Housework is not just for the girls, since most men live on their own before they marry. It's terrible when parents haven't trained their young men. Won't your daughter-in-law just love you when she has her first baby and her husband is able to keep the home clean and all the laundry done? Boys who are about 9 or 10 can easily learn this. If you wait until they are in their teen years, you have waited too long.

Suggestion: Drop the title of "teenager" from your vocabulary. It connotes rebellion. They are "young men" or "young ladies," and you should expect them to act like it.

Spiritual

Talk about God. Talk to your children about God, your Lord, and how He plays a part in your everyday life.

Daily prayers. Pray with them about their needs and fears. Ask them to pray for your needs, especially during a family trial. *Daily prayers are the best remedy for daily cares.*

Share your trials. You're not "shoving religion down their throats" when you share your trials and how the Lord helped you through them all. Don't hide all that you go through as an adult so they are unprepared for life. But, at the same time, don't bring them into your confidence and into details that they should never have to face as a child.

Caution: Children have ears and they hear everything! Be careful what you say in their presence and especially watch your tongue when you are on the phone. Your children are not your best friends. They need you to be the parent and to protect them while they are young! Don't impart fear to your children.

God answers prayers. Use a prayer tree to show how God answers prayers. You will find this at the end of Chapter 2, "Your First Love."

See your joy! Live your faith! Let them **see your joy in the Lord!** Another thing Erin did with our small children every day was to have them put on their *armor of God*. They acted it out as if they were putting on each piece of armor. Our little boys used to make their own armor with helmets and swords. They would proclaim in a loud voice, "This is my sword of the Spirit—the Word of God!" "I'm wearing sandals of peace, so I can be a peacemaker when I see trouble!" "This is my shield of faith, so I can put out all the fiery darts of the devil when he shoots them at me!"

Lead them to the Lord at an early age. (Don't leave this blessing to a Sunday school teacher or someone else.)

Hiding God's Word in their hearts. Have them memorize Scripture every day. By hiding God's Word in their hearts, they will have the foundation they need for a truly great and godly character. You will find some tips on Bible memorization in *Workers at Home: Making the Most of Your Time*.

Disciplining and training. By following God's Word by disciplining, training, and correcting your children, you are setting an example for them to do the same with your grandchildren.

Respect

"Honor your mother and your father" (Eph. 6:1). This should be the first Scripture every child should memorize at two or three years of age.

Follow your example. Be careful how you speak about your parents in front of your children; your children will follow *your* example. Be sure you treat or speak about *your* parents in the way that you want to be treated when you get older.

Glorify disrespectful children. Don't allow your children to be disrespectful to other adults. If you allow television in your home, you are training them to be rebellious. Disrespect for adults is being emphasized on *all* the sitcoms they watch and the movies they view. It's very popular these days to glorify these disrespectful children.

Talking back. Do you allow your children to talk back to you? If they answer anything but "Yes, Ma'am" or "No, Sir," they are talking back. *Never* allow your children to talk back to you.

How many times do you call before your children come? Never call twice. Children know how many times you are willing to call for them. Every child waits to come until just before they know that you will "blow up."

Here I come! Teach them to answer on your first call with *"Here I come!"* This begins by teaching your toddler to say, "Here I come, Daddy," and then taking his hand and bringing him back to you, praising him along the way.

Suddenly unable to walk. If they get "weak in the knees" and are suddenly unable to walk, they get a little switch on the leg.

Come along willingly. By the time they are able to say the words "Here I come, Daddy," they think it is *their idea,* and they come running along willingly.

Are you too lazy? Don't call them if you are too lazy to go get them after your *first call*. Remember, delayed obedience is disobedience!

*Testimony: "I was telling one of my friends last week that I am working with my kids on obeying me **immediately,** without waiting to be told a second time. My friend honestly couldn't see why it was so important, and I admitted that at times I did still give them a second chance. Within just a day or two of my telling her this, Evan (my two-year-old) put a penny in the CD player in the car and shorted out the entire electrical system—the dash lights were out, and I even got pulled over because I didn't realize the taillights were out also! When I saw what he was about to do, I told him 'no,' and he looked right at me, probably to see whether I had my 'last chance' look on . . . which I must not have, because he put the coin in anyway. This made me realize why it was so important for my kids to know they have to obey the **first** time. Expensive lesson, but I am praising God for making it so obvious that I couldn't miss it!"*

Base every lesson on a Scriptural foundation. Don't speak badly about others, and don't tolerate it from your children. My wife and I always try to base every lesson on a Scripture. There are many Scriptures on the subject of slander.

Show respect. Show respect for other people's belongings and property. Investing in others will teach this.

Manners

Introducing themselves. Teach your children the polite way of introducing themselves. Have them say, "It's nice to meet you" with a smile (and a handshake for the boys).

Proper phone etiquette. Teach them proper telephone etiquette. Have them identify themselves and ask, "Who's calling, please?" Then teach them to cover the phone, or go and get you—never yell for you!

Make eye contact. Look your children in the eyes so they will learn to do the same. If your child does not make eye contact when speaking, it may affect how others perceive his sincerity.

Do you allow your children to interrupt? Are you encouraging interruptions by allowing your child to get what they want when they interrupt? Never allow them to interrupt when you or others are speaking. **Stand quietly.** Teach them to stand next to you *quietly*. After a short wait, pardon yourself and ask them quietly what they need.

Go away and come back. If they interrupt, make them go away and come back and do as you have asked—over and over if necessary! And don't listen to what they want or you are just breeding interruptions!

A proper attitude should be life-long. Don't use the phrase "As long as you are in my house you'll . . ." Your goal should be to develop a godly man or godly woman. Good behavior and a proper attitude should be life-long. It is important to develop your children's character, not just suppress their fleshly response.

Don't. Don't speak badly about your children, ever! Don't call them brats or worse. Don't say that you can't wait until they go back to school or grow up. You will reap what you have sown. That same attitude will return to you later.

Home Schooling

Many people think it's strange that we educate our children at home. The Lord knows that it is not merely a commitment but a conviction. Here are our reasons for educating our own children. If you are not educating your children at home, I hope that after reading this you will feel it is something you would like to pray about and discuss with your wife.

And *you* shall teach them diligently. God gave your children to you to train until they are adults. As adults, they need to know, among other spiritual things, how to read, write, and do math. One only needs to turn on the news, read a newspaper, or pick up a magazine to see that those who are graduating from high school are unable to perform these basic skills. Major companies are now having to spend money to teach remedial skills to our nation's young adults because they didn't learn the basics in their twelve *plus* years in school. **"And you shall teach them diligently** to your sons and shall talk of them when you sit in your house and when you walk by the way and when you lie down and when you rise up" (Deut. 6:7).

God *gave them* knowledge and intelligence. You spend years building into this little child morals and wisdom, and then school unravels all that they have been taught. To top it off, then they turn your own children against you and toward their peers. Daniel never could have stood alone had his parents not trained him as a young boy. We claim this Scripture in Daniel 1:17, which says: "And as for these four youths (Daniel, Hananiah, Mishael, and Azariah), *God gave them* knowledge and intelligence in every branch of literature and wisdom; Daniel even understood all kinds of visions and dreams."

Make up your mind. As with all promises, there are conditions that must be met. God's condition, which these youths met, was that they remained undefiled. "But Daniel **made up his mind** that he would not defile himself . . ." (Dan. 1:8). If we keep our children undefiled as these youths' parents kept them, then we can trust that God will give our children what they will need.

Ask yourself these questions: If your children are surrounded by evil, will they remain undefiled? Is the world's knowledge more important than the condition of their souls? Do you want your children to learn a different religion? Secular humanism is taught in all public schools and is intermingled with *every* subject they take. "For I will remove the names of the Baals from her mouth" (Hos. 2:2).

Our days. Have you considered how much time your children spend in school versus the time they spend at home with you and their mother and brothers and sisters? ". . . Our days on the earth are like a shadow . . ." (1 Chron. 29:15).

A friend of the world is an enemy of God. Do you want their peers to have first place in their lives? Do you want their peers to be the persons they most want to please? Wouldn't you rather it be *you* and the Lord who are first in their lives? Don't you want them to want to please *God* most? "Therefore, whoever wishes to be a **friend of the world** makes himself an **enemy of God**" (James 4:3).

Disgraceful even to speak of the things. We all know the problems in school: peer pressure, drugs, sex, drinking, and violence. Not only are our children exposed to these evils, but the schools are now *educating* our children in evil! They are teaching your children about AIDS, homosexuality, birth control, turning parents in for child abuse, and the list goes on. "And do not participate in the unfruitful deeds of darkness . . . for it is **disgraceful even to speak of the things** which are done by them in secret" (Eph. 5:11–12).

Turn away. Instead, teach them to ". . . **turn away from evil** and do good" (1 Pet. 3:11). Our five-year-old boy, Cooper, is learning to be a gentleman. If Erin is or any of his sisters are dressing, he turns away and sings to the tune of "Dixie": "Look away, look away, look away, godly man!"

Leave the presence of a fool. Let's heed God's Word when He warns, "Leave the presence of a fool or you will not discern words of knowledge" (Prov. 14:7).

Lest he fall. Would you like it if your wife worked in a bar or somewhere else where immorality, drugs, violence, and alcohol were rampant? How long could she "stand" before it started to affect her? "Therefore let him who thinks he stands take heed **lest he fall**" (1 Cor. 10:12).

Bad company corrupts good morals. Your children have less power to resist an evil influence than a grown man or woman does. "Do not be *deceived,* **bad company corrupts good morals**" (1 Cor. 15:33).

Cause one to stumble. If you put your children into an environment that is evil and that will corrupt their good morals, you may find this to be a sobering Scripture: "It is inevitable that stumbling blocks should come, but woe to him through whom they come! It would be better for him if a millstone were hung around his neck and he were thrown into the sea, than that he should **cause one of these little ones to stumble**" (Luke 17:1–2).

Here are just a few more of the benefits of educating your children at home:

A mother's teachings. Since your wife is your child's teacher, you can be sure that your son or daughter will learn everything he or she needs to know. She's not trying to teach 30 children, so she can take the time to explain to each child what he or she may not understand. She will not have to go on to a new lesson until they have mastered the previous skill. This is one-on-one tutoring, a method in which *all* children excel. ". . . Do not forsake **your mother's teaching;** indeed, they are a graceful wreath to your head" (Prov. 1:8).

Wisdom will enter your heart. Your children will be learning "academics" instead of wasting time learning about birth control, child abuse, recycling, or worshiping "mother earth." Their time will be spent wisely. They also will have the skills to be leaders since God separated those He chose for leadership, i.e., Abraham, Joseph, Moses, John the Baptist, and Jesus. "For **wisdom will enter your heart,** and knowledge will be pleasant to your soul" (Prov. 2:10).

Seek ye first the kingdom of God. You will be able to put Bible reading and memorization first. If you place the most importance on these subjects, then you can claim the Scripture: "Seek ye first the kingdom of God and **all these things shall be added unto you"** (Matt. 6:33).

Imperishable quality of a gentle and quiet spirit. Your goals for your daughters should be different than your goals for your sons. Each of your girls should be capable of teaching her own children and helping her own husband. You should encourage them not to pursue careers, which would jeopardize their marriage. Teach them to manage a home, care for children, sew, and do a ministry from their home. Use Proverbs 31 as your guide. "Let her works praise her in the gates" (Prov. 31:31). But most importantly, you can guide your daughters to have "the **imperishable quality of a gentle and quiet spirit,** which is precious in the sight of God" (1 Pet. 3:4). A gentle and quiet spirit will only be learned from *your wife's* example.

Without the spirit. My goals for my sons are to be mighty in spirit, diligent, and to have a strong work ethic. "For the body **without the spirit** is dead" (James 2:26).

He will exalt you. Both your daughters and your sons need to learn to live their lives for the Lord. "Humble yourselves in the presence of the Lord, and **He will exalt you"** (James 4:10).

Destroy the soul. The way to direct our children's lives is not toward college or a good job where they'll make a lot of money. A recent survey reported that, of those who professed to be Christians (our sons and our daughters) and went to college (secular as well as Christian colleges), 80 percent of them turned away from their faith! Parents, is a college degree more important than your child's eternal soul? "And do not fear those who kill the body, but are unable to kill the soul; but rather fear Him who is able to **destroy both soul** and body in hell" (Matt. 10:28). The pursuit of money should not be the goal. All of us must seek the Lord to find out what "call" is on our children's lives.

My God shall supply. Many times it is the parents' "pride" that has them sending their children on to college. Beware of all colleges, especially when they are out of town. You may be paying for your impressionable son (or daughter) to be carried away into lust and other sins such as drinking or drugs. Jesus didn't leave His parents' authority until He was 30! Many perverse teachings have been planted in the minds of young men and women, even in Bible colleges, and have given forth "bad fruit" later in life. Interestingly, Charles Darwin, the father of evolution, had a degree in theology! "For **my God shall supply** all my needs according to His riches in glory" (Phil. 4:19). *Note of caution: Erin has personally counseled women whose husbands have learned some unimaginable, actually perverted, theories from their professors in Bible colleges.*

Number our days. The most important benefit is the **"quantity,"** *not* quality, time that you spend with your children. Do you remember older people telling you "how fast time flies," and "enjoy your children while they are young"? Take that advice, because they are right. "Teach us to **number our days,** that we may present to Thee a heart of wisdom" (Psalms 90:12).

Benefits of Home Schooling

Well-behaved children. Taking the time to develop well-behaved children will bring praise from others, instead of shame. Also, your children are your testimony and witness to others, whether they are with you or out on their own. "You will know them by their fruits . . ." (Matt. 7:16).

I have no greater joy than this. If you spend more time "disciplining, teaching, and training," there will be less need for correcting. Catch bad behavior quickly. Remember, "A switch in time saves nine!" You will have children who are helpers, not burdens. But most importantly, they will be strong in faith. **"I have no greater joy than this,** to hear of my children walking in Truth" (3 John 1:4).

Tough love. If you love them enough to train them early, you won't have to use "tough love" on them when they reach their teens. "Tough love" is needed by parents who didn't discipline and train their children when they were young. They were afraid to use the rod because they did not fear the Word of God, but instead feared man. *And yes, we do recommend "tough love" for teenagers even though we don't agree with it for the marital relationship. Parents are commanded to punish and control their children; however, neither the husband nor the wife is instructed to respond to their spouse's actions with anything but love and respect.*

Warning: "Tough love" is *never* to be used on your wife. This is unscriptural and the consequences are disastrous!

Love and respect for you. When you love, teach, train, and discipline your children, they will be part of your life even after they are married. Because you have instilled in them love and respect for you, they will choose to be close to you as adults.

Financially supporting them. Another blessing is that you won't be financially supporting them in their adult life if you have trained them diligently in good work ethics.

Let us as Christians make a mass exodus from our public schools and take our children back for Jesus Christ!

Personal commitment: To love, teach, train, discipline, and use the rod with my children with all diligence. "Based on what I have learned from God's Word, I commit to following God's plan for parents that is outlined in Proverbs. I will remember always that these children are the Lord's and have been entrusted to me. I am to train and discipline them in love so they will be ready for God's service and willing and able to obey Him."

Date: _____ Signed: _____

Homework

"My people are destroyed for lack of knowledge. Because you have rejected knowledge, I also will reject you from being My priest. *Since you have forgotten the law of your God,* **I also will forget** *your children"* (Hos. 4:6). We have seen the destruction of our youth. Let us take heed to this verse. It is speaking to us as fathers of this forgotten generation.

1. **3x5 cards.** Men, I hope that you have been faithful to write down the verses from *each* chapter that has touched your heart. Continue to keep these cards with you and bring them out **regularly** until you have completely and totally renewed your mind in Christ Jesus!

2. I want to encourage you to not only renew *your* mind, but also teach these same verses to your children.

3. Share the wisdom from *this* chapter with *one other father* who needs help with his children. However, make sure your children are in line! Also, be sure you are honest about how your children are not *always* perfectly well behaved.

Test Your Wisdom

1. What must be the foundation of our relationship with our children? _____ (1 John 4:19).

2. All of our activities keep us too busy. We must remember that they are only _____; therefore they have only temporal value. Instead we must devote our time to things, which are _____ (2 Cor. 4:18).

3. As believers anointed with the Holy Spirit our **touch has** _____ and _____ (Luke 6:19 and Luke 8:46).

4. Are we to comfort our children when they cry or are distressed? Yes / No (2 Cor. 1:3).

15. Father's Instructions

5. Many parents, even Christian parents, fail to express their love for their children by taking the time and energy to _____ and _____ them (Rev. 3:19).

6. What has caused many of our children to go astray? A lack of _____ (Prov. 5:23).

7. What does Scripture tell us to use when correcting our children in Proverbs 23:13, Proverbs 23:14 and Proverbs 13:24? The _____. Please take the time to mark these verses in your Bible.

The answers to Homework questions are at the end of this workbook.

Chapter 16

Empty Talkers and Deceivers

*"For there are many rebellious men,
empty talkers and deceivers . . . who must be silenced
because they are upsetting whole families,
teaching things they should not teach for the sake of sordid gain."
—Titus 1:10–11*

In our society, everyone, even Christians, seek out "experts" to help them in marriage, especially the young man who is just starting a family. These young men, for the most part, have been deceived. They unknowingly are being taken in by "empty talkers and deceivers" all for sordid gain.

"They profess to know God, but by their deeds they deny Him, being detestable and disobedient and worthless for any good deed" (Titus 1:16), the opening verse goes onto say.

Often they prey not on the husband, but instead go after the weaker one— their wife. "For among them are those who enter into households and captivate weak women weighed down with sins, led on by various impulses, always learning and never able to come to the knowledge of the truth" (2 Tim. 3:6–7). Men don't know how to lead their family or protect their wife because no one has ever taken the time or energy to teach them. The book of Titus has a lot to tell us about men (and women) encouraging (or teaching as it says in some Bible versions) the younger men (and women).

"*Older* men are to be temperate, dignified, sensible, sound in faith, in love, in perseverance. *Older women* likewise are to be reverent in their behavior, not malicious gossips nor enslaved to much wine, teaching what is good, so that they may *encourage the young women* to love their husbands, to love their children, to be sensible, pure, workers at home, kind, being subject to their own husbands, so that the word of God will not be dishonored. Likewise urge the young men to be sensible..." (Titus 2:2–6).

Titus 2:6–8 says, "Likewise urge the young men to be sensible; in all things show yourself to be an example of good deeds, with purity in doctrine, dignified, sound in speech which is beyond reproach, so that the opponent will be put to shame, having nothing bad to say about us."

These verses explain that the older women are to encourage (or teach as it is stated in some Bible translations) the younger women in the things of God; therefore, the husband is not alone, but should encourage his wife to seek out women who show the fruits of righteousness in regard to the way she speaks of and responds to her husband and also those whose children are well-behaved and living a life that honors God.

Though the verses do not specifically command that the older man to encourage (or teach) the younger man, it is implied. There is no doubt that you, as an older man, can greatly influence a younger man in the ways of God. And if you are thinking you are not old enough, no matter what your age, you are an older man to someone. Even a young man in his twenties can influence a boy in his teens. And if we don't take the time to encourage and teach these young men, what else are they to do but seek out the world's view and standards and/or be taken in by those whose motivation is "sordid gain"?

Many of you are encouraging and teaching younger men and you don't even know it. You are teaching them by your example. The young men in your church, your neighborhood, your place of work, and family members (your sons, nephews, and younger brothers)—they are all watching. What do they see in your life? Are you an example of a godly man or a man who claims to be a Christian?

"You are our letter, written in our hearts, known and read by all men" (2 Cor. 3:2).

"Ye are our epistles written in our hearts, known and read of all men" (2 Cor. 3:2, KJV).

Your life is an epistle or letter, which is being read by men who know you and also men who you may not know that are watching you from afar. Is your life bringing glory to God?

If it is not, then what are you going to do about it?

What to Teach

There are many things that we could teach the younger men, but does God give us any guidance or directions as to what or how we are to teach? God doesn't leave it up to our favorite subjects or our passions or our preferences. The Bible clearly gives us a specific outline in Titus 2:6–8 (NIV):

Encourage the young men to be self-controlled . . .

In everything set them an example by doing what is good.

In your teaching show integrity,

seriousness,

soundness of speech

that cannot be condemned,

so that those who oppose you may be ashamed

because they have nothing bad to say about us.

Know–Live–Speak

Whether or not you want your life to speak to others is not your choice. Our lives are our letters "known and read by all men." Erin and I don't know about you, but we want our lives to show Jesus. People aren't impressed with your Christian bumper sticker or the fish on your car.

They are *not* impressed with the cross you wear around your neck or the Bible you carry with you. They are looking at your life, your attitude, and your love (or lack of love) for others. It is our prayer that these verses have brought conviction to your heart and that you will take the next step toward a life that whispers or even shouts "Jesus!"

To change your life you will need to do these three things in this order:

Know the Word of God.

Live the Word of God.

Speak the Word of God.

Know It

"**Study** to show thyself approved unto God, a workman that needeth not to be ashamed, rightly dividing the word of truth" (2 Tim. 2:15, KJV). Until you know something, you cannot live it. If this is your first time through this book, you have seen how learning the Truth has set you free in many areas where you were once bound. That is *not* the power of this book; it is the power of His Word.

Dear friend, you have already taken the first step toward a life that will encourage the younger men. By taking this course, you have begun to study the Word of God as it relates to men and the issues men face. Most of us, if not all of us, built our houses on sinking sand. Our opinions and lifestyles were a result of not knowing what God thought; instead we ignorantly accumulated teachers that "tickled our ears" (2 Tim. 4:3).

But now we are all at the same place; we are all at the glorious point in our lives where we are open and searching for the Truth. We know because you have sought after this book that is convicting and very difficult to swallow, especially in today's world. We know that as we have renewed our minds on just a few of God's principles that we were once ignorant of, we have seen tremendous changes in our lives. This motivates us to want more.

Once you know the Truth, then you need to replace your old thoughts and old opinions with the Truth. As you have been reading through this book, if you have been making those 3x5 cards as we have suggested, then you are well on your way to a new life that will change the lives of others.

"And do not be conformed to this world, but be transformed by the *renewing* **of your mind,** that you may prove what the will of God is, that which is good and acceptable and perfect" (Rom. 12:2). God's way of changing us is simple and perfect. He tells us in this verse that by renewing our minds we will be transformed. On top of all that, we also prove, by our lives, what the true will of God is for a man—that which is good, acceptable, and perfect! Hallelujah!

How often have we tried to change ourselves? And every time we try, we once again are defeated. Then we add more defeat to our lives as we try and change others, which has an even higher rate of failure. God's ways are different. His ways are far above our ways and our reasoning.

"For as the heavens are higher than the earth, so are My ways higher than your ways, and My thoughts than your thoughts" (Isa. 55:9).

"Trust in the Lord with all your heart, and do not lean on your own understanding" (Prov. 3:5).

The only way for us to change ourselves is to renew, or make new, our minds. The only way to change others is to live with them in love that is patient, kind, etc. As we mentioned before, using the 3x5 card method works. We know because in our minds are hundreds of Scriptures that replaced our thoughts and the way we used to think. And without any effort on our part, our lives started to change because of the Scriptures that we read over and over again. Many men and women who now have restored marriages have told us that this method changed their lives. In addition, many write to tell us that they have literally worn out their books, reading them over 50 times! Putting that much of God's Word in your mind will undoubtedly result in a totally transformed life!

Live It

Once your mind is renewed by a particular principle, then your life will naturally begin to reflect the change. In addition, we must also be willing to make the changes necessary and not compromise the will of God that has come to reside in our minds. The changes will appear in the ways that we act and react to things, the priorities in our lives, and even our desires or goals. All of these things will begin to reflect our newly renewed minds. However, if we try to hang on to our old habits or friendships that don't fit in with our new minds, then we fall into the trap of double-mindedness.

James 1:6–8 says, "But let him ask in faith without any doubting, for the one who doubts is like the surf of the sea driven and tossed by the wind. For let not that man expect that he will receive anything from the Lord, being a double-minded man, unstable in all his ways."

When we continue to associate with those who are now not like-minded or hold on to old habits, doubts enter our minds. We begin to doubt the validity of the principle. We must instead not hesitate to take our renewed mind to the next step by making the changes in our lives that we have been prompted to make by the Holy Spirit.

Unfortunately, too many make the mistake of hesitating to obey the leading of the Holy Spirit by not making changes in our lives. It is in the midst of this hesitation that we find ourselves in the very dangerous state of double-mindedness. This unfortunate state is where, we believe, most Christians of today live. It is why they don't receive abundant blessings from God and do not live His abundant life as He promised. God tells us that those who are double-minded should expect nothing from God (James 1:8). It all began with *knowing* the Truth, but then failing to *live* the Truth.

We see it often in our ministry. When someone finds out the Truth about trusting God in a particular area of his life, through the renewing of his mind, he comes under conviction. But because of fear, rebellion, or apathy, he fails to line his life up with his conviction. Soon there is a pattern of failure, and confusion follows—the "double-minded" man principle explained in James 1:8 is activated.

At this point, many men write and ask us what they should do about their newfound convictions when their wife does not yet share those convictions. This is when the principles in "Manages His Own Household" should be followed. If you are careful not to manipulate or pressure your wife and have stopped trying to get your own way by demanding, and if you have shown your wife a spirit of love and understanding, then when a situation arises, you will not only be able to share your newly found conviction with your wife, but because of the love and understanding of your spirit, she will very likely want to act on your newly found conviction.

If you are so radically and wonderfully changed in your attitude toward your wife, your wife, as was mentioned in the very beginning of this book, will want to get a copy of the women's book *A Wise Woman*. This will put you in a perfect position for your entire family to be that "epistle read by all men." Your positive influence can have a radical effect on the world around you when it is not only you who has changed, but your change has spilled over into the lives of your wife and your children. It happens all the time in our ministry—may it happen in your life!

Speak It

Once your mind is renewed and your life reflects your renewed mind, then God will begin your ministry to other men. One of the greatest needs of today is for men to minister to other men. There are many young men who are going into seminary to become preachers. Personally, I am not interested in what they have to say as much as a man who has lived the life he has been called to live (as a husband, father, and provider) and has come through it victoriously. No one wants someone to *point* the way; we want them to have built a bridge over the deep rivers and valleys they have crossed personally.

When Erin had to face caring for her father who was dying, she looked to an older woman who had cared for her bedridden mother. She knew that woman knew what she was feeling and the hardship that she was facing. Knowing she had done it, and had not only survived but was greater for the experience, gave Erin the fortitude and example to accomplish that difficult task. Erin could not tell you how many times that woman's example helped her to go on, not only to make it through caring for her father, but then again when she was caring for her dying mother. There are very few who will live a radically different life, a life that whispers or even shouts "Jesus!" But those who do are the ones who change the course of the world and never really know it.

God will begin your ministry, most likely, in the confines of your family, friends, church, and community. Later, if you continue to grow, God will expand your territory. Who would have ever dreamed that the Lord could take a heartbroken person like Erin and allow her to minister around the world? Certainly not Erin, nor I either!

"For the eyes of the Lord move to and fro throughout the earth that He may strongly support those whose heart is completely His" (2 Chron. 16:9).

God is looking for you. He wants to use you. Just one person like you can change thousands of lives if you just search for the Truth, get outside your area of comfort, allow your convictions to change you, and begin to line your life up with your newly found principles. God will do the rest.

We don't know about you, but we want God to ask the devil to consider us like he considered Job. We want God to take this frightened man and woman who are hiding behind these computers and make them "mighty warriors" like Gideon. We want to have such faith that we could be like Abraham and be a friend of God's. We want to be after God's own heart like David and walk with God like Enoch had the pleasure of doing.

We want to have the wisdom of Solomon to minister to the men and women of this world. We want to be a leader like Moses to deliver God's people from the bondage of the world and lead them through the wilderness to the Promised Land. We want our lives to be so pleasing to God that because of us our children will be blessed like David's children and lineage.

You may say "impossible," but we know it is possible. God said it and we believe it.

"Jesus said, 'With men it is impossible, but not with God; for all things are possible with God'" (Mark 10:27).

Fruits!

"You will know them by their fruits. Grapes are not gathered from thorn bushes, nor figs from thistles, are they?" (Matt. 7:16).

"So then, you will know them by their fruits" (Matt. 7:20).

How do the younger men find you? They find you by your fruits! When men look to us for personal help in training their children, we tell them to look for the men in their church who have well-behaved children. They are there, yet sometimes they are hard to find. These are the children who often sit in church with their parents rather than going to children's church, but you may not notice them because they are not disruptive. You don't notice them because they are not running around with the other children up and down the aisles. But when you find them, you know it.

Though Erin and I totally messed up in our marriage because of our ignorance of the principles of marriage, we did a bit better with our parenting (thanks to Erin and her mother's example) and now we have a lot of fruits! We are continually praised for our children and for their behavior. These are the fruits in the area of children.

Young men need to see a happy man in order for them to want what he has. This is a powerful evangelism tool. Erin's older and younger sister, who both just recently became powerful, on-fire Christians, told her that she was the greatest influence that led her to the Lord. Erin's sisters said quite frankly, "I wanted what you had!" They both said they saw our children, Erin's life, and the blessings she lived in and said, "Why not me!?" Then, as Erin talked to both of them, her sisters realized *Who* was at the center of Erin's life and *Who* was the giver of these blessings. This is real evangelism that works!

So many men and women talk and lecture to their family members until they are blue in the face, and are puzzled why they don't want to accept the Lord or any of their counsel. But if we are unhappy, miserable in our marriage, constantly complaining about our job, and act angry or are always ready to become unglued, who would want what we had to offer? However, if you can live a life not free from trials, but rather with the blessings that follow a man who praises the Lord in the *midst* of those trials, that's a life worth wanting.

It doesn't happen overnight. It is a process. You may begin by looking like a complete nut, a moron, a fool—but you'll turn out to be a "fool for the Lord"! God in His infinite wisdom "has chosen the foolish things of the world to shame the wise, and God has chosen the weak things of the world to shame the things which are strong" (1 Cor. 1:27, KJV).

When you stop debating or trying to make them understand why you do what you do—like Erin and I did when our family kept confronting us on the number of children we were *continuing* to have, the way we disciplined our children, our decision to teach our children at home rather than sending them to school, and our non-dating practices for our teens who are now in their twenties—but instead *live it,* you, too, will see them coming to you for help. It didn't take long for us to see that we were not going to convince them or anyone else by what we said—we had to live it long enough to produce fruits.

Jeremiah 17:7–8 says, "Blessed is the man who trusts in the Lord and whose trust is the Lord. For he will be like a tree planted by the water, that extends its roots by a stream and will not fear when the heat comes; but its leaves will be green, and it will not be anxious in a year of drought **nor cease to yield fruit."**

I love the way that verse reads: "who trusts in the Lord and whose trust *is* the Lord." If your trust is in Him and in His Word and in His promises, then we promise that in the end you will not be ashamed.

Fulfilling Your Call

When our fourth child was born, Erin was in her early thirties. This child, a girl, Erin says will forever change her life. She knew that someday that little girl would look to her and emulate her as she grew to womanhood. She knew she needed help. When she discovered the passage in Titus 2 about the "older women teaching the younger women," she went to our pastor at the time and asked him where she might find an "older woman" to teach her. His reply was simply, "I don't know." If a man came to your pastor, today, and asked the same question in regard to finding an "older man," what would be his response?

Unfortunately, most young men don't even know that the Bible tells them where they are to get help, and even if they did, would they find you? It has been Erin's heart since that day her house fell to be an older woman who helps younger women prevent their houses from falling. She tells everyone that she made so many mistakes that could have been avoided had she just had a godly woman willing to show her what the Bible said and to love her enough to tell her when she was making a fatal mistake, as with her contentiousness, which she humbly tells everyone resulted in our marriage being destroyed.

In this day and age, it now complicates matters that most young men and women don't want to listen to *anyone* about *anything*. They seek out "experts" in child training rather than a man or woman of God who has well-behaved children. They listen to talk shows to get "advice" from other foolish, arrogant men who are in the world and follow that fatal advice with their wives. And often they listen and seek advice from the men and women their own age for advice and counsel, as Rehoboam (Solomon's son) did to his destruction and that of his nation. (See 1 King 12.)

This book, we feel, is just one of the ways that the Lord has given us "the desires of our hearts." Our ministry, for the most part, is spent helping desperate men and women who have just found out that their spouse has been sleeping with their best friend, has moved in with him or her, or has just filed for a divorce. But our heart *for years* has been to be able to somehow **prevent** the pain and heartache that Erin had to endure. Rather than waiting for the problem to arise, let us all fulfill the call on our lives as the "older man" and invite men we know to study *A Wise Man* with us.

Most groups are born when just two like-minded friends get together to go through the book. Then, lo and behold, they meet someone who would benefit from the information and they invite him to join them. Their group grows by word of mouth and the fruits are incredible: men are getting saved and marriages are being restored. Soon they find that they are older men ministering to the real needs of the men in their church, neighborhood, and circle of friends.

God's way often doesn't happen through a board of directors or a vote. His way begins with men, like you and maybe your friend, who want more of God in their lives. They want their lives to be different, and they stumble on *A Wise Man,* which they find different than anything they've ever read or heard. Its message is tough to swallow, but soon after a "peace" sets in. They are forever changed by the *power* **of God** and by the *principles* and *promises* **of His Word.**

Has God placed a burden on your heart for the men in your life, church, and community? Then I would urge you to begin praying about opening your home to the men the Lord will send you. If you have just a few minutes a week to spare and a pot of coffee to offer, then you are ready to begin to change the world around you. This may be just the first step in your ministry to reach men with the gospel and to heal the brokenhearted in the church. Will you fulfill the call the Lord has on *your* life?

I Shall Not Be Ashamed

God promises that if we look to Him, if we trust Him, if we follow His commandment about how to live and set our faces like flint, not allowing criticism and controversy to cause us to compromise what we know is true, then we too, will not be ashamed.

"They *looked to Him* and were radiant, and **their faces shall never be ashamed**" (Ps. 34:5).

"Then **I shall not be ashamed** when I look upon *all* Thy commandments" (Ps. 119:6).

"How blessed is the man whose quiver is full of them [children]; they shall not be ashamed, when they speak with their enemies in the gate" (Ps. 127:5).

"For the Lord God helps me; therefore, I am not disgraced; therefore, I have *set my face like flint,* and I know that **I shall not be ashamed**" (Isa. 50:7).

It's not an easy road being a powerful Christian man today and following the teachings of the Lord and His Word, but it is rewarding. It's not about living a "religious" life. Being *religious* does more to run people off from God than to win them to Him. It's living a fruit-bearing life that comes from a *renewed* mind followed by a life of dying to self. It's a life that shows through by the way you radiate the love of the Lord and exhibit the fruits of a life devoted to loving Him. It's about living the gospel, not just in word but in deed. "For I am not ashamed of the gospel, for it is the power of God for salvation to everyone who believes, to the Jew first and also to the Greek" (Rom. 1:16). Will you join us?

"Therefore, do not be ashamed of the testimony of our Lord, or of me His prisoner; but join with me in suffering for the gospel according to the power of God . . ." (2 Tim. 1:8).

May Your Life Encourage and Teach the Younger Men!

Personal commitment: To make my life a living epistle that will glorify God. "Based on what I have learned from God's Word, I commit to learning, living, and speaking the Truth to the younger men in my life. I will begin in my home and move out from there as the Lord leads."

Date: _____ Signed: _____

Homework

1. Please, write down the verses from *this* lesson on your 3x5 cards.

2. Gentlemen, you've got a ministry that is just waiting for you to embrace. "Do you not say, 'There are yet four months, and then comes the harvest'? Behold, I say to you, **lift up your eyes, and look on the fields, that they are white for harvest**" (John 4:35).

3. Share this information with *one other man* whom you believe would want to host *A Wise Man* with you. Make a call today to someone you know who is also hungering for the truth and make a date to meet and study to show yourselves workmen, unashamed.

Write his name on this line _____ _____ and then pray.

Test Your Wisdom

1. How should we set an example for the young men? "In everything set them an example by doing _____ _____ _____" (Titus 2:7).

2. What are they to **"encourage"** the young men to do? ". . . To be _____ _____" (Titus 2:6)

3. "Blessed is the man who trusts _____ _____ Lord and whose trust _____ _____ _____" (Jer. 17:7).

4. "In your teaching show _____, _____, and _____ of _____ . . ." (Titus 2:7).

5. Why are they to do all this? ". . . So that those who oppose you may be _____ because they have _____ _____ ____ _____ _____ _____" (Titus 2:8).

6. How will you know these older men? "So then, you will know them _____ _____ _____" (Matt. 7:20).

7. When a man looks to the Lord to fulfill this call, how will he look? "They looked to Him and were _____, and **their faces shall never be ashamed**" (Ps. 34:5).

The answers to Homework questions are at the end of this workbook.

Chapter 17

Opening the Windows of Heaven

"Test me now in this," says the LORD of hosts,
"if I will not open for you the windows of heaven,
and pour out for you a blessing until it overflows."
—*Malachi 3:1*

This is a pretty powerful statement from God. Nowhere else in Scripture does God tell us to test Him, except here in this verse. What is it that God says will cause Him to open the windows of heaven, pouring out His blessing on us until it overflows?

"'Bring the whole tithe into the storehouse, so that there may be food in My house, and test Me now in this,' says the Lord of hosts, 'if I will not open for you the windows of heaven, and pour out for you a blessing until it overflows'" (Mal. 3:10).

Did you see it? It's tithing. Tithing will cause God to open the windows of heaven and shower His blessings over your life!

Many Christians shy away from learning as much as they can about this important principle, but please don't miss this! God wants us to be faithful and obedient in **all** things, and when we neglect or choose to be disobedient in one area of our lives, it spills over into other areas as well. **What exactly is tithing?** It is giving back to God ten percent of the first of your increase.

Our society as a whole is ignorant of this principle. Many churches fail their people by neglecting to teach the importance of tithing. Why is it so serious? Because God is angry when we fail to give back to Him what is rightfully His. "The earth is the Lord's, and all it contains, the world, and those who dwell in it" (Ps. 24:1). Tithing is an act of worship.

There are too many Christians who either live in poverty or are in as much debt as the unbeliever. But God wants to make every believer "the head and not the tail." He wants you to be "above" and "not be underneath" debt or anything else that will rule or control your life (Deut. 28:13). We are told, "Owe nothing to anyone except to love one another . . ." (Rom. 13:8). "The rich rules over the poor, and the borrower becomes the lender's slave" (Prov. 22:7).

Most Christians in the United States are blessed with so much, especially if we look at other nations and the level of poverty at which most people of the world live. We spend our earnings on pleasures while our churches, missionaries, and ministries struggle to make ends meet. Why? Because we try to hold onto what is not rightfully ours to keep.

We take but give little. "Now this I say, he who **sows sparingly** shall also **reap sparingly**; and he who **sows bountifully** shall also **reap bountifully**. Let each one do just as he has purposed in his heart, not grudgingly or under compulsion, for God loves a cheerful giver" (2 Cor. 9:6).

We ask and wonder why we don't receive. "You ask and do not receive, because you ask with wrong motives, so that you may **spend it on your pleasures**" (James 4:3).

God wanted to **bless** His people, but He did not because they were unwilling to give into His storehouse. He tells them in Hag. 1:6–7, "'You have sown much, but harvest little; you eat, but there is not enough to be satisfied; you drink, but there is not enough to become drunk; you put on clothing, but no one is warm enough; and he who earns, earns wages to put into a purse with holes. Thus says the Lord of hosts, 'Consider your ways!'"

"'You look for much, but behold, it comes to little; when you bring it home, **I blow it away.** Why?' declares the Lord of hosts, 'Because of My house which lies desolate, while each of you runs to his own house'" (Hag. 1:9).

Understanding Tithing

It is ironic that so many Christians erroneously believe that they are not able to "afford" to tithe and bless God through offerings. The truth is that they are simply caught in a vicious cycle that only obedience and faith can cure. They can't afford to give because they rob God to pay men, thereby robbing themselves of being blessed!

As a matter of fact, it is when we are in deep poverty that God asks us to give. The Christians in Macedonia understood and applied this principle of giving: "Out of the most severe trial, their overflowing joy and their extreme poverty welled up in rich generosity" (2 Cor. 8:2). Sounds a bit like many of us, doesn't it?

Why 10%?

The word tithe in the Hebrew is **"ma'asrah,"** which translates to "a tenth." So, whenever God speaks to us in His Word and says to "tithe," He is saying to give Him a tenth.

Why should I give my tithe first, before paying my bills?

This is the principle of "first fruits" of our labor. Deuteronomy 18:4 tells us, "You shall give him the **first fruits** of your grain, your new wine, and your oil, and the first shearing of your sheep." Then, in Exodus 34:24 and 26, God says, "For I will drive out nations before you and enlarge your borders.... You shall bring the **very first** of the **first fruits** of your soil into the house of the Lord your God..."

This also is confirmed in the New Testament when Jesus tells us in Matthew 6:33, "But seek **first** His kingdom and His righteousness; and **all** these things shall be added to you."

Where should I tithe?

Malachi 3:10 tells us, "'Bring the whole tithe into the **storehouse**, so that there may be food in My house, and test Me now in this,' says the Lord of hosts, 'if I will not open for you the windows of heaven, and pour out for you a blessing until it overflows.'"

Your **storehouse** is where you are spiritually fed. Many Christians make the mistake of giving where they are **not** spiritually fed but would rather give where they see there is a need—but this is foolishness. It is like going to a restaurant, ordering a meal, but when the check comes telling the cashier that you would rather give to the restaurant down the street that is not doing too well!

If you are attending a church where you are being spiritually fed, then you should be tithing at least a tenth of your income to your home church. That means that if you attend church and feel led to sow financially into our ministry (or any other ministry or missions), then this would be an offering "above and beyond" your tithe. We don't want you to steal from your church to sow into our ministry "for this would be unprofitable for you" (Heb. 15:17).

However, many of our fellowship members who are **not** attending a church (for a variety of reasons) *and* are being fed through our ministry tithe by sowing into restoring marriages, since this is where they are being spiritually fed.

Again, as we have encouraged you throughout this book—seek **God**. This goes for everything, including your finances. Then be obedient and faithful to **Him**!

Don't make the mistake of diligently following all the principles for restoring your marriage yet fail to tithe, lest you find your marriage unrestored because you are stealing from God.

Remember, Malachi 3:8–10 tells us, "**Will a man rob God**? Yet you are robbing Me! But you say, 'How have we robbed Thee?' In **tithes *and* offerings**. You are cursed with a curse, for you are robbing Me, the whole nation of you!"

But since I am not under the law and I live by grace, 10% is no longer required, is it?

God's grace warrants giving more, not less. When we have experienced His forgiveness, His mercy, His compassion, and His sacrifice of His shed blood whereby we become partakers of His glory, it will increase our willingness to give more, certainly not less.

". . . Freely you received, **freely give**" (Matt. 10:8).

"He who did not spare His own Son, but delivered Him over for us all, how will He not also with Him **freely give** us all things?" (Rom. 8:32).

However, ". . . he who *sows* **bountifully** shall also *reap* **bountifully**. Let each one do just as he has purposed in his heart, not grudgingly or under compulsion, for God loves a cheerful giver" (2 Cor. 9:6).

But if we are doubleminded and don't really trust that God will provide for us, "let this man expect that he will receive nothing from the Lord." When we hold onto what we have to try to take care of ourselves, we will never see God's awesome power on our behalf.

God's desire is to pour His power and His blessings into our lives. When we tithe, we are being obedient. But when, out of utter gratitude and worship, we freely give offerings beyond what is commanded, we are truly opening the door for God to pour out His blessings and do His pleasure in our lives.

We know He "is able to do exceedingly and abundantly above all that we ask or think, according to the power that worketh in us" (Eph. 3:20, KJV).

"Seek ye first the kingdom of God and His righteousness, and all these things shall be added unto you" (Matt. 6:33, KJV). Do we take God at His Word or not?

Principles of Stewardship

As we have seen, tithing is an important principle in the Bible. God expects us to tithe back to Him a portion of what He has so generously given to us. Indeed, all that He has given us is still His—we are stewards that He has entrusted to care for the earth and all that is in it. How we handle what He has entrusted to us—our money, our talents, our time and our family—demonstrates our obedience to His Word, our trust in His promise to provide, and, most importantly, our faith in Him.

17. Opening the Windows of Heaven

The way you view and handle your finances is basic to your Christian growth and understanding God's principles of stewardship will enable you to mature in your spiritual walk and inherit the blessings God has for your life.

As you have read thus far in this book, God deals with many areas in our life that indirectly affect our marriage. It is not enough to concentrate on marriage principles exclusively, but again God is using this trial in your marriage to transform you more into His image as He draws you out of the world's destruction and shows you the pathway to life.

The riches of God are not in order for us to "get rich" in the way the world seeks riches, but instead His blessings are part of our heritage. God wants to prosper us (Jer. 29:11) as long as He knows that we will use our inheritance wisely, without allowing prosperity to bring us to ruin. Giving a car to a child who is too young will most certainly end in tragedy. It is not until a parent sees maturity is he willing to turn over the keys of the car.

God wants us to have a mature attitude toward money, for it has the power to affect our ability to make wise decisions: "Two things I asked of You, do not refuse me before I die: keep deception and lies far from me, give me neither poverty nor riches; feed me with the food that is my portion, that I not be full and deny You and say, 'Who is the Lord?' Or that I not be in want and steal and profane the name of my God" (Prov. 30:7–9).

It is clear, though, that it is God's desire to bless His children. Here are more verses that show God's heart toward you as one of His:

"It is the *blessing of the Lord* that **makes rich**, and He adds no sorrow to it" (Prov. 10:22).

"The *reward of humility* and the *fear of the Lord* are riches, honor and life" (Prov. 22:4).

"And by *knowledge* the rooms are filled with all precious and pleasant **riches**" (Prov. 24:4).

"A *faithful man* will *abound* **with blessings**, but he who makes *haste to be rich* will not go unpunished" (Prov. 28:20).

These verses maintain that there are conditions to financial blessings (spiritual maturity) and that this is truly a heart issue (an absence of greed).

All of us want God's blessings upon our life, but did you know that how you handle your financial blessings has a great deal to do with how you grow in the Lord and to what degree God is able to work in your life?

"No one can serve two masters; for either he will hate the one and love the other, or he will stand by and be devoted to the one and despise and be against the other. You cannot serve God and mammon (deceitful riches, money, possessions, or whatever is trusted in)" (Matt. 6:24, AMP).

"Whoever can be trusted with very little can also be trusted with much, and whoever is dishonest with very little will also be dishonest with much. So if you have not been trustworthy in handling worldly wealth, who will trust you with true riches?" (Luke 16:10–11).

To grow in our ability to be used of God, which is spiritual wealth, and gain the *greater* things (having the power and presence of God in our lives) depends in part on how we handle our finances.

To prove this further, there are roughly 500 references in the Bible to faith and 500 to prayer, but there are over 2,000 verses that refer to our finances! In addition to the spiritual laws that were set in place when God created the universe (see chapter 1), God has also established financial laws, which He has shared with us in His Word. We benefit from following the laws or suffer the consequences if we don't. It doesn't matter if we are ignorant of them or have chosen to reject them; these laws, like gravity, exist and cannot be debated.

Principle #1: We reap what we sow.

One of the most important principles of stewardship is sowing and reaping. To reap a harvest, we must sow seed first. There are many

Scriptures that give us insight into of the subject of sowing and reaping. Here a just a few:

"Now this I say, he who **sows sparingly** shall also **reap sparingly**; and he who **sows bountifully** shall also **reap bountifully**" (2 Cor 9:6).

"Those who sow in tears shall reap with joyful shouting" (Ps. 126:5).

"Do not be deceived, God is not mocked; for whatever a man sows, this he will also **reap**" (Gal. 6:7).

"For the one who **sows to his own** flesh shall from the flesh **reap corruption**, but the one who **sows to the Spirit** shall from the Spirit **reap eternal life**" (Gal. 6:8).

"And let us not lose heart in **doing good**, for in due time we **shall reap** if we do **not grow weary**" (Gal. 6:9). When we sow with the understanding of this principle and with faith in the Lord and His Word, we should **expect** to reap a harvest in and where we have sown! This is really exciting!

No farmer would take the time or the money to sow seed if he did **not** expect to **reap** a harvest. In addition, if he wanted to **reap** a harvest of corn, he would **sow** corn. If he wanted to **reap** wheat, he would **sow** wheat.

Therefore, if you want to reap kindness, sow kindness. If you want to reap forgiveness, forgive! If you want to reap restoration in your marriage, then **sow** into **restoration** by ministering and/or sow financially—then **anticipate** a harvest, since God's principles and His promises are true and He is faithful!!

We can also believe God's promise that sowing into His work means we are investing in our eternal future. "Do not store up for yourselves treasures on earth, where moth and rust destroy, and where thieves break in and steal. But store up for yourselves **treasures in heaven**, where neither moth nor rust destroys, and where thieves do not break in or steal; where your treasure is, there your heart will be also" (Matt. 6:19–21). More importantly, what we do with money here on earth is a true indicator of where our hearts are.

"Now He who supplies seed to the sower and bread for food will supply and multiply your seed **for sowing** and increase the harvest of your righteousness; you will be enriched in everything for all liberality, which through us is producing thanksgiving to God" (2 Cor. 9:10–11).

In other words, when God gives us a bountiful harvest, it is not so we can keep it selfishly for ourselves but so we can sow even more into the kingdom of heaven.

The very wealthy Christians of today are the channels that keep ministries going, send missionaries to foreign lands, and keep our churches flourishing so that they can reach the lost for the Lord. They do not use their finances for their own pleasures but have found that in sowing into the things of God they have true joy and contentment.

However, we must also remember that poverty and prosperity are relative terms. What we call the "poverty level" in the United States would seem like affluence to those in many other countries.

As Christians, we must find contentment in any and every situation. The apostle Paul reminds us in Philippians 4:12: "I know how to get along with *humble means*, and I also know how to live in **prosperity**; in any and every circumstance I have learned the **secret** of being filled and going hungry, both of having **abundance** and suffering *need*."

Indeed, there are times when God calls His saints to suffering, martyrdom, or poverty (like the poor widow who gave two coins—all she owned) in order to glorify Himself. When He calls us to poverty or suffering, though, He gives us the grace to bear it with joy and thanksgiving—without grumbling or complaining.

While we can't understand all of God's reasons for allowing poverty, we can trust that His ways are higher than our ways. "Out of the most severe trial, their overflowing joy and their **extreme poverty** welled up in **rich generosity**. For I testify that they gave as much as they were able, and even beyond their ability" (2 Cor. 2:8). Sometimes those who suffer the greatest need become the most generous! And for someone with a love of money, a loss of riches may be one of the ways God breaks us, draws us to Himself, and teaches us to rely solely on Him.

However, in our country, poverty and debt do not usually draw the interest or attention of your family, friends, and neighbors. If we have been blessed with much, we must witness to others not by self-righteously preaching to them or condemning their lifestyle but by allowing them to "read" **God** in our lives! "You are our letter, written in our hearts, known and read by all men . . ." (2 Cor. 3:2). We must exhibit the fruits of who our Father is. We must be at peace in the midst of troubles, bless our enemies, freely forgive, and walk in whatever prosperity the Lord allows. Our generosity should glorify Him and may be the very kindness that God uses to draw others to Himself!

". . . And let them say continually, 'The *Lord* be magnified, **who delights in the prosperity of His servant**" (Ps. 35:27).

Principle #2: God owns everything.

Psalm 24:1 (NIV) says simply, "The earth is the Lord's, and **everything in it** . . ." Everything we have belongs to God.

"Yours, O Lord, is the greatness and the power and the glory and the majesty and the splendor, for **everything** in heaven and earth is **Yours**" (1 Chron. 29:11).

"'The silver is **Mine** and the gold is **Mine**,' declares the Lord Almighty" (Hag. 2:8).

All we have, whether much or little, is on loan to us—we are stewards. Again, it is how we handle what has been entrusted to us (as explained in the Luke 16 parable) that will determine whether He blesses us with more or if He takes away what we already have.

Principle #3: God provides everything.

"Otherwise, you may say in your heart, 'My power and the strength of my hand made me this wealth.' But you shall remember the Lord your God, **for it is He who** *is giving you power* **to make** *wealth*, that He may confirm His covenant which He swore to your fathers, as it is this day. It shall come about if you ever forget the Lord your God and go after other gods and serve them and worship them, I testify against you today that you will surely perish" (Deut. 8:17–19).

"But who am I and who are my people that we should be able to offer as generously as this? For **all things** come from **You**, and from **Your** hand we have given You. For we are sojourners before You, and tenants, as all our fathers were; our days on the earth are like a shadow, and there is no hope. O Lord our God, **all this abundance** that we have provided to build **You** a house for Your holy name, **it is from *Your* hand, and all is *Yours*"** (1 Chron. 29:14–16).

"And **my God** will supply all your needs according to *His riches* in glory in Christ Jesus" (Phil. 4:19). Whether you earned it in your job or it was given to you, who was the Source of everything that you have? God.

Principle #4: God wants the first portion of what He gives you.

Many Christians give to their church and other charitable organizations but are not blessed because they don't understand this very important principle. God is clear throughout the entire Bible that He wants to be **first** in every area of your life.

If you pay your bills before returning the first back to Him, God is not first in your life and you will have missed the blessing. We learned in chapter 5, "First Love," that God removes from us what we have put ahead of Him.

"Honor the Lord from your wealth, and from the **first** of all your produce; so your barns will be filled with plenty, and your vats will overflow with new wine" (Prov. 3:9). The principle is clear; we **must give to God first**.

Often when Christians begin to consider tithing, they cannot see how they can possibly tithe since they are barely making ends meet. This is because they are also ignorant to what has been happening in their finances. Haggai 1:9 says that God "blows away" what you bring home and He also allows the **devourer** come and take what was rightfully His.

"'Bring the whole tithe into the storehouse, so that there may be food in My house, and test Me now in this,' says the Lord of hosts, 'if I will not open for you the windows of heaven, and pour out for you a blessing until it overflows. *Then* I will **rebuke** the **devourer** for you, so that it may **not destroy** the fruits of the ground; nor will your vine in the field cast its grapes,' says the Lord of hosts" (Mal. 3:10–11).

Every month non-tithing Christians are met with "unexpected" expenses, things like repairs or other needs they did not foresee. But it is only because they are ignorant of this principle. For if God is **first** in your life— first in your heart, first in your day, and first in your finances— then (and only then) will God "open for you the windows of heaven, pour out for you a blessing until it overflows," and faithfully "rebuke the devourer for you."

Those who humble themselves by giving God their tithe and offerings will delight themselves in **abundant** prosperity! "But the *humble* will inherit the land, and will delight themselves in **abundant** *prosperity*" (Ps. 37:11). His Word tells us, "Adversity pursues sinners, but the *righteous* will be **rewarded** with prosperity" (Prov. 13:21).

Principle #5: What you do with the first portion determines what God does with the rest.

When God asked Abraham for His son, he did not withhold him; as a result, God tells him, "for now I know that you fear God, since you have not withheld your son, your only son, from Me. . . . because you have done this thing and have not withheld your son, your only son, indeed I will **greatly bless you** . . ." (Gen. 22:12, 17).

God told the army who took Jericho that they were not to take the spoil of the first city, then God would give them the rest. God always wants to see if we put Him first to test our hearts. "The refining pot is for silver and the furnace for gold, but the Lord tests hearts" (Prov. 17:3). However, one of the soldiers, Akin, could not resist and took some of the spoil. When they were to take the next city, Ai, in a battle that was much smaller and should have easily been won, they were defeated. (See Joshua 6.)

This principle is not just in your finances, or in your restoration, but in every area of your life. When we fail to give to God first, then we are robbing God of what He has asked for. He wants no other gods before Him: not our money, our spouses, our marriages, or our careers. What you do with the first of everything will determine what God will do with the rest—bless it or curse it.

Are you in a financial crisis?

"But seek first His kingdom and His righteousness, and all these things will be added to you" (Matt. 6:33).

Have you sought the Lord about your finances? In Philippians 4:19, the Bible clearly teaches that the Lord is the One who will supply **all** our needs. However, if we go to others with our needs rather than seeking the Lord—if we fail to "seek Him **first**"—then "all these things" will *not* be "added unto" us.

Are you following the principles for financial security in the Lord? The Scriptures teach us that we are to tithe in order to be "filled with plenty" and "overflow" (Prov. 3:9–10). We are also encouraged to "sow" if we want to reap (Gal. 6:7, 2 Cor. 9:6). Have you been sowing and faithfully tithing? Take the time to read these passages of Scripture again and again, then pray for how the Lord wants to change the way that you are trusting Him while fulfilling His command to all believers, beginning by giving a portion back to Him.

If you are tithing faithfully and still in a financial crisis, make sure that you are following all of God's statutes. There are many references in Scripture to actions that lead to poverty, including not asking (James 4:2), asking with wrong motive (James 4:3), adultery (Prov. 6:26), heavy drinking or gluttonous behavior (Prov. 21:17, Prov. 23:21), laziness (Prov. 10:4, Prov. 14:23, Prov. 28:18–20), not accepting rebuke or correction (Prov. 13:18), making hasty decisions (Prov. 21:5), oppressing the poor (Prov. 22:16), living treacherously with your wife (Mal. 2:14–16) or failing to honor her (1 Pet. 3:7) and, of course, withholding from God what is rightfully His.

While we are giving back to God in tithes and offerings, we also need to be sure we are giving our wives the honor they deserve. "You husbands likewise, live with your wives in an understanding way, as with a weaker vessel, since she is a woman; and grant her honor as a fellow heir of the grace of life, so that your prayers may not be hindered" (1 Pet. 3:7). Has your wife been the one who has tried to live within your means but you were irresponsible with your spending? Have you shamed your wife to others or joked about her spending? Be sure you are pure in heart and faithful to your wife in every way.

When Erin was in financial ruin as a single mother of four young children, she learned the principle of tithing. Even though she lived close to poverty level, she began tithing for the first time in her life (being raised as a Catholic she had never even heard of the principle). Not only did she sow by tithing ten percent of the meager amount of the money she received, but she also sowed into the lives of women who were experiencing tragedy in their lives (telling them about God's ability to restore their marriages).

Erin's obedient heart that learned to tithe to the Lord set the standard in our home when I was gone. God honored her by leading me to tithe soon after I came home without her even telling me!

Men, if you are still struggling with giving, it may help you to know that God owns everything we have, and it is only because of Him that we have been given the "power to make wealth, that He may confirm His covenant" with us. (Deut. 8:18). Therefore you need to make sure that you give to Him **first** to confirm that He is **first** in your life!

Will you serve God or mammon (money)?

Too many shy away from teaching on giving because of the abuses and because they don't want to be considered "money seekers," but it doesn't eliminate the truth in the message. Search for the truth yourself. Test Him to see if He is faithful to His promise. Give to God first, tithe to your storehouse (where you are spiritually fed), and see if your life changes and you are blessed in all areas of your life.

God is the one who provides for our ministry and for our family. We sow into the lives of those who are brokenhearted and water with ongoing support through our fellowship, but it is God who brings the increase. We look to no one to supply our needs but God alone.

Failing to properly teach such an important principle would be to neglect to feed the sheep and shepherd those who are coming to us for help, support, and direction.

Jesus said to feed His sheep, and God said in Hosea that His people perished for a lack of knowledge (Hos. 4:6). Many who come to us are new Christians or have been attending a church where this principle, and other principles of restoration, are not taught. Our job is to make disciples of the Lord, to give them the tools they need to transform their lives.

For those of you who have never given God His tithe, may God prove to you that you can do more with 90% of your income than the 100% than you used to control. It will take a step of faith, but, just like when you chose to restore your marriage rather than moving on, your life will never be the same.

For those of you who do give (but God is not first), may you rearrange your priorities in every area of your life to show God that He has first place.

God is a God who longs to be gracious to us; He longs to bless us! ". . . And let them say continually, "the Lord be magnified, **who delights in the prosperity of His servant**" (Ps. 35:27).

Let me close with this wonderful **promise**: "Those who **sow** in tears shall **reap** with joyful shouting" (Ps. 126:5). **Hallelujah**!!

Personal commitment to give: "Based on what I have learned in Scripture, I commit to trusting and blessing the Lord with my finances. I will seek the Lord regarding how and where to tithe. I will sow into restoring marriages through sharing the good news about restoration with those whom God brings into my life and through my giving financially as God leads and faithfully provides for me."

Date: _____ Signed: _____

Homework

Every verse in this chapter proves one thing. That God wants to open the windows of heaven and shower His blessings over your life! So, the question is: Will you remain like so many Christians who chooses to ignore what God wants and longs to do in your life—in your family? Will you live in poverty or prosperity?

1. **3x5 cards.** Men, this is the final to write down the verses from *this* important chapter that has touched your heart. Keep these cards with you and bring them out **regularly** until you have completely and totally renewed your mind in Christ Jesus!

2. I want to encourage you to not only renew *your* mind, but also teach these same verses to your wife and children by living them.

3. Share the wisdom from *this* chapter with *one other man* who needs help with his finances—boasting about your own weakness so that the power of Christ may dwell in you. (2 Cor. 12:9).

Test Your Wisdom

1. Where does God tell us in Malachi 3:10 to give our tithes "'Bring the whole tithe into the _____"?

2. What's the warning in Malachi 3:8–10 regarding tithes and offerings "Will a man _____ God? Yet you are _____ Me! ... In tithes _____ offerings."

3. "'You look for much, but behold, it comes to little; when you bring it home, I _____ it away. Why?' declares the Lord of hosts, 'Because of My house which lies desolate, while each of you runs to his _____ house'" (Hag. 1:9).

4. What does the Lord actually tell you to do? "_____ Me now in this" (Mal. 3:15).

5. Why aren't we more blessed? "You ask and do not receive, because you ask with _____ motives, so that you may spend it on your _____" (James 4:3).

6. Should you tithe before or after paying bills? "For I will drive out nations before you and enlarge your borders... You shall bring the very _____ of the _____ fruits of your soil into the house of the Lord your God..." (Ex. 34:24 26).

7. "Now this I say, he who sows _____ shall also reap _____; and he who sows _____ shall also reap _____. Let each one do just as he has purposed in his heart, not grudgingly or under compulsion, for God loves a cheerful _____" (2 Cor. 9:6).

The answers to Homework questions are at the end of this workbook.

Answer Key for Test Your Wisdom

Chapter 1

1. by their fruits 2. tested, add, reprove, liar 3. firmly planted, fruit, prosper 4. free 5. His, Word, healed them, delivered them, doers, spit us out

Chapter 2

1. obedient, heart, committed 2. love, father, mother, son, daughter 3. detestable, disobedient, worthless, Jesus, By the things He suffered

Chapter 3

1. yes, 2. tax-gatherer 3. choice, tough, never having to say you're sorry 4. kindness of God 5. of reconciliation 6. a) because God forgave me, b) because of His shed blood, c) comfort, reaffirm d) take advantage, e) forgive, transgressions, 70, 7, 490

Chapter 4

1. blows 2. gently, soft tongue 3. The heart of the righteous 4. folly, shame 5. content 6. rottenness 7. devil, father, devil

Chapter 5

1. Christ, man, woman, God 2. slaves, slaves, righteousness 3. keys, heaven, bind, loosed 4. without a word 5. everyone, will, practice lawlessness 6. firm in your faith, same experiences, faith, hoped for

Chapter 6

1. corner of the roof 2. constant dripping 3. no one can control her 4. These will be personal testimonies. 5. Honest answers accompanied with confession and repentance. 6. yes or no 7. yes or no

Chapter 7

1. behavior, chaste, respectful 2. turn away, fears the Lord, blameless 3. profane 4. bitter, sharp, unstable, entices, flattering, seduces, boisterous, rebellious, remain, home, no, the world, enemy, God 5. ring of gold, swine's snout 6. shames, joyful heart

Chapter 8

1. word, evil, evil 2. authority, remain quiet 3. revile, threats 4. teachers, own 5. grace, humble 6. the Lord, blasphemed or dishonored

Chapter 9

1. believing wife 2. saved 3. pray to your Father 4. household 5. harden, broken, remedy 6. tested 7. everything

Chapter 10

1. permission, permission 2. three 3. all, love, His 4. justice, victory 5. decision 6. heart, He, all, any, God

Chapter 11

1. knowledge, 2. ears tickled, 3. fruit, produce (or bear), cut down, 4. one flesh, 5. adultery, 6. dead, in the Lord, 7. great

Chapter 12

1. labor in vain 2. smitten, curse 3. bearing, children 4. continually, My Father 5. Lord 6. temptation, ruin, destruction, harlot, increase

Chapter 13

1. us 2. for Christ 3. lack of knowledge 4. seems 5. ceased to pray 6. superficially 7. did not send

Chapter 14

1. your own, your own, your 2. at home, at home 3. strongly support, heart 4. learned to be content, be content 5. weary, consideration, wings 6. wives, everything, love of money, love of money, love of money

Chapter 15

1. Love 2. temporary, eternal 3. healing and power 4. yes 5. reprove and discipline 6. their lack of instruction, rod

Chapter 16

1. what is good 2. self-controlled 3. in the, is the Lord 4. integrity, seriousness, soundness of speech 5. ashamed, nothing bad to say about us 6. by their fruit, radiant

Chapter 17

1. storehouse 2. rob, robbing, and 3. blow, own 4. test 5. wrong, pleasures 6. first, first 7. sparingly, sparingly, bountifully, bountifully, cheerful

As we conclude this workbook, let us quote John 21:25.

"And there are also many other things . . . which if they were written in detail, I suppose that even the world itself would not contain the books which were written."

Resources

First a warning: We who have gone through difficult marriages, separation, and/or divorce want to warn you about books, ideas, or other people who will sway you to go the way of the world, which always ends in disaster. It may seem like the easiest road, but in the end it is the road to even more sadness, trials, difficulties, and heartache than you are already experiencing. Please be careful what you read! Those books whose foundation is in philosophy, or those written by psychologists or marriage counselors, will fill your mind with destructive thoughts.

We do not recommend reading books that cover the following topics: "spicing up your marriage," "tough love," and "co-dependency." We have seen the damage these ideas have done in destroying marriages and the men and women who looked to them in their desperation.

Look to God and to those of like mind to encourage you. Please go to the Counselor (God's Word), which is free, and save your money and your marriage. Stay away from the "professionals." If you cannot find the books listed below in your church library, ask if they might order them from your local Christian bookstore. The ISBN number will help them to order the correct book. All of these are in paperback and most are very inexpensive.

The Bible. New American Standard Bible. The verses in this workbook have been taken from this version. Some have asked us why most of our books use the NASB and not the King James Version. The reason is that when I left Erin, I left my Bible behind, an NASB. Erin used my Bible for about 20 months before I asked for it back. Erin lived every Scripture that is in this manual (except the chapters written exclusively for men). When we began attending a new church where they read from the KJV, I began using that version too and Erin got one as well! Currently our new pastor uses an NIV that we both now use. We have both come to **love** the Bible—period! The version doesn't matter to us! Finally, we have broken away from being Pharisees—hallelujah!

How God Will Restore Your Marriage: There's Healing after Broken Vows for the marriage that has crumbled or that looks a little shaky. This book is just for men and it is offered through Restore Ministries. This one book has restored more marriages and given hope when it was desperately needed in a "seemingly" hopeless situation. *"ALL the things in this book are true. My spouse has not only returned home, but our marriage is better than when we first met." —M.H.*

How to Save Your Marriage Alone. This book by Dr. Ed Wheat helped Erin when her husband was gone and gave her the first glimmer of hope. ISBN 0-310-42522-0

Streams in the Desert. Mrs. Charles Cowman wrote her thoughts, quotations, and spiritual inspirations which helped to sustain her during her difficult years as a missionary and particularly the six years she nursed her husband while he was dying. This has been a devotional classic for more than 70 years! A must if you are living in the midst of trials! I lived in this book for more than two years! ISBN 0-310-22420-9

Hinds Feet on High Places by Hannah Hurburt: This is available in most Christian bookstores. It is a story about the character "Much-Afraid" and her journey to perfect peace. Her struggles and fears will make you cry and her triumphs will inspire you to continue your difficult walk. I have read this many times alone and to my children. ISBN 8423-1433-4

Come Away My Beloved. The poems and short stories are written as though God was speaking to you Himself. This is a wonderful book for meditation and comforting thoughts. ISBN 0-932814-02-6

My Utmost for His Highest by Oswald Chambers: This is a wonderful daily devotional as well as a place to journal your growth in the Lord. ISBN 1-57748-737-5

Workers@Home: Making the Most of Your Time by Erin Thiele for your wife or if *you* are alone with your children. This book will help you to run your home effectively and efficiently. *"This book has totally changed my life." —D.T. "This book is the best book I have ever read bar none!" —K.D.* This book is offered through Restore Ministries.

Enter by the Narrow Gate: HomeSchooling by Conviction: Workbook by Erin Thiele: *"This taught me not only about homeschooling, but about being a better wife and mother. My home is now a happy home!" "What I liked best was the great and practical information, but the very best was*

Erin's total focus on the Lord." "*This is the best book ever!*" Offered through Restore Ministries.

Who Will Rock the Cradle? by Phyllis Schlafly: Each chapter is written by a different expert in the area of childcare, from pediatricians to the actual owners of a multitude of daycare institutions. Surprisingly, all agree that the phenomenon of daycare is destroying our children and our society. The book, I found out, is currently out of print. However, large book distributors can still get them.

Supernatural Childbirth by Jackie Mize: This book is full of Scriptures and is an awesome and powerful testimony to the Word of God and His promises. Jackie was told as a young girl that she would never be able to have a baby, but when she met her husband who knew the promises of God, their awesome testimony began. Not only did they discover how to conceive and carry a baby to term, together they discovered the secret of having a totally pain free labor and delivery!

Dr. Pohl and Dr. Rawson in Houston, Texas, who specialize in microsurgical vasectomy reversals and tubal ligation reversals (respectively). Contact Dr. Pohl's at 713.Reverse or **vasectomyreversal.com**. Contact Dr. Rawson at 281.363.4445 or **fertility.com**.

Restore Ministries International

POB 830 Ozark, MO 65721

USA

For more help

Please visit one of our Websites:

EncouragingMen.org

RestoreMinistries.net

HopeAtLast.com